Competitive Advantage

Third Edition

Fixing Small Business Security And Safety Problems

Bill Wise CPP

Published By

SWG®
Security Wise Group LLC

"A Fool And His Money
Are Soon Parted"

Thomas Tusser
(English Farmer and Writer.
1524-1580)

The information and recommendations in this book are necessarily general in nature and do not guarantee results. The actions and recommendations we describe are considered common security and safety practices that can be beneficial in reducing loss exposure. However, no book or program can guarantee results.

A loss prevention program for your business can be most effective when it is prepared by Certified Protection Professionals, board certified by ASIS International, after an exhaustive study of each businesses individual risk exposure. The content and process of this book is the copyright of Security Wise Group LLC® and may not be duplicated in any way without the express written permission of the author.

By purchasing this book, the buyer agrees to the above disclaimer. Business owners may use the procedures and forms found in this book for their own internal company use only.

© 2009 Security Wise Group LLC
http://www.securitywisegroup.com

ISBN: 978-0-578-00469-3

Table Of Contents

Introduction

- Welcome to the *Third Edition* of Competitive Advantage.
- Why putting your hard earned profit dollars in your pocket makes more sense than writing them off.
- Stop managing by crises.
- What's new in this edition?

Chapter 1
Securing Your Business After A Loss .... Page 13

- A first Lesson From Losses.
- Learn what happens when a crime loss occurs.
- Learn about risk analysis and how to look at your business vulnerability.
- Learn how you can perform a basic loss prevention survey to match strategies the experts use to your own business.

Chapter 2
Get Some Expert Advice .... Page 35

- Choose the experts with the best credentials to partner with.
- Find systems integrators and avoid hardware installers that are not full service.
- An additional 6 reasons to get the best help.
- Get help knowing your crime risk exposure.

Chapter 3
Secure Your Cash .... Page 53

- The experts tell you the best way to secure your cash.
- Find out what safe you should buy....and why.
- Know who was in the safe when the money went missing.
- Learn what policies and procedures you need to control access to your cash.
- Put it where it belongs.
- Lessons From Losses ... Insecure Old Safes.

Chapter 4
A New Key Control System .... Page 69

- Planning a new access control system.
- What lock hardware should you buy?
- What policies do you need to control it all?
- What else do you need to lock up and how should you do it?

Chapter 5
A New Burglar Alarm System .... Page 87

- Love them or hate them … you need them.
- What you need to know to select the best system to meet your needs.
- Where and what to install for the best results.
- Policies that you need to prevent false alarms.
- Should you outsource alarm response?
- Testing your system to make sure it works.

Chapter 6
Camera Systems .... Page 101

- What CCTV equipment should you buy?
- What should you avoid to reduce exposure to lawsuits?
- Best practices and procedures from the experts.
- Why you need to go digital.
- Where should you put them?
- Lessons From Losses … Can you find your stolen stuff at auction?
- More.

Chapter 7
Controlling Loss Exposure Using Rules, Policies and Procedures .... Page 117

- Selecting the right people.
- Lessons From Losses … Selecting the wrong people.
- What's the best screening process to keep out the crooks.
- Six reasons to do it right.
- Another Lesson From Losses … A bad job of hiring.
- It's about Opportunity, Risk and Reward.
- It's not a policy until it's in writing.
- Holding your people accountable.
- Rules and policies you need to control losses.
- Yet another Lesson From Losses … Unwritten rules.

Chapter 8
Your Cash Controls .... Page 139

- Planning your system.
- Follow the money.
- Learn about "Critical Control Points".
- Policies and procedures you need to hold your people accountable.
- More.

Chapter 9
Using Armored Car To Move Your Money .... Page 155

- Learn how to manage the process of moving your cash to the bank.
- Use our tools to document the deposit and reduce investigative time.
- Handle disputes the right way.
- Watch that contract language.
- Bag and tag your money to prevent losses.
- Cash Management programs you can use.

Chapter 10
Some General Policies that We Recommend .... Page 167

- Turn your loss prevention program into a "core competency".
- Program considerations.
- Loss reporting and communications to those that need to know.
- Dealing with customer and employee personal property.
- How should you deal with outsource security services?
- Why you need a crime loss reporting system.

Chapter 11
Employee Dishonesty .... Page 179

- It's mostly an inside job.
- Why do people steal?
- The Embezzlers
- Lessons from Losses …Bad habits.
- Learn how you should investigate losses.
- What about polygraph and employee searches?
- Manage the behavior.
- Even more Lessons From Losses.
- What about Workers Compensation fraud?

Chapter 12
External Threats - Criminals Out To Get You. .... Page 207

- Preventing armed robbery and how to deal with it if you can't.
- Lessons From Losses … When things go wrong.
- Are you vulnerable to burglars?
- What to do to defend against shoplifters.
- Another Lesson From Losses … Other things that can go wrong.
- What about short change artists and counterfeit crooks?
- Vandals just want to destroy your property.
- Crimes against your customers.
- Lesson From Losses - Inventory loss and vendor theft- is it really missing?

Chapter 13
Recover More Profits With A Well Designed Safety Program .... Page 233

- A top down commitment.
- What about OSHA and what is a MSDS anyway?
- Learn about what policies and procedures you need to succeed.
- My aching back and other common plagues that can hit your employees.
- Putting together an action plan that involves your employees that works.
- Learn about claims management issues that can hit you at any time.
- Business safety surveys - find hazards, make some changes and reduce losses.
- What is a Hazard Communication Program and why do I have to have it?
- Learn how to conduct an accident investigation.
- How do you handle customer General Liability claims?
- Much More.

Chapter 14
Crisis Management ... Page 267

- When things seriously go wrong.
- Why should you go through the process of creating a disaster plan?
- My own Lesson From Loss.
- What are some basic causes of a business crisis?
- A smoldering crisis - you can see it coming.
- Prepare your SMART Plan now.
- More Lessons From Losses.
- The best communications in a disaster.
- When things get put right by your best actions.

Chapter 15
Connecting The Dots .... Page 293

- Lessons From Losses ... Work outside the box.
- What have you learned and what have you fixed?
- One more Lesson From Losses ... Having a new "partner".
- You can do it.

Chapter 16
Famous Last Words .... Page 303

- Some things about resistance to change.
- About the author-that would be me.
- More ways that we can help.
- How to find us if you get stuck.

"*I should have no objection to go over the same life from its' beginning to the end: requesting only the advantage authors have, of correcting in a Third Edition the faults of the first.*"

Benjamin Franklin
US author, diplomat, inventor, physicist, politician, & printer (1706 - 1790)

Introduction
Third Edition

Welcome to the <u>Third Edition</u> of **Competitive Advantage** where you can learn how the loss prevention policies, procedures and programs used by large international corporations can be adapted to fit any sized organization…even yours. Can your business gain a Competitive Advantage through a Loss Prevention Program?

Every business with employees, retail customers, deals with cash and inventory; factors in "shrink" as an ordinary business write-off. This "planned loss" can be greatly minimized through proper loss prevention tactics and tools. The result is an increase in dollars to the bottom line. Businesses that generate more profits gain a **Competitive Advantage.**

For example if the average independent stand alone convenience store is generating $500,000 in sales and is losing the industry average of 3.27% of gross sales, specifically due to shrink, on an annual basis, the business is writing off $16,350.00 in loss.

Since the profit is generally 5% or $25,000.00 on the $500,000.00 C-Store, this means of the $41,350 potential in Net Profit, the loss is actually 39.2% of potential net profit dollars.

If you could reduce that loss by just fifty percent each year, would the $8,175.00 help you gain a competitive advantage? Could you invest in better in-store displays? Could you buy more promotional advertising? If you took these fundamental steps would your business be better off? What if you could reduce it further?

Putting your hard earned dollars in your pocket makes more sense than writing them off. You can positively take a proactive stance and implement policies, procedures, processes and programs to minimize risk and control loss.

All businesses can experience losses due to customer and employee theft, poor safety practices and bad or incomplete accounting procedures. Many businesses, just like yours, are leaving a nickel of profit on the table for every dollar of sales and walking away.

The need to address common problems that can result in business profit losses often arises due to a crises response for many owners of small to medium sized companies. That is, a crime loss or an incident has occurred that has seriously affected operations negatively and a solution is needed to address the loss and hopefully prevent future incidents of the same type.

Sometimes, however, a business owner will consult with a loss prevention expert such as a Certified Protection Professional before a serious loss occurs. Okay, nothing major has happened yet, but a bunch of really annoying small losses have occurred that clearly represents a pattern that needs to be addressed before it becomes serious.

That's where we come in. This book will offer some solutions to some of the problems encountered in twenty-five years as a corporate regional loss prevention manager and for the last few years as an independent consultant.

Most large companies employ Loss Prevention Managers to help reduce shrinkage of cash, inventory and other assets. Loss Prevention Managers reduce employee theft, Workers Compensation costs, ensure compliance with company rules and procedures, life safety code compliance and help more profits flow through to the bottom line.

Large companies pay an average of over 1/2 % of gross sales for Security hardware and loss prevention personnel. That investment average exceeded .65% on average in 2007. Small to medium sized companies simply cannot afford this. Or can they?

By the way, big company loss prevention problems are often the same as those that are encountered by small and medium cap companies like yours. They just happen quicker, in greater numbers and cost more money.

What we hope you will do with the information that you will find in this book is to use the loss prevention program survey tools that you find to assess your vulnerability to losses. You can use that information and other analysis tools to catalogue your risks and create goals and action steps to reduce your loss exposure. The biggest losses we've seen to life, property, business assets and your good reputation are either due to or made worse by failure to plan, act and change the business environment from "Reactive" to "Proactive". These days, being reactive is risky behavior and you are betting the farm that nothing negative will happen!

We think that the tools and ideas that you will find will help you to adopt some proactive strategies that you compile into a blueprint designed to put the loss dollars that you are experiencing back into your pocket and be able to prevent a potential smoldering crisis or at least use the strategies to minimize losses and speed the business recovery back to normal.

What we will attempt to do in this Third Edition, is to present a series of common loss examples and give you some solutions to respond to the crime or claim loss. We call these examples "Lessons From Losses". They represent some of the loss scenarios that we have personally had to solve along with some unusual losses found while researching this book.

Our purpose with this approach is to open a dialog that allows you to be aware of and to try some responses that should help keep your profits from flying away or at least provide a framework to help you diagnose what went wrong.

New elements in the Third Edition include protecting your company's proprietary information. The value of how you provide products and services to your customers can often be worth as much as your physical products themselves to you competition. Protecting your customer's personal and financial information can impact your business profitability especially if you do not treat it with a high degree of care and wind up exposing it to identity theft.

You will see expanded information related to access control and electronic surveillance methodology. Throughout the book we will attempt to give you solutions to your loss exposures using Basic, Better and Optimal choices. We will point out that often the most expensive and elaborate exposure fix is not necessarily the best. We will also use our crystal ball to share with you what we think will be available in the future as affordable protection to prevent losses like "data mining" using exception based reports.

We have gone into a lot of detail about screening new employees and why it is really important to your bottom line to spend a lot of time and effort to find the very best people.

We have expanded the chapters that help you to figure out what your business exposure to loss really is and what some effective barriers can do to stop the criminals from selecting you as their next victim.

The safety chapter has been expanded to include several new topics such as claims management and how to create a hazard communication program that OSHA requires for all businesses.

As soon as you can figure out what can and will go wrong, it's all about using people, policies, procedures and systems to protect your business from preventable crime and claims losses. For this reason, we have added a chapter about Crisis Management and how to plan for the worst case scenarios that happen all to often.

You can increase your business bottom line profits through anticipation and prevention of losses with a proactive controllable approach. You can gain a major **Competitive Advantage** for your business and increased profits. You control your pricing advantage not just in how you buy and sell, but how you save, just like the large companies do. They manage all of their cost centers.

This book does not intend to provide all of the answers but will hopefully point the reader in the right direction. Sometimes, however, you just need to pick up the phone and call someone that may have the answers to your specific issue. A number of resources and some examples of common forms may be found through out the book as an offer of further help. If you really get stuck, our E-mail address is listed in the last chapter.

Bill Wise CPP

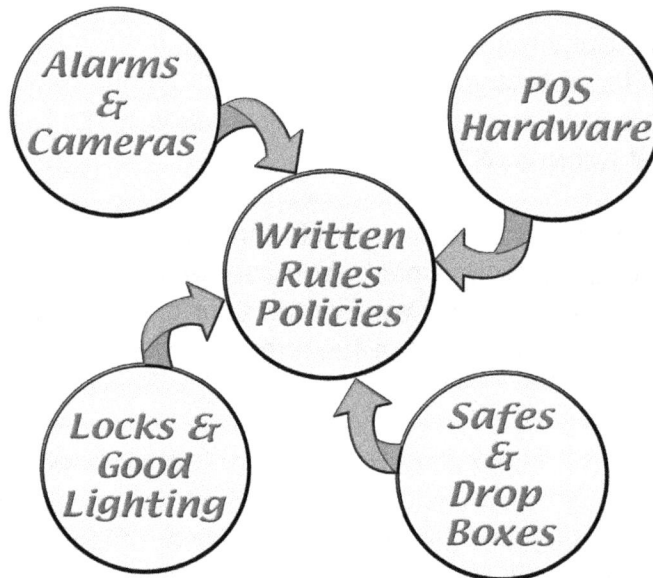

Synergy

An effective Loss Prevention Program consists
of a variety of hardware tools that are managed
by a series of rules, policies and procedures.

All entities of the program must be designed
to work together to create the whole

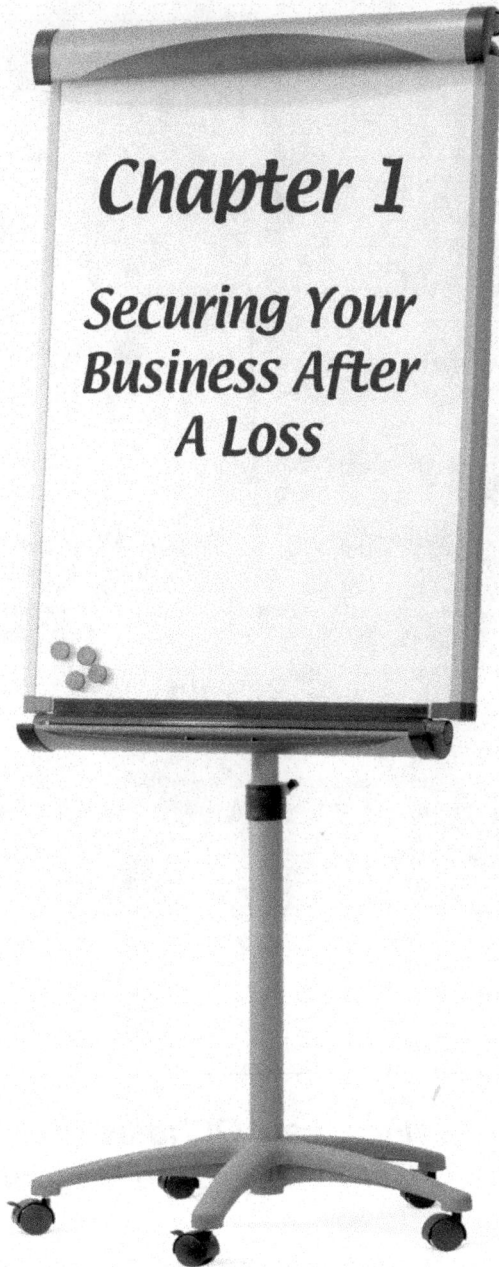

Chapter 1

Securing Your Business After A Loss

*"First Law Of Holes: If You
Get In One, Stop Digging*

(Anonymous)

A SERIES OF UNFORTUNATE EVENTS

Imagine your surprise this morning as you arrive at your business at 6:00 AM and notice your back door is propped open and the store hand truck is laying in the drive-way. Since you know that none of your managers are due to arrive until 7:00 o'clock, you have a nagging suspicion that you may have had a burglar visit during the night. Pushing back a rising feeling of panic, you rush inside and your worst fears are realized. The back room is trashed and when you walk into the office, the safe...is...**gone!**

You call 9-1-1 on you cell phone because the office phone was smashed and you tell the operator that there has been a break-in and the safe was stolen. You tally up the loss from last nights sales records and wait for the police to arrive.

What the police find when they investigate:

- There is no forced entry.
- They were unable to lift any latent fingerprints.
- The safe was loaded on the store hand truck and it and the $12,657 inside was wheeled out the back door.
- There were no witnesses.
- Store locks had not been changed for years. Many current and former managers potentially had access.
- They think it was an inside job but do not have a suspect.

WHAT WENT WRONG?

Among the first things you realize is that trying to protect your business from bad people trying to break in is sometimes less of a priority than protecting it from the people already inside. Your employees!

Okay, let's go back to the details of the burglary and review what you know so far.

1. You don't have a system in place to control building access.
2. You don't have a system in place to detect or deter intruders at night.
3. You may need to review your hiring practices.
4. You need a new safe.
5. You need to review all policies and procedures related to security and cash handling.
6. There is a lot of money missing and no suspects.

What you just found out is that it is very possible for a current or ex-employee to get into your business when it is closed and cause damage and take your hard earned cash. You have lost both the money and your trust.

HOW DO YOU FIX ALL THIS?

So, how should you proceed to fix the problems that you have discovered as a result of this loss? You do know that it is time to look at your current business operations and practices and decide what steps you need to take right away and what things can be positioned on an implementation time-line.

First, you need to get your business open and running. Today! You arrange for some register cash and call a security expert that you heard speak at a recent Chamber of Commerce meeting who is a loss prevention professional (more on these guys later) to get advice about what to do.

You get started on cleaning up the mess and call in your management team for a meeting. It's time to sit down with a pencil, paper and some trusted people to think about and discuss what happened and what you are going to do about it.

Risk Analysis

The starting point for considering the adequacy of your security procedures and policies is to conduct an analysis of what your risk of loss is and what potential effects any given loss event could have on the survival of your business. The security expert arrived in time for the meeting and after hearing your explanation about what happened and asking a lot of questions regarding the makeup of your company begins the process by leading the group through a "What If" exercise.

Worst Case Scenario

As bad as a major theft can be, worse things really can happen. Some questions each business needs to respond to and formulate a plan can include:

• How likely are we to experience an armed robbery with a potential injury or death of employees or customers?

• What is the likelihood of a major cash theft or embezzlement of occurring?

• If a burglary occurred at one of our retail stores or warehouse facilities, how long will it take us to recover?

You know that the second item has occurred so how many smaller losses occurred before this? Is there a pattern of a lot of small losses that you have written off in the past?

Risk is the Probability and Severity of loss from exposure to a hazard, claim or crime.

SEVERITY

Catastrophic: Complete business failure due to crime loss resulting in deaths, loss of reputation and civil and or criminal liability.

Critical: Major business degradation resulting from crime related employee/ customer injury and significant business interruption.

Moderate: Minor business degradation due to crime loss and some business interruption.

Negligible: Less than minor business degradation and disruption.

The loss described in our first scenario is somewhere between moderate and critical depending how much money was in the safe. Most small to medium size business enterprises can ill afford major cash losses since profit margins are narrow and extensive cash reserves are not available to cover losses. What amount of loss would be critical to your business?

PROBABILITY

Frequent: Occurs often and business is continuously exposed.

Likely: Occurred several times in recent years and business is exposed regularly.

Occasional: Will occur periodically and has occurred sporadically in the past.

Seldom: May occur if the right conditions are present and occurred infrequently in the past.

Unlikely: So unlikely you can assume it will not occur.

Most business like yours will experience a probability factor from seldom to occasional depending on whether you have systems and controls in place to reduce exposure to loss.

ANALYZE RISK CONTROL MEASURES

After you have determined your tolerance and probability for risk, you should investigate specific strategies and tools that reduce, mitigate, or eliminate the risk. Effective control measures reduce or eliminate one of the three components (probability, severity, or exposure) of risk.

OPTIONS

Transfer:

You can buy insurance. Risk transference does not change probability or severity of the hazard, but it may decrease the probability or severity of the risk actually experienced. Risk is greatly decreased or eliminated because the possible losses or costs are shifted to another entity. Because of cost, most companies only insure for the most serious losses.

Reduce:

The overall goal of risk management is to plan operations or design systems that do not contain hazards or loss exposure. A proven order of precedence for dealing with hazards and reducing the resulting risks is:

1. Plan or Design for Minimum Risk. Design the system to eliminate hazards.

Without a hazard there is not probability, severity or exposure.

2. Incorporate Security Equipment and Devices. Reduce risk through the use of design features or devices. These devices usually do not effect probability but reduce severity. An example is that an automobile seat belt doesn't prevent a collision but reduces the severity of injuries. That's why their use is the law in most states.

3. Provide Warning Devices. Warning devices may be used to detect an undesirable condition and alert personnel. An example is to incorporate an internal audit process. If you are a public company, Sarbanes-Oxley requires audit compliance. "Inspecting what you expect", is a great prevention program, in any case.

4. Develop Procedures and Training. Even in situations where it is impractical to eliminate hazards through design selection or adequately reduce the associated risk with security equipment and warning programs, written procedures and training should be the basis of all loss barriers used.

But let's get back to the immediate need time-line. Let's face it. If you are the business owner in our loss example above, your previous planning and execution related to protecting company assets hasn't gone too well. You really need to look for some expert advice!

Along with your need for some expert advice, you can also engage in an introspective analysis to attempt to determine some of your options that you will need to explore to reduce your exposure to the loss that just occurred. And to develop a strategy to put in place systems and barriers that you need to prevent exposure to future losses.

Crime occurring at your business just did not come at you like a bolt out of the blue. It is highly likely that you have been experiencing and tolerating numerous small losses perhaps for years. For instance if you have been tolerating shrinkage in cash or assets for a significant period of time without developing programs and cost controls, you have walked away from your losses accepting them as a cost of doing business. It's your profit margin that we are talking about here.

We think that your next step in developing a cure for your loss exposure problem involves getting help from experts such as Certified Protection Professional™ loss prevention consultants and security systems hardware integrators who can help you develop a tactical response and help you prioritize what needs to be done first.

Loss prevention pros typically use business survey tools to identify whether you are missing common security hardware devices and systems known to assist prevention efforts and policies and procedures to manage them. The pros will take this data derived from answers that you provide and assist you to "connect the dots" that form a comprehensive loss prevention program including training in the effective use and management of all of your program elements.

Survey tools can take many forms, but we have identified a series of questions based on published survey standards from ASIS International that can be used by business owners to start the process by asking themselves the right questions. The devil is in the details of the interpretation of your answers to the questions, knowing what else to ask in answer follow up and determining what systems and management tools will most likely experience success in your unique business environment and culture. After all, what works for business giants like Wal-Mart may not be appropriate for your small chain of grocery stores or restaurants.

For now, we need to concentrate on the questions you need to consider and why they are important to solving the problem of loss exposure.

You Can Survey Yourself!

Here is a tool that you can use to get a good idea where you stand when it comes to systems, policies and procedures that you need and are commonly used by companies of all sizes to reduce loss exposure. You have got to start being proactive. Reactive is where you may have been and you need a plan to change direction.

The Loss Prevention Survey was developed by Security Wise Group LLC modeled on one created by ASIS International. I use this form with all new clients to get a snapshot of their crime loss vulnerability.

We like to start the process by filling in personal contact information. This information is important to us to know who's who in your company and how we can find the key decision makers when needed. When we do a survey, we are basically using it to create a profile of your company in order to get a handle on what you do, how you do it and who is in responsible charge. So our contact information page gives us the "go to" person in the organization that makes the decisions and establishes whom our primary relationship will be with.

We also use this section to identify which is the best way to communicate with our customer. We have found that many companies are very comfortable with E-mails and phone consultations. On the other hand, we have found others who will simply not reply to E-mail so it's important to make sure that the preferred lines of communications are wide open.

How do you prefer to communicate?

Our form section asking for contact information looks like the following:

Name of Company:		Primary Address:		
Type of Enterprise:		Number of Locations:		Date of Survey:
Sponsor:		Sponsor Number:		Completed by:
Name, Title, Address and Phone # for primary and secondary contacts:				
Name:	Title:	Phone:		Cell:
Address:	City:	State:	Zip:	E-Mail:
Name:	Title:	Phone:		Cell:
Address:	City:	State:	Zip:	E-Mail:

The next step after identifying those items, we begin the actual process by asking a question that is at the heart of the inquiry process. It asks you to state in terms of percentage of gross sales, how much shrinkage or inventory variance is occurring in your operations. This question is vitally important because it gives us an idea about what profits you are losing that may be available for recovery to your bottom line. Note that inventory shrinkage dollars are profit dollars.

Any percentage of sales lost to shrinkage that you can recover flows directly to your bottom line. This is so because you have already paid for the raw material or inventory acquisition, cost of production for labor, occupancy costs and everything else.

In order to serve you better, we need to know more about your existing systems.
* Your Average Unit Volume = $_____ per year.

Retail store percentage of gross sales you estimate to be "shrink" or loss. For restaurants food cost variance between actual usage (beginning vs. ending inventory) and theoretical (what you sold).
    1%   2%   3%   4%   Over 5%

What is really incredible is that when you recover shrinkage losses, top line sales numbers also grow as you are now receiving credit for the retail sales of your finished product.

Survey questions 1 - 4 asks you to determine if the business access controls are adequate to keep out unauthorized persons during periods when the business is closed and controls the access to cash and stock areas when the business is open. This section is a major opportunity for your loss prevention professional interpreting the survey to create a teaching moment with the business owner to inform them regarding state of the art key control and electronic access control systems that are available and are becoming increasingly affordable to all businesses regardless of size.

I. Physical Security
1. Describe exterior door access locks for all locations. (Electronic access control? Keyed dead bolt? Crashbar inside, cylinder outside etc.)

   _____

   _____

2. Does the ingress/egress hardware meet local and state fire code?   Yes   No
3. List all exterior door lock system corrections.   None

   _____

4. List any missing/malfunctioning interior door locks, closers, crashbars etc.

   _____

You will need to take detailed notes on a separate piece of paper regarding the current store lock systems and determine whether the systems that are being observed are the same in all of the business locations.

Take pictures or draw a diagram of all access control points. The importance here is to determine answers to the questions of whether there exists a consistent and suitable physical control of your business premises at all locations regardless of other risk factors.

It is amazing how some companies expand the number of business units and do not integrate access controls with their existing locations but simply accept whatever hardware is included in the new location. Integration of access control systems is a major tool you need for your business security and helps you get preventative maintenance program costs under control. Written policies are needed to set rules and expectations needed to maintain the integrity of the system. No sense in locking the doors, if you don't know where all of your keys are. Worse, they may be in the possession of a dishonest ex-employee.

Question 5 asks whether you have written procedures in place to manage your key control systems. We have provided some examples in the lock related sections of this book and you're either in control or your not.

---

5. Written polices are in place to enforce key control and access rules.   Yes   No

---

Questions 6 & 7 pertain to money safes. A "rated safe" means a UL rated safe that is burglary rated and not just fire rated. Electronic time delay safes have paid for themselves many times over, in our experience, by allowing the programming of individual combinations, unauthorized lock-out windows and an audit feature that allows the owner/operator of the business to identify who entered the safe and when. Protecting your cash and high value inventory with the proper equipment is a key loss prevention element when correctly managed by well-designed written policies and procedures.

---

6. A burglary rated safe is in each location that handles money or valuables.   Yes   No
7. All safes are electronic time lock that are programmed to allow individual combinations.   Yes   No

---

Questions 8 - 10 ask about burglar alarm protection, a basic need in all businesses. Unfortunately, in our experience, many of these systems are improperly installed and maintained creating virtual havoc in the form of false alarms and monitoring company calls to the business owner at 3:00 AM. False alarms are a huge expense to public law enforcement and many police departments will eventually not respond to alarm calls if you have many false alarms. In fact, the owner usually starts receiving citations and fines if the problem is not corrected.

8. Is there a burglar alarm in each location?   Yes   No
9. Does the system adequately protect the building interior after close?   Yes   No
10. List the name of the alarm monitoring company for all locations.

Your security professional can help you determine if the system is functional and protects the areas of the buildings where cash and valuables are kept. Our rule of thumb is that protection should start at the money safe and radiate outward from that point and include detection sensors covering pathways leading to the safe.

Exterior doors should be contacted and large open areas covered by PIR (passive infrared) sensors. A strobe light and siren should be located near the front of the building to alert passerby and police.

Each business has different protection requirements and some alarm service providers are proficient and some are not. We recommend that you obtain the name of the current provider along with information about when any existing contracts expire. We go into a lot of detail in a later chapter about alarm service providers.

Installing, upgrading and replacing the company alarm system often becomes necessary over time as electronic systems reach the end of their useful life. It is certainly time to reevaluate your system if you have experienced a loss and the intrusion detection and notification tasks failed. If you have contractual agreements with an alarm service provider and wish to switch alarm companies, your security professional will advise you whether it is feasible depending on who owns the system and when contracts are scheduled to expire.

Questions 11 - 15 addresses the fact that there is no question that if your business handles cash, a point of sale cash register system is a must. The equipment can be virtually worthless, however, if written policies and procedures are not in place governing how cash is to be handled. The implementation of rules is necessary in order to set expectations and to create an audit trail so that individuals can be held accountable in the event of a shortage or loss.

II. Cash Controls
11. The business has an electronic POS system to record sales activity.   Yes   No
12. The business has written cash control policies.   Yes   No
13. Managers and employees are trained and acknowledged written policies.   Yes   No
14. Register sales activity flows to a back of the house manager's workstation.   Yes   No
15. All operators have their own cash drawer.   Yes   No

Questions 16-20 are related to your use of CCTV systems which are another basic business system needed to protect store assets and can be a deterrent to theft, robbery and false accident claims. It needs to be stated that there are a lot of poor quality camera systems hanging on company walls out there. Unfortunately some companies think they can save money by installing "dummy" or non-working cameras that are worthless at prevention and actually increase your liability exposure. If poor equipment is used, improperly installed or not maintained, the systems are a huge waste of money and can expose you to expensive litigation in the event that a customer injury occurs on your property and the presence of the surveillance equipment provides an expectation that the system is monitored.

---

16. Each location has a CCTV system.   Yes   No

17. Cameras and recording is digital (DVR).   Yes   No

18. List what locations are viewed. (i.e. Registers, back door, office, sales area, outside lots etc.)

_____

19. List locations not covered that should be.

_____

20. Written procedures are in place related to the use of CCTV equipment and operation of the DVR/Recorder.   Yes   No

---

You can see for yourself whether the system is working and whether recorded records are maintained for a sufficient time frame needed to review incidents that occur on your property that may not be reported in a timely manner.

The good news is that there are many very good affordable digital camera systems available that will make you very happy the first time you are able to use the system to catch a thief or thwart a false slip and fall claim. The key opportunity here is to take the plunge and make use of this tool to better manage your business.

The purpose of the next 3 **questions 21 - 23** is to determine if the business has written security procedures governing employee actions in the event of theft, burglary, robbery, altercations, trespassers etc.

---

21. This business has written security procedures. (i.e. theft, burglary, robbery prevention and response, disturbances, trespass, etc.)   Yes   No

22. Does this company employ security personnel?   Yes   No

23. If Yes, are they in-house or contract. If contract, name of company providing service.

_____

Without these policies in place, the business is exposed to civil liability if reasonable care is not performed to protect customers and employees. Your loss prevention experts have a number of programs available to help you establish a security procedures and response plan.

Identified use of security personnel, such as guards, in any of the business' locations, will be responded to with a recommended review by our company when we make our recommendations to our customers. Guards are expensive, often inefficient and can cause more problems then they solve if not managed properly.

There are many cost effective alternatives such as remotely monitored interactive video systems that have personnel respond verbally online and view any reported disturbance when an alarm button is pressed.

The HR Section **questions 24 through 32** is another important place where you need you to look at some issues that you may not have addressed before. This section relates to specific issues that will make or break a security and loss prevention program. Most of the losses occurring in your business are due to employees' actions or omissions. If you're not paying attention to HR basics and employees are not accountable due to lack of policies and procedures, losses will surely occur.

III. Human Resource issues

24. Does this business have a person assigned to HR/Benefits?   Yes   No
25. If Yes, are HR issues handled in-house or with a contract company. List contract company.

_____
26. The business has issued an employee handbook.   Yes   No
27. Is there a written disciplinary action policy?   Yes   No
28. The company conducts new hire orientation where all company policies, procedures and rules are explained.   Yes   No
29. Employees and managers receive a copy of the rules and sign an acknowledgement form.   Yes   No
30. A back ground investigation is conducted on all new employees.   Yes   No
31. A background investigation is conducted for managers/supervisors.   Yes   No
32. Workers Compensation and customer claims are centrally reported to an assigned person and logged.   Yes   No

---

As loss prevention experts, our response to a "No" answer to any of these questions will be to offer the needed resources to correct the problem.

The last two **questions 33 and 34** relate to business safety programs. This is another area that you may not have addressed previously that is a business cost control opportunity of enormous proportions.

Customer Liability and Workers Compensation claim cost is an immediate hot button for every business regardless of size. Claims costs and insurance premium costs are out of control continuing in an upward spiral at a rate of 20% per year. There are a number of solutions that you will find in the safety section of this book that you can use to rein in some of these costs.

33. The business has a written safety policy/program in place.   Yes   No
34. Safety hazards are identified and corrected using an inspection report process.   Yes   No

We will be providing you, for instance, with some solutions to high Workers Compensation claims frequency through organized safety programs. This effort typically reduces claims significantly and eventually can reduce your insurance costs. Organized safety inspections that we will show you, can identify hazards that when corrected, reduce loss exposure and finally you will learn that the camera system that you may find hard to justify for crime loss is on an easy pay back track when used to dispute phony claims.

After you have written down all of the information that we have asked on our survey, you probably have a pretty good idea by now about the direction your loss prevention experts will be taking as they analyze what you need to do to start doing a better job of protecting your people and assets. It will also be pretty obvious to you, as well, after you complete the exercise.

Asking and answering a lot of questions about your vulnerability to crime loss is an important beginning to the process of creating the barriers to loss that you need to incorporate. The hard part is the art of interpreting the answers and determining if the lack of a particular piece of equipment or a policy really can impact your ability to protect your business.

You can see the actual complete form that we use for all of our initial site surveys on the next two pages. Feel free to tear it out of the book and photo copy it. Or drop me a request through our website (www.securitywisegroup.com), and I will E-mail a copy to you as a PDF file.

Invite your management team to survey the business with you. They will likely be more objective and thorough versus you doing it alone!

SWG® Security Wise Group LLC
Loss Prevention Consultants

Loss Prevention Survey© (Rev. 1/2009)

Organization Information:

Name of Company:	Primary Address:	
Type of Enterprise:	Number of Locations:	Date of Application:
Application Sponsor:	Sponsor Number:	Completed by:

Name, Title, Address and Phone # for primary and secondary contacts:

Name:	Title:	Phone:		Cell:
Address:	City:	State:	Zip:	E-Mail:
Name:	Title:	Phone:		Cell:
Address:	City:	State:	Zip:	E-Mail:

In order to serve you better, we need to know more about your existing systems.
* Your Average Unit Volume = $_____ per year.

Retail store percentage of gross sales you estimate to be "shrink" or loss. For restaurants food cost variance between actual usage (beginning vs. ending inventory) and theoretical (what you sold).

1% ☐   2% ☐   3% ☐   4% ☐   Over 5% ☐

I.   Physical Security

1. Describe exterior door access locks for all locations. (electronic access control? Keyed deadbolt? Crashbar inside, cylinder outside etc.)

_____

2. Does the ingress/egress hardware meet local and state fire code?   Yes ☐   No ☐
3. List all exterior door lock system corrections.   None ☐

_____

4. List any missing/malfunctioning interior door locks, closers, crashbars etc.

_____

5. Written polices are in place to enforce key control and access rules. Yes ☐   No ☐
6. A burglary rated safe is in each location that handles money or valuables. Yes ☐   No ☐
7. All safes are electronic time lock that are programmed to allow individual combinations. Yes ☐   No ☐
8. Is there a burglar alarm in each location? Yes ☐   No ☐
9. Does the system adaquately protect the building interior after close? Yes ☐   No ☐
10. List the name of the alarm monitoring company for all locations.

_____

II.   Cash Controls

11. The business has an electronic POS system to record sales activity. Yes ☐ No ☐
12. The business has written cash control policies.   Yes ☐ No ☐

13. Managers and employees are trained and acknowledged written policies.   Yes ☐ No ☐
14. Register sales activity flows to a back of the house manager's workstation?   Yes ☐ No ☐
15. All operators have their own cash drawer.   Yes ☐ No ☐
16. Each location has a CCTV system.   Yes ☐   No ☐
17. Cameras and recording is digital (DVR).   Yes ☐   No ☐
18. List what locations are viewed. (i.e. Registers, back door, office, sales area, outside lots etc.)

_____

19. List locations not covered that should be.

_____

20. Written procedures are in place related to the use of CCTV equipment and operation
    of the DVR/Recorder.   Yes ☐   No ☐
21. This business has written security procedures. (i.e. Theft, burglary, robbery prevention and
    response, disturbances, trespass, etc.)   Yes ☐   No ☐
22. Does this company employ security personnel?   Yes ☐   No ☐
23. If Yes, are they in-house or contract. If contract, name of company providing service.

_____

III.   Human Resource issues

24. Does this business have a person assigned to HR/Benefits?   Yes ☐   No ☐
25. If Yes, are HR issues handled in-house or with a contract company. List contract company.

_____

26. The business has issued an employee handbook.   Yes ☐   No ☐
27. Is there a written disciplinary action policy?   Yes ☐   No ☐
28. The company conducts new hire orientation where all company policies, procedures and
    rules are explained.   Yes ☐   No ☐
29. Employees and managers receive a copy of the rules and sign an acknowledgement form.
    Yes ☐   No ☐
30. A back ground investigation is conducted on all new employees.   Yes ☐   No ☐
31. A background investigation is conducted for managers/supervisors.   Yes ☐   No ☐
32. Workers Compensation and customer claims are centrally reported to an assigned person
    and logged.   Yes ☐   No ☐
33. The business has a written safety policy/program in place.   Yes ☐   No ☐
34. Safety hazards are identified and corrected using an inspection report process.   Yes ☐   No ☐

This survey is general in nature since no survey can address all of the vulnerabilities of various types of business enterprises. However, many businesses experience losses due to common reasons. The purpose of this survey is to identify possible control weaknesses that may be decreasing profits. Security Wise Group®, will provide a written response outlining the control issues we find, along with programs available that can help you recover some of your profits. The survey is for planning purposes only, and no other warranties or guarantees are made or implied that you will recover losses and no survey can address all of the loss prevention issues facing your business.

As part of our continuing service to our SWG® member companies, an in-depth system audit is available on a fee per service plus expense basis.

Signature of Business Representative: _____ **Date:** _____

Signature of Security Specialist: _____ **Date:** _____

When you have completed the survey, you may have identified a number of missing or perhaps incomplete loss prevention systems, policies, procedures or electronic systems that have been found to be key elements of any loss prevention program. Your next steps include listing these items under the proper heading in the following exercise.

An exercise you can use to identify and analyze your organization positives and negatives is called a "SWOT" analysis. This model is very basic but can ask some very important questions that you need to have answered before you can identify all of the elements of a successful loss prevention plan. It can be especially effective when operations management and your key employees get involved in the process. You will find that the results can give you a lot more information that you need to make planning changes that your organization may need to move forward in order to be more competitive and profitable. It's called working together or "Synergy" a combined effect greater than their separate effects. It fact this process is a useful tool for a lot of business planning purposes like sales and marketing strategy sessions.

We suggest that you and your assembled management team each take out a piece of paper and pencil and answer the following questions. Write this down, it's important.

In fact you may find it best to use the "Brainstorming" approach of completing your lists on flip chart paper and tape the completed sheets on the wall for reference while you consider the action plan that you need to complete.

SWOT = Strengths – Weaknesses – Opportunities – Threats

The "S" represents the question where you make a list of your "Strengths". What do you do really well? For instance, do you have detailed and written policies and procedures that you use to guide employee behavior and identify accountabilities? How about a written employee manual that is used for every new hire orientation? Do you have well maintained physical barriers like an access control system, cameras and good lighting? What do you have in place now to protect yourself against criminal acts? List them all now on the flip chart.

List your technical skills and those within your organization. What are you really good at? Have you leveraged your skills to position your business ahead of the competition in the areas of employee development and training? Do you have good accounting and point of sales information?

When you are done with this first section, most of you will have a pretty extensive list of all of the things that you know how to do really well. The list represents your competitive advantage in the marketplace. The question is "Does all of this translate into a viable defense against losses?" The answer will shape what you need to focus on in your loss prevention plan.

The "W" is the question of what your competitive weaknesses are. We have every hope that this will be the shortest list in your analysis, but you really need to be brutally honest with yourself when writing down what your weaknesses are. Think, "worst case scenario". Can you prevent a catastrophic loss from occurring? If not, can you rapidly respond to mitigate further losses and damage?

This list will certainly include any barriers that exist that prevent you from being able to effectively protect your organization from criminal attack. Perhaps it is an issue of financing or lack of necessary training, equipment or knowledge of how to execute protection strategies. What are you not doing that is allowing your risk exposure to continue?

The answers to your negative attributes will prompt you to ask important questions. Is it time to analyze how your capital is allocated? Should you be spending more or less on purchasing, replacing and upgrading security equipment? Should you be looking at what needs to happen to grow your businesses loss prevention skills to be able to respond to technological changes that will benefit the safety of your employees? Should your next hire be a specialist in skills that your organization does not currently have in the area of systems audit and information technology? Does your management team need to acquire more personal management skills or technical skills?

The "O" asks you to identify what unrealized Opportunities exist on your radar. Even the most mature organization in terms of longevity and experience can develop a blind side and miss obvious opportunities. The missed opportunity can actually be telegraphed to our customers and our employees with some undesired results,

For instance, we know several companies that perform a stellar job of attracting good employees but often fail to provide the right amount of skills training in a new hire orientation program. Others spend extravagant amounts of money on security equipment that a salesman made them fall in love with but then fail to use it in a systematic way expecting it to work on it's own by Magic. If you have the tools in place are you making them work for you? Are all of your tools capable of being integrated into other operating systems to become part of the whole?

We have noticed businesses that simply do not want to deal with electronic security components. Whether it is a skill based issue – a little phobia about computers - or just is outside of the normal work comfort zone and they do not want to take the time to use it. The opportunity list, hopefully, will be as long and varied as your strengths list and should urge the question of "If we're not going after protecting a significant piece of the business profit pie, why not?" Missed opportunities beg for a complete analysis of whether current resources can be used to go after the prize. Has the enterprise developed the flexibility to change when they need to on their own initiative or are they forced to try new processes and technology as a survival mechanism?

The "T" asks the question to identify all of the Threats that can make the enterprise fail at worst and merely show modestly declined revenue and profits at best. The list of what can go wrong can be endless and tedious but must be recognized so that a countering strategy can be put in place. It is rather like investing in the financial market. A good balance of stocks and bonds can protect your assets from large swings in the marketplace.

You should always start an organizational threat list with the worst-case scenarios. Start with catastrophic loss due to a fire, a robbery with injuries involved, and a major theft of assets or weather event like a flood. Don't forget to add the entire next tier of possible losses due to potential exposure to traffic accidents involving one of your trucks, serious Workers Compensation or customer liability claim, a crime loss to your business, liability exposure resulting in your being sued for either something that you did, or worse, failed to do.

So you have completed the four lists and surrounded by your managers and trusted key employees you can now ask the necessary questions about what you need to do to create an environment where change isn't quite as frightening and progress to a specific list of potential actions and list multiple activities that address what needs to be done, who will do it and when the activity will be completed.

By the way, did you know that 30% of all business bankruptcies are a result of employee theft or embezzlement? This list should give the business owner pause to consider whether potential losses are either insured against _and_ exposure reduced through sound company policies, procedures and work rules that you have initiated to protect your investment. You have done that, right?

"Fidelity/Crime Insurance" sometimes referred to as "Bonding", protects organizations from loss of money, securities, or inventory resulting from crime. Common Fidelity/Crime insurance claims allege employee dishonesty, embezzlement, forgery, robbery, safe burglary, computer fraud, wire transfer fraud, counterfeiting, and other criminal acts.

These schemes involve every possible angle, taking advantage of any potential weakness in your company's financial controls. From fictitious employees, dummy accounts payable, non-existent suppliers to outright theft of money, securities and property. Fraud and embezzlement in the workplace is on the rise, occurring in even the best work environments.

Any business employer needs to be concerned with Employee Dishonesty or any business handing cash or securities needs protection from robbery or theft will need Fidelity/Crime Insurance. Because crime-related losses are not typically covered by most property insurance policies, crime protection insurance is a necessary component for any business.

Unfortunately, the majority of businesses don't purchase enough crime protection. If yours is like the average U.S. business, you can expect to lose 6 percent of your total annual revenues to employee fraud. And most business insurance policies either exclude or provide only nominal amounts of coverage for loss of money and securities as well as employee dishonesty exposures.

According to a recent study by the Association of Certified Fraud Examiners (ACFE). It estimates the average business is losing six percent of its total annual revenue from losses involving employees — that's on average more than $9 per day per employee.

Fraud and embezzlement in the workplace is on the rise, occurring in even the best work environments. Some of these frauds that we talk about in this book went on for years, and when discovered the ultimate impact was enormous. Smaller companies and non-profits as we will show you, are especially vulnerable to Fidelity crimes.

White collar crime can have serious financial consequences, even threatening a private company's survival. To put it bluntly: it is the loyal, long term, conscientious and trusted employee whose dishonesty can put you out of business. The programmer who never takes a vacation and is never sick. The long term employee who is "just like family." Let's face it. Only employees like this really have the opportunity steal over a long period of time. Only employees like these can take enough to jeopardize the financial survival of your firm.

The prevention programs that you put in place will determine whether this can happen again!

The liabilities covered by fidelity insurance coverage are:

* Money and Security Coverage - Covers losses due to burglary and destruction.
* Employee Dishonesty Coverage - Covers losses due to dishonesty of employees.

Many insurance policies combine both these categories. Business can opt for either a mono line policy for customized liability coverage or a package policy offered by insurance agencies. The premium for crime insurance coverage is decided by the insurance agencies based on the crime loss track record of the organization. A small-to-mid-sized organization pays an average premium of about $1000 for a $100,000 insurance coverage. Most of the insurance agency's that provide this type of coverage have websites and online forms, where details of the business can be entered for the approximate premium to be calculated.

It's good to remember, however, that insurance is just a component of your loss prevention program. There is no single strategy "Silver Bullet" to protect your business.

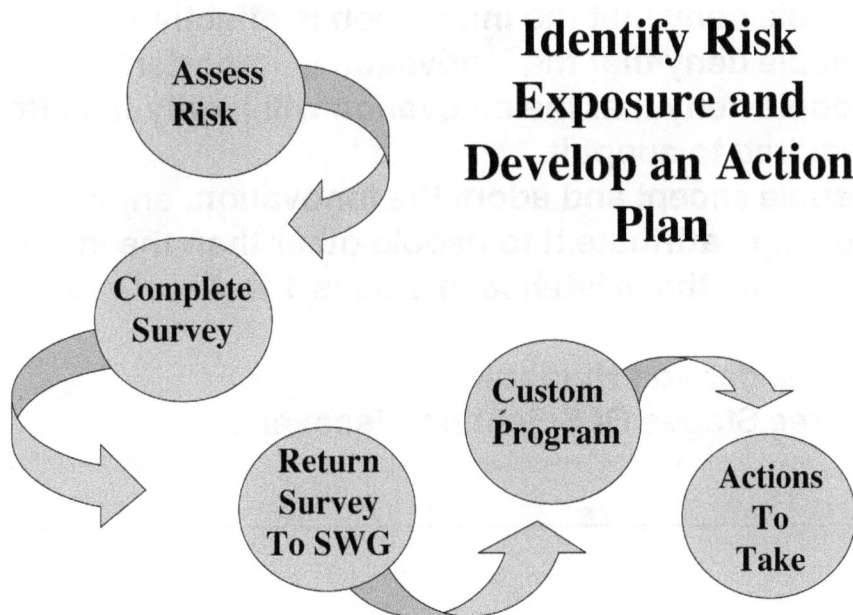

Identify Risk Exposure and Develop an Action Plan

Assess Risk

Complete Survey

Return Survey To SWG

Custom Program

Actions To Take

The five stages of innovation

1. People deny that the innovation is required.
2. People deny that the innovation is effective.
3. People deny that the innovation is important.
4. People deny that the innovation will justify the effort required to adopt it.
5. People accept and adopt the innovation, enjoy its benefits, attribute it to people other than the innovator, and deny the existence of stages 1 to 4.

Alexander von Humboldt
'Three Stages Of Scientific Discovery'

"An investment in knowledge always
pays the best interest."

Benjamin Franklin
US author, diplomat, inventor, physicist,
politician, & printer (1706 - 1790)

When we tell you to get some "Expert" advice, we mean that you need to locate a Certified Protection Professional (CPP) who has been board certified by the American Society For Industrial Security (ASIS-International). This organization is over 50 years old and has been recognized as the leading creator of national standards related to loss prevention management and has created the CPP certification to recognize education and experience achievement for security professionals.

ASIS International (ASIS) is the largest organization for security professionals, with more than 33,000 members worldwide. Founded in 1955, ASIS is dedicated to increasing the effectiveness and productivity of security professionals by developing educational programs and materials that address broad security interests, such as the ASIS Annual Seminar and Exhibits, as well as specific security topics. ASIS also advocates the role and value of the security management profession to business, the media, governmental entities, and the public.

Staff loss prevention managers in large companies are generally expected to have the CPP designation and provide the expertise that they need to reduce crime losses and claims. You probably need one too but cannot afford the $150 thousand a year to have one of these people on your staff.

Not to worry. You can acquire the expertise on an outsource basis when you need it, for as long as you need it, for a lot less.

In 2007, ASIS International, the preeminent society for security management professionals, was awarded accreditation by the American National Standards Institute (ANSI), the U.S. member of the International Organization for Standardization (ISO). This prestigious endorsement confirms that ASIS's international certification programs adhere to the highest professional standards.

The accreditation for the Certified Protection Professional Program confirms that ASIS complies with ISO/IEC 17024, a voluntary international standard for organizations responsible for certification of persons. It is a means of providing assurance that certified personnel meet the published requirements of a given certification program. More than 300,000 professionals around the world currently hold certifications from organizations accredited under ISO/IEC 17024.

Aside from the initial rigorous process of obtaining the ANSI accreditation, ASIS's certification programs must be annually assessed, audited and undergo a thorough on-site review of its management systems and procedures.

Thousands of security practitioners have earned ASIS's CPP certification, the highest recognition accorded a security professional, since its introduction in 1977. The CPP exam is now administered in 30 countries around the world.

In addition to obtaining the ANSI accreditation, ASIS's professional certification program is the first and only program of its kind to be awarded a coveted designation by the U.S. Department of Homeland Security under the Support Anti-Terrorism by Fostering Effective Technology Act of 2002 (SAFETY Act).

The ASIS certification program is the first and only program of its kind to be awarded a coveted Designation by the U.S. Department of Homeland Security (DHS) under the Support Anti-Terrorism by Fostering Effective Technology (SAFETY) Act of 2002.

What is the SAFETY Act?

The purpose of the SAFETY Act is to ensure that the threat of liability does not deter manufacturers of anti-terrorism technologies from developing and commercializing new products that could significantly reduce the risks or effects of terrorist events. Companies that supply products and services that can be used to detect, defend against, or respond to acts of terrorism can apply for and receive coverage under the law.

Although this legislation was largely intended for product manufacturers, ASIS took the unprecedented step of convincing DHS that the legislation also should apply to non-traditional products and services, specifically ASIS guidelines and certification programs. This ground breaking initiative on behalf of ASIS members and other security practitioners has had beneficial outcomes in both arenas, with guidelines receiving the SAFETY Act Designation in May 2005; certification in July 2006 after two years of effort.

What does this mean?

The SAFETY Act Designation gives ASIS board-certified professionals, their employers, and their customers immediate protection from lawsuits involving ASIS certification and the ASIS certification process that arise out of an act of terrorism. Not only does it limit the types of liability claims that can be brought against a certificant, but it also entitles the certificant to immediate dismissal of those specific types of claims. Employers of ASIS certified practitioners also gain protection against terror-related liability claims that can include a presumption of dismissal from a lawsuit.

What does this mean for employers of ASIS board-certified personnel?

In addition to the many benefits of having ASIS board-certified practitioners on staff, the scope of liability protection granted by DHS is a significant corporate benefit that can be used as an integral part of business strategy.

While the SAFETY Act will not prevent all terror-related claims against employers of personnel holding an ASIS certification, it should limit the types of claims that can be brought against them, thereby reducing the threat of onerous lawsuits.

The Certified Protection Professional educational program bestows these security experts with a significant ability to help those that employ them reduce liability exposure when defending against allegations of inadequate security in the context of premises liability litigation. While the act relates to acts of terrorism, it is clear that utilizing the certification defense as stated in the description of The SAFETY Act of 2002, will certainly extend to cases where criminal attacks have occurred on private property.

In our opinion, this all means that if you have your company Loss Prevention Program designed by a Certified Protection Professional, you will be able to mitigate a lot of liability exposure against allegations of negligent security claims. At the least, your due diligence in employing expert advice will be difficult to dispute and you usually get sued for what the plaintiff says you did not do versus what you did in many of these third party liability cases.

We will refer to these people a number of times through out this book and it is now time to offer you an important piece of advice related to installing and using security equipment. Namely, who should you trust to install your locks and electronic security solutions?

You really don't have the time, patience and skill to find people with all of these lock, camera, safe and alarm skill sets and check the quality of their work. With a little diligence and the help of your CPP loss prevention consultant, you can find a company that provides systems integration service that addresses all of your security issues. They will take the responsibility of all installation and repair project management.

A number of assumptions apply.

First of all, they recognize that your installations must be done by a competent company that understands your business and shares your sense of urgency and budget sensitivity.

Secondly, your vendors must be competent to install and service all of your systems and understand how they can fit together to further enhance your security program.

Finally they should be considered a trusted partner company that has demonstrated that they will be around for a while and are always readily available to respond to emergencies and supply workable solutions that make sense in a timely manner.

The independent local locksmith that you may have used in the past for emergency repair or re-key can fix your locks, service your safes and install mechanical hardware but may not be able to provide you with an integrated patented key-control system and manage the key records for all of your locations.

While some locksmith firms can install a camera system or a stand-alone electronic access control, they typically do not work on alarms. They may not have the systems expertise that you need to put a total program together and be able to train your staff.

On the other hand, like the locksmith trades, alarm companies install and monitor your burglar and fire alarm systems and many will often install cameras and card readers, but most cannot fix your locks or handle safe emergencies. They may also not be in the position of being able to package the systems that you need and provide training.

Your CPP loss prevention professional has the experience to help you to identify your best alternatives for addressing loss vulnerabilities and give you assistance in developing a time line plan to put the program into motion so you can coordinate the efforts of various providers.

Most importantly, your CPP has the expertise to help you to write and implement policies and procedures that you need to ensure the best use of your equipment and to hold your employees accountable for maintaining and supporting your company loss prevention efforts.

One topic that has to be addressed for due diligence, is to try to determine who could have used a key to your building and carted your safe away. If you do not have a key register of all former and existing key holders, your primary resource is the local police department whom you have called to solve the case.

A few words about your expectations related to the results of their investigation. In our scenario, there was little in the way of physical and forensic evidence to aid in closing the case. Failure to enforce a key control policy has resulted in a broad list of suspects and the investigating detective may not even be able to find them all in order to question them. It doesn't look good. You case will soon gravitate to the back burner of the detective's case-load if some results are not forthcoming in a short period of time.

Your CPP can assist by contacting the local police to determine if they need assistance or can otherwise share information about possible suspects. Your expert can also interview employees to determine whether they have knowledge about the crime or of other vulnerabilities in you business that have not been addressed yet.

Your loss prevention professional can assess your company operations and give you, on a fee for service basis, a major jump-start by:

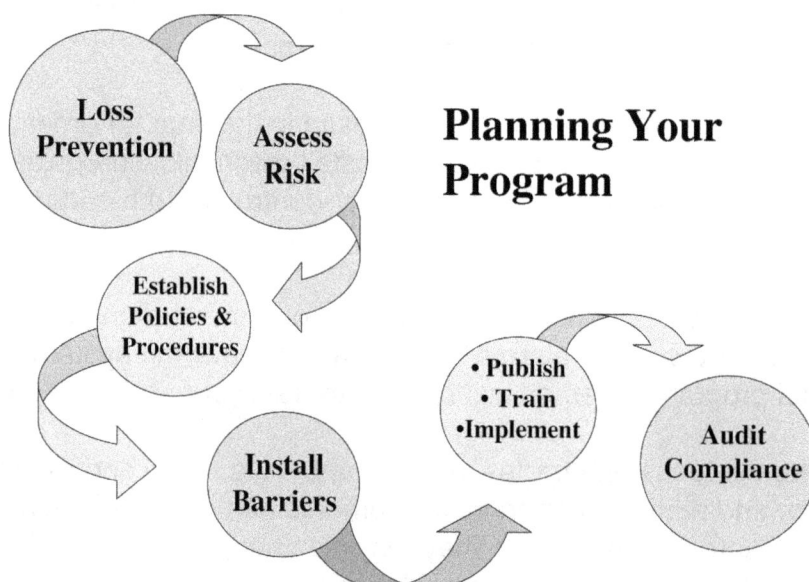

Planning Your Program

1.   Conducting a loss prevention survey observing the latest industry guidelines to identify missing, outdated or ineffective programs, policies and equipment.

2.   Presenting recommendations for the creation of policies and procedures and recommendations regarding security hardware that you need.

3.   Helping you to create an implementation plan that you can use to introduce the needed components of a new loss prevention program using a cost effective and affordable time-line.

4.   Assisting you with the creation of the program written elements such as manuals and handbooks and assist your people with implementation.

5.   Acting as the project manager, if required, to assist you or directly participate in the program roll-out.

6.   Provide you with on-going expertise that you need if your program hits a snag or you experience a loss and need advice regarding how to proceed. You need this support for the same reasons that you need the expertise of accountants and human resource experts.

Assessing Crime Risks

Part of the task of getting expert help in dealing with a crime loss problem that you are having is getting information about crime statistics in your area. The existence and availability of crime trends is a key piece of information that you need to proceed with your loss prevention plan.

If you have already had a serious violent or property crime at one of your operating units or company owned property, you now have the additional knowledge of "forseeability". That means, if you never saw a crime loss coming at you before, now you do. In other words, the conditions that could have contributed to the event such as poor lighting, poor cash controls or lack of cameras and other deterrents, now have to be addressed and corrected. The last thing that you need is to have one serious crime loss become a pattern of losses and potentially have to defend why you didn't fix the problem after the first time.

A major question that you will be asked and have to defend at any premises liability claim or litigation, was whether the crime was foreseeable, that is did you know or should you have known it could happen and did you provide reasonable care to prevent it from occurring. The average business is usually able to defend their efforts to protect customers and employees in a reasonable manner because for the most part they have not experienced serious violent crimes on their property.

You will be asked whether you were aware of the crime rate in your immediate neighborhood, especially if the rate of violent crime is relatively high in your area. In the case of a liability litigation, the plaintiffs attorney will likely show you a print out a mile long showing every call that the local police precinct responded to at your business and maybe throw the net out even wider and include everything within a mile of your business. The plaintiffs' attorney will have every police response to a crime call highlighted (in red).

If you have a fairly high number of calls to the police for assistance for help with shoplifters, vagrants or disturbances, Plaintiff will attempt to link these incidents both minor and otherwise as proof of a high crime rate and the requirement therefore of a higher level of protection and care. The purpose of this maneuver is to show that the proximate cause of their injury was your failure to meet the standard of care established by the existence of a high crime rate.

However, even if you have never been a crime victim, how about the surrounding businesses in your area? It is more than possible to end up being tarred by the same brush because if the neighborhood has a crime problem, you should have known that it could happen to you as well.

All the more reason to find out what your risk level is in comparison to your immediate area as well as your city and state and the national average rates for comparison. There are a number of ways that your CPP loss prevention professional will proceed to get this information.

General numbers for national, State and city crime rates are available as part of the FBI's annual numbers round up called the "Uniform Crime Report" (UCR). You can go online to the website: www,fbi.gov/ucr and go right to all of the information about both violent as well as property crimes.

To find your city crime rate, select the city option and on the next page select your state, and finally you can scroll down the list and find your city or town. For instance, we selected the city of Philadelphia and found the following listing of crime for the year 2005. The crime stats are updated each year and the numbers run a year behind current trends.

Population	1,472,000
Total violent crime	21,609
Homicide	377
Rape	1,024
Robbery	10,069
Aggravated Assault	10,139
Total Property Crimes	60,419
Burglary	10,960
Larceny	38,039
Motor Vehicle	11,420

The UCR reports are a treasure trove of other information such as where the crimes occur and under what circumstances.

For instance this about robbery:

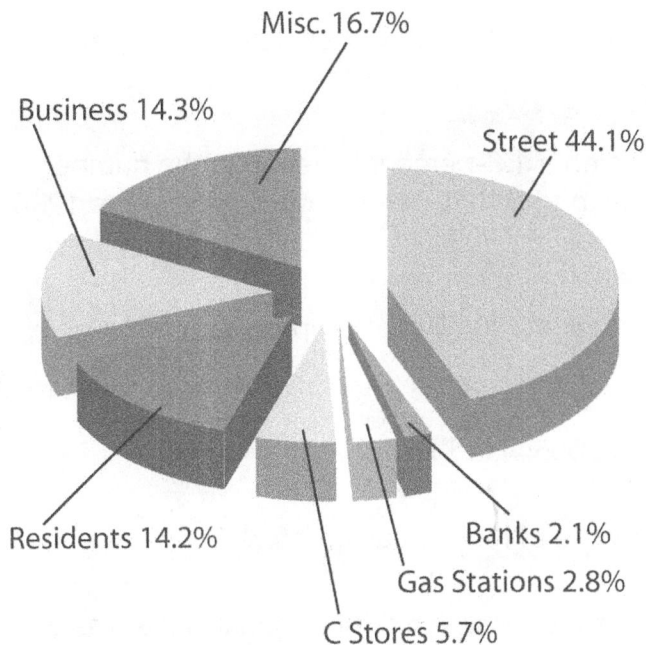

Misc. 16.7%

Business 14.3%

Street 44.1%

Residents 14.2%

Banks 2.1%

Gas Stations 2.8%

C Stores 5.7%

Definition

The Uniform Crime Reporting (UCR) Program defines robbery as the taking or attempting to take anything of value from the care, custody, or control of a person or persons by force or threat of force or violence and/or by putting the victim in fear.

Overview

• Nationwide in 2005, there were an estimated 417,122 robbery offenses.

• In terms of robbery trends, robbery had the largest percentage increase, 3.9 percent, in the estimated number of offenses when compared with the 2004 estimate. The estimated number of robbery offenses declined 22.1 percent in a comparison with the data from 10 years earlier (1996 and 2005).

• By location type, most robberies (44.1 percent) were committed on streets or highways.

• Firearms were used in 42.1 percent of reported robberies.

• The average dollar value of property stolen per robbery offense was $1,230. By location type, bank robbery had the highest average dollar value taken—$4,169 per offense.

And about the crime of burglary:

Definition

The Uniform Crime Reporting (UCR) Program defines burglary as the unlawful entry of a structure to commit a felony or theft. To classify an offense as a burglary, the use of force to gain entry need not have occurred. The Program has three sub-classifications for burglary: forcible entry, unlawful entry where no force is used, and attempted forcible entry. The UCR definition of "structure" includes, for example, apartment, barn, house trailer or houseboat when used as a permanent dwelling, office, railroad car (but not automobile), stable, and vessel (i.e., ship).

Overview

- In 2005, law enforcement agencies reported an estimated 2,154,126 burglary offenses—a 0.5-percent increase compared with 2004 data.

- An examination of 5- and 10-year trends revealed a 1.8-percent increase in the number of burglaries compared with the 2001 estimate, and a 14.1-percent decline from the 1996 number.

- Burglary accounted for 21.2 percent of the estimated number of property crimes committed in 2005.

- The average dollar loss per burglary offense in 2005 was $1,725.

- Of all burglary offenses in 2005, 65.8 percent were of residential structures.

- Most (62.4 percent) of residential burglaries in 2005 for which time of occurrence was known took place during the day, between 6 A.M. and 6 P.M.

- Among burglaries of nonresidential structures when time of occurrence was known, 58.0 percent occurred at night.

And this about Larceny:

Definition

The UCR Program defines larceny-theft as the unlawful taking, carrying, leading, or riding away of property from the possession or constructive possession of another. Examples are thefts of bicycles, motor vehicle parts and accessories, shoplifting, pocket-picking, or the stealing of any property or article that is not taken by force and violence or by fraud. Attempted larcenies are included. Embezzlement, confidence games, forgery, check fraud, etc., is excluded.

Overview

- There were an estimated 6.8 million (6,776,807) larceny-theft offenses nationwide during 2005.

- An examination of 2 and 10-year trends revealed a 2.3-percent decrease in the estimated number of larceny-thefts compared with the 2004 figure, and a 14.3-percent decline from the 1996 estimate.

- Two-thirds of all property crimes in 2005 were larceny-thefts.

- During 2005, there were an estimated 2,286.3 larceny-theft offenses per 100,000 inhabitants.

- From 2004 to 2005 the rate of larceny-thefts declined 3.2 percent, and from 1996 to 2005, the rate declined 23.3 percent.

- The average value for property stolen during the commission of a larceny-theft was $764 per offense.

Some Variables about how to interpret crime statistics

Until data users examine all the variables that affect crime in a town, city, county, state, region, or college or university, they can make no meaningful comparisons.

Each year when the Federal Bureau Of Investigation publishes the UCR in a document called Crime in the United States, many entities such as the news media use reported figures to compile rankings of cities and counties. These rankings, however, are merely a quick choice made by the data user. You need to be aware, that they provide no insight into the many variables that make up the true picture of crime in a particular town, city, county, state, or region.

Using these rankings by themselves can lead to a simplistic or incomplete analyses that often create misleading perceptions just like the plaintiffs attorney has used to try and convince the jury that you are located in a crime ridden area and you have not done the required job to protect his client from harm. The reality can be quite different when you add in other important information

You need to consider other characteristics

As the FBI puts it: "To assess criminality and law enforcement's response from jurisdiction to jurisdiction, one must consider many variables, some of which, while having significant impact on crime, are not readily measurable or applicable pervasively among all locales. Geographic and demographic factors specific to each jurisdiction must be considered and applied if one is going to make an accurate and complete assessment of crime in that jurisdiction. Several sources of information are available that may assist the responsible researcher in exploring the many variables that affect crime in a particular locale. The U.S. Census Bureau data, for example, can be used to better understand the makeup of a locale's population. The transience of the population, its racial and ethnic makeup, its composition by age and gender, educational levels, and prevalent family structures are all key factors in assessing and comprehending the crime issue."

Local chambers of commerce, planning offices, or similar entities provide information regarding the economic and cultural makeup of cities and counties. Understanding a jurisdiction's industrial/economic base; its dependence upon neighboring jurisdictions; its transportation system; its economic dependence on nonresidents (such as tourists and convention attendees); its proximity to military installations, correctional facilities, etc., all contribute to accurately gauging and interpreting the crime known to and reported by law enforcement.

As we all know instinctively almost, certain parts of every town appear to be more dangerous than others. If your business is surrounded by liquor stores, bars and tattoo parlors and you are in a generally disadvantaged part of town lacking services and amenities enjoyed elsewhere, you know that it may not be safe to travel alone at night for most people. We know it instinctively because poverty and lack of opportunity breeds crime.

However, take the same neighborhood and plant a local police precinct in the middle along with new street lights and the crime rate will be greatly reduced or modified as the usual group of suspects are displaced outward by all of the police activity.

That means that the strength and the aggressiveness of your local law enforcement agency are also key factors in understanding the nature and extent of crime occurring in that area. Although information pertaining to the number of sworn and civilian employees can be found in the UCR publication, it cannot be used alone as an assessment of the emphasis that your community places on enforcing the law.

For example, one city may report more crime than a comparable one, not because there is more crime, but rather because its law enforcement agency through proactive efforts identifies more offenses. Conversely, we can tell you that in the past, some agencies have purposely either miss- categorized or otherwise under-reported certain crimes that the local politicians have deemed to be bad for the city's reputation.

In Philadelphia in the 1970's under Mayor Frank Rizzo, it was common to underreport violent crimes. More recently the Philadelphia Police Department was scandalized when it became apparent that rape crimes were being categorized as unfounded or "other" and were subsequently unsolved.

Attitudes of the citizens toward crime and their crime reporting practices, especially concerning minor offenses, also have an impact of the volume of crimes known to police.

Making better judgments about your crime rate

You need the help of your CPP loss prevention expert to become as well educated as possible about how to understand and quantify the nature and extent of crime in your own environment in order to make rational decisions about how to protect yourself, your employees and your assets.

Valid assessments are possible only with careful study and analysis of the various unique conditions affecting each local law enforcement jurisdiction.

Historically, the causes and origins of crime have been the subjects of investigation by many disciplines. Some factors that are known to affect the volume and type of crime occurring from place to place are:

- Population density and degree of urbanization.

- Variations in composition of the population, particularly youth concentration.

- Stability of the population with respect to residents' mobility, commuting patterns, and transient factors.

- Modes of transportation and highway system.

- Economic conditions, including median income, poverty level, and job availability.

- Cultural factors and educational, recreational, and religious characteristics.

- Family conditions with respect to divorce and family cohesiveness.

- Climate.

- Effective strength of law enforcement agencies.

- Administrative and investigative emphases of law enforcement.

- Policies of other components of the criminal justice system (i.e., prosecutorial, judicial, correctional, and probational).

- Citizens' attitudes toward crime.

- Crime reporting practices of the citizenry.

This means that while the UCR is all very interesting information, it really doesn't tell you much about your own neighborhood. You're going to need to boil it down to a number that is relevant to your own situation.

You could go to the local precinct and speak to the officer in charge of community policing but the number may not be available in a relative format. Furthermore, the numbers by themselves can be misleading in the same way that the printout of crime calls to your store and neighborhood are misleading. For instance, Wal-Mart has one of the highest rates of calls for service in most communities where they are located but have one of the lowest loss rates of any other large big box enterprise. One store that I'm aware of actually has it's own police substation located next door to cut down on travel to all of the reported shoplifter calls, vehicle break-ins and traffic accident calls.

The good news is that you can get very good crime statistic numbers from a number of commercial sources. The company that we have used with good results is called Cap-

Index. The company is located in Pennsylvania and specializes in providing crime risk maps that show the relative total crime rate as a numerical score that is compared to a national average number score of 100. You are then designated as either above or below the national average for purposes of planning your loss prevention program. While we generally do not give commercial endorsements, we have had very satisfactory response and results from this company. In the interest of full disclosure, we have no financial interest or benefit in identifying this service company. They have just performed well when their services were used.

Do You Know Your
Neighborhood Crime History?

The cost of obtaining this information, which shows the crime rate of a mapped area of concentric circles around your business address, has usually cost us less than $200 per site address. The most cost effective information is contained in their Crimecast page program.

"CRIMECAST® scoring methodology involves the creation of two concentric circles around the site in question: the first circle at a maximum radius of one (1) mile or a population threshold of 25,000 people; and the second circle at a maximum radius of three (3) miles or a population threshold of 100,000 people. Both circles are shown on the Site Map, along with the CRIMECAST scores for each census tract that falls within these circles."

Site Maps can enhance the interpretation of a CRIMECAST® assessment. For example, a map can show whether a high CRIMECAST® score is derived from a high crime risk in the immediate vicinity of a site or whether it is due to avenues of high crime vulnerability from more distant neighborhoods.

The standard Site Map shows "CAP Index" scores in comparison to the national average for the current time period (year requested by customer). However, other types of CRIMECAST® scores and a full range of demographic data can be mapped. Also, customized maps can be provided for areas much larger than the standard three-mile radius and for other geographic units such as; zip codes, counties, states, etc. Maps much larger than the standard 8 1/2-by-11 inch formats are available.

We think obtaining this data is an enormous help in determining risk exposure and developing defensive measures. However you go about it, it's information you really need to know in order to conduct proactive planning on your loss prevention program.

We thought that you would like to know some interesting statistics that we came across in the FBI's Uniform Crime Report...

ARRESTs

The Uniform Crime Reporting (UCR) Program counts one arrest for each separate instance in which a person is arrested, cited, or summoned for an offense. The Program collects arrest data on 29 offenses. Because a person may be arrested multiple times during the year, the UCR arrest figures do not reflect the number of

Expert Advice Should Be Part Of Every Business Toolbox!

individual people who have been arrested. Rather, the arrest data show the number of times that persons are arrested, as reported by law enforcement agencies to the UCR Program.

In 2007, the FBI estimated that 14,209,365 arrests occurred nationwide for all offenses (except traffic violations), of which 597,447 were for violent crimes, and 1,610,088 were for property crimes. Nationwide, the 2007 rate of arrests was estimated at 4,743.3 arrests per 100,000 inhabitants; for violent crime, the estimate was 200.2 per 100,000; and for property crime, the estimate was 544.1 per 100,000.

The number of arrests for violent crimes decreased 1.1 percent in 2007 when compared with arrest data from 2006. The number of arrests for property crime increased 5.4 percent in 2007 when compared to 2006 arrest figures.

Arrests of juveniles (under 18 years of age) for murder rose 2.8 percent in 2007 when compared with 2006 arrest data.

In 2007, 75.8 percent of all persons arrested were male, 81.8 percent of persons arrested for violent crime were male, and 66.6 percent of persons arrested for property crime were male.

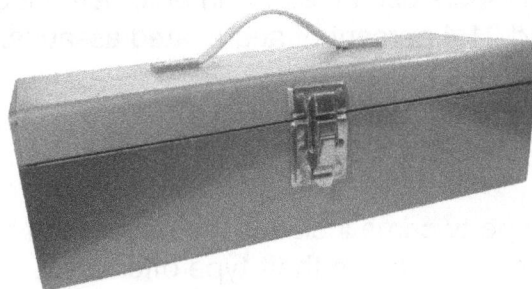

VIOLENT CRIMES

Violent crime is composed of four offenses: murder and non-negligent manslaughter, forcible rape, robbery, and aggravated assault. According to the Uniform Crime Reporting (UCR) Program's definition, violent crimes involve force or threat of force.

According to 2007 Crime In The United States Report figures released in September 2008, violent crime in 2007 was down 0.7 percent from 2006. An estimated 1,408,337 violent crimes occurred nationwide in 2007.

Aggravated assault accounted for the majority of violent crimes, 60.8 percent. Robbery accounted for 31.6 percent and forcible rape accounted for 6.4 percent. Murder, the least committed violent offense, made up 1.2 percent of violent crimes in 2007.

Offenders used firearms in 68.0 percent of the nation's murders, 42.8 percent of robberies, and 21.4 percent of aggravated assaults. (Weapon data are not collected for forcible rape offenses.)

PROPERTY CRIME

Property crime includes the offenses of burglary, larceny-theft, motor vehicle theft, and arson. The object of the theft-type offenses is the taking of money or property, but there is no force or threat of force against the victims. The property crime category includes arson because the offense involves the destruction of property; however, arson victims may be subjected to force. Because of limited participation and varying collection procedures by local law enforcement agencies, only limited data are available for arson.

According to 2007 Crime In The United States Report figures released in September 2008, property crime in 2007 was down 1.4 percent from 2006. There were an estimated 9,843,481 property crimes in the nation in 2007. The 10-year trend, comparing 2007 with 1998, presented a 10.1-percent drop in property crime.

In 2007, the rate of property crime offenses was estimated at 3,263.5 property crimes per 100,000 inhabitants.

Larceny-theft offenses accounted for over two-thirds (66.7 percent) of all property crimes in 2007.

Property crimes accounted for an estimated $17.6 billion dollars in losses in 2007.

LAW ENFORCEMENT EMPLOYEES

City, county, state, and tribal law enforcement agencies reported that, collectively, they employed 699,850 sworn officers and 318,104 civilians and provided law enforcement services to more than 285 million inhabitants nationwide, The rate of full-time law enforcement employees (civilian and sworn) per 1,000 inhabitants in the Nation for 2007 was 3.6; the rate of sworn officers was 2.4 per 1,000.

2007 data on law enforcement officers killed in the line of duty will be available in mid-October.

In 2006, 48 law enforcement officers were feloniously slain in the line of duty, and 66 officers died in accidents in the performance of their duties. The state that had the most felonious deaths of officers was California, where 6 officers died in 2006.

DRUGS & YOUTH

A special supplement to the 2004 report showed that the volume of juvenile arrests for drug abuse violations involving all drug types, collectively, increased 22.9 percent in the 10-year period from 1994 to 2003 (no update was provided in the 2005 report).

When an individual is arrested for a drug abuse violation, the reporting agency indicates the type of drug in one of four categories:

- Opium or cocaine and their derivatives
- Marijuana
- Synthetic narcotics
- Dangerous non-narcotic drugs

The number of arrests of juveniles for three of the four drug types increased, except for opium or cocaine, which decreased 50.9 percent.

**Parents...do you know where
your kids are at?**

"entia non sunt multiplicanda
praeter necessitatem"
or:

"The simplest explanation
tends to be the right one."

Occam's Razor

William of Occam
c. 1288-1348

"Trust but verify".

Ronald Reagan
40th President of US
(1911 - 2004)

Let's return to your problem that you have following the burglary in Chapter 1, your loss prevention professional can identify a safe vendor who can provided you with a "loaner" safe until you decide on what you need moving forward. Since for the purpose of our example loss scenario, you have determined that all of your companies safes are long past write off and their useful life is limited, here are some considerations related to securing your money. These ideas can apply, even if you are replacing just one of your safes and plan to change others later.

PLANNING A SAFE PURCHASE

In our example loss scenario, you lost the last one because it was determined that it wasn't bolted down to the floor. You made a note to make sure all of your company safes are secured to the floor in order to prevent burglars from jacking them up and removing them.

Let's discuss some basics that you need to consider when buying a safe for your business.

If you have multiple managers needing access, then an old style dial safe is out of the question since it only allows one combination at a time, which must be shared. Given your current circumstances, anybody can come in at night, open the safe, take money and you will not be able to identify who it was. Remember, you have already established that you have a trust issue and you need to segregate responsibility and accountability.

Most businesses need to have space in their safe to store a number of cash drawers that are set up with coin to quickly bank on a register operator. If not, then interior space may not be as much of a concern.

The safe should be at least "B" rated and be bolted securely to the floor. UL tool rated safes may be required by your insurance carrier, so now would be a good time to check.

What is "Underwriters Laboratories" or "UL"?

This product testing company claims to have the best safecrackers in the business.   UL has been testing and certifying safes for more than 80 years. The first safe tested for burglary resistance was in 1923 and the first bank vault in 1925.

Chisels, wenches, screwdrivers, power saws, cutting torches, crowbars, abrasive cutting wheels, jackhammers, even specified amounts of nitroglycerin are just a few of the "tools" UL technicians use during a safe attack. The idea is to test safes to worst-case scenarios. They use tools that could be found at any construction site or hardware store. They also analyze blueprints as if the burglar might have blueprints of the design and attack its weakest points to evaluate the safe for certification.

A two-person crew conducts UL's safe attack tests. The object is to create an opening large enough to withdraw "valuables" (anywhere from 2 to 6 square inches on a safe and up to 96 square inches on a vault), activate the locking mechanism so the door opens or to cut as many bolts from the door as necessary to pry it open before the time specified in the rating requirement expires.

Safes are rated for their resistance to attack against specific tools for a set period of time. There are a dozen different ratings, everything from ATM machines, to gun safes to bank vaults. For example, a safe that bears a Class TRTL-15x6 rating, which might be found in a jewelry store, should resist a hand tool and torch attack for a minimum of 15 minutes. A TRTL-30x6-rated safe, which would protect important documents or store money, should withstand an attack for 30 minutes. The ultimate safe rating — a TXTL60 — should withstand an hour's worth of attack that includes the use of 8 ounces of nitroglycerin.

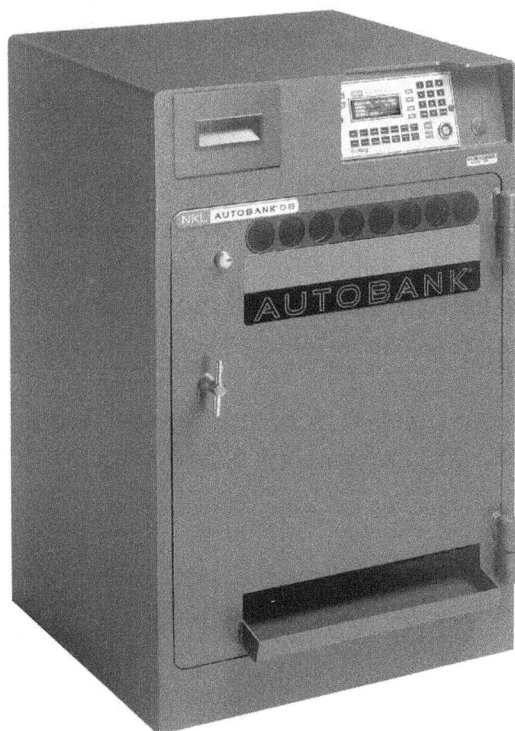

In addition to burglary protection ratings, UL also rates safes for their fire resistance protection. Class 350 safes protect paper documents, Class 150 safes protect magnetic tape and photographic film, while Class 125 safes protect floppy disks. In addition to the Class Rating, safes obtain an hourly rating for fire resistance — anywhere from 30 minutes to four hours.

Another test UL runs on safes is an impact test. This test simulates a safe falling though multiple stories of a building — resulting from a fire that has weakened the structure. After the safe is heated to 2,000 degrees Fahrenheit in a furnace, it's raised three stories and dropped onto a pile of bricks. In order to meet the requirement, the safe can't pop open. Temperatures inside can't rise to above 300 degrees Fahrenheit and sample papers left inside have to be readable.

A number of manufacturers offer electronic locks for their safes. Since the technology is constantly changing, do some online research as well as get recommendations from your CPP loss prevention professional.

A typical set up should allow each authorized user to have an electronic key which usually has a round disk to touch the lock keypad and a pin number that is enrolled into the safe system using a higher level key/permission than the users. Note that some of the new biometric locks require each user to enroll a thumbprint that is scanned instead of using a fob or card proximity reader.

This may sound confusing, but it really isn't. It simply means that the safe has a minimum of three levels of key/permissions. The general user, such as your managers, will all have the same level. A higher key/permission level key, usually held by the senior manager at the location, is used to

enroll these subordinate keys. These users are usually prompted to change their pin numbers regularly by the system. The only access function for these two levels is to open the outer door of the safe and inner drop compartments at times programmed into the system.

Note that many other useful functions are possible with these locks including a complete audit of all user access by time and date of each entry.

The lock can be programmed to allow managers access only during normal business hours and not allow access during non-business hours, at the discretion of the owner. As an available programming alternative, specific key holders can be denied off hour's access. While we do not recommend this function, some locks allow for a time delay that requires a wait of several minutes following activation for the bolt to throw and allow access. The purpose is to deter robbery.

If you have one of these, and you have more than one authorized user...

It really is time for digital electronic access

All of the decisions regarding how the lock will operate are determined by a programming level key/permission. An owner or manager level that does not need access to the contents for their own safety holds this level key.

This is the key /permission level with access to the safe audit, can change the date and time and set the various functions, but does not allow this person access to the safe contents.

If the store location uses armored car banking services, some other considerations apply. You must order a special safe for this purpose.

This type of safe has an exterior drop slot that allows deposit drops to be placed in a separate compartment that is controlled by both the manager key/pin and an armored car key that has been enrolled in that unique safe/location. The armored car company only possesses this key. Any spare keys must be held off-site. Keys are useless until they are enrolled in a specific safe location but should non-the-less be controlled and kept in a secure location.

Just a few more comments about the installation and use of electronic lock safes.

Safes should always be located in a private area where cash counts and other banking functions can occur away from public view. The purpose here is to avoid "impulse" robbery. However, new cash management safes are now available whereby each bill is fed into the slot and instantly accounted for with the money dropping into a cassette that an armored car company can retrieve at appropriate intervals. In this case, the safe can be located in close proximity to the register operator or in the office when used specifically to organize deposits.

Electronic locks should be plugged into an isolated circuit or preferably it's own interruptible surge protected power supply. A $300 investment in a UPS can save lots of money in repairs because a power surge can blow out a lock circuit board. If that happens, plan on at least a day out of service.

By the way, unlike your old insecure dial safe, without a back up power supply, the safe won't open.

A final thought is to consider that the useful life of these safes is about six or eight years. All safes will eventually break depending on how hard and how frequently your manager's slam the door shut. Not a good idea, especially considering how many fingers get crushed in safe door slamming accidents!

Safe warranties are typically a year making the need for extended warranties an issue to consider. A typical emergency repair that may require drilling can cost $1,000 if the problem goes beyond circuit board replacement. It also means more than a day out of service.

You may want to talk to your CPP loss prevention professional about a lease deal for all of your locations that includes all service and repairs for a monthly cost that spreads to each location and frees up your capital for other things. At the end of the lease, get a new one.

I have to put you on notice that the best safe in the world cannot protect you from theft unless you have written policies and procedures that specify how the safe will be used, how money will flow in and out, get to the bank, who is accountable to insure that all policies and procedures are followed and what are the consequences for failure to follow the policy.

POLICIES AND PROCEDURES YOU NEED

This is our first opportunity to talk about policies and procedures that every company needs to fully utilize security hardware. Without written and acknowledged policies, the hardware systems that you expect to protect your assets will fail to meet your expectations. You will lose money and be forced to start all over again trying to protect your profits. Here are some issues for your consideration.

*   Policies must be specific and written. Expecting to have everyone know what accepted practices are in your organization cannot be "Unwritten Rules" if you expect specific behaviors. So called unwritten rules are subject to everybody's personal interpretation and are unenforceable.

*   You must train all employees whose performance is impacted by the policy.

*   Failure to follow policies must have very specific consequences.

*   A copy of the policy must be given to your employees.

- You must obtain a signed acknowledgement from your employees that they have been trained, received a copy of the policy and understand the consequences of failure to comply. Keep the acknowledgement in the employee's permanent file.

- Policies that require unnecessary written paperwork are doomed to fail. Never require a signature on a piece of paper when you can achieve the same result by swiping a key card and entering a pin number.

Your safe is the last place that you keep money at the end of your cash control program before it is transported to the bank and your account receives credit. The safe is a component of your cash control system that includes your POS system.

Point Of Sale cash register systems are constantly changing and will not be addressed in this book other than to state the absolute requirement that all business must have an acceptable system to record sales data and produce reports that allow the business owner to establish accounting controls.

Policies specific to the security of your safe storage of money should include some of the following. The list is not all-inclusive; you may need to be more specific.

- Include a prohibition that managers are not allowed to share electronic safe keys `and pin numbers with anyone.

- Only one manager per shift, the designated cash manager, is allowed to enter the safe to make change, prepare deposits or issue cash drawers.

- Each cash manager is required to balance the safe fund at the beginning and end of their shift.

- Lost or stolen safe keys or codes must be reported immediately

Most other policies related to the usage of the safe really fall into the category of cash controls and will be explored in Chapter 8.

LOCATING SAFES IN YOUR BUSINESS

The next few pages will discuss the placement of safes in 3 different types of business enterprises: a fast food restaurant, a convenience store and a wholesale parts distribution business. Your business may be similar to the ones depicted, but all businesses are different and should be surveyed by a professional looking at the actual buildings, locations and crime loss history. Just remember that our three examples are made up!

Each of these enterprises have different floor plans, products and crime exposure depending on the location, demographics and whether the business has taken adequate steps to reduce exposure using barriers, policies and procedures. Let's take a look at the three fictional examples and see where we recommend that you position your safes.

Gordo's Fast Food Restaurant:

Gordo's is a 54-seat restaurant part of a twelve-store chain featuring Southwest American food in a shopping center lot located in front of a large home improvement store in a commercial neighborhood.

A four-lane highway connects the shopping center to a major interstate highway located a mile away. The Gordo's chain has been in business twenty years and has experienced a few robberies over the years and a half dozen serious deposit thefts. There are two entrances in the dining room and a back door all leading to adjacent parking lot shared in common with other shopping center businesses.

The store features a walk up counter in the dining room with three register stations. There is

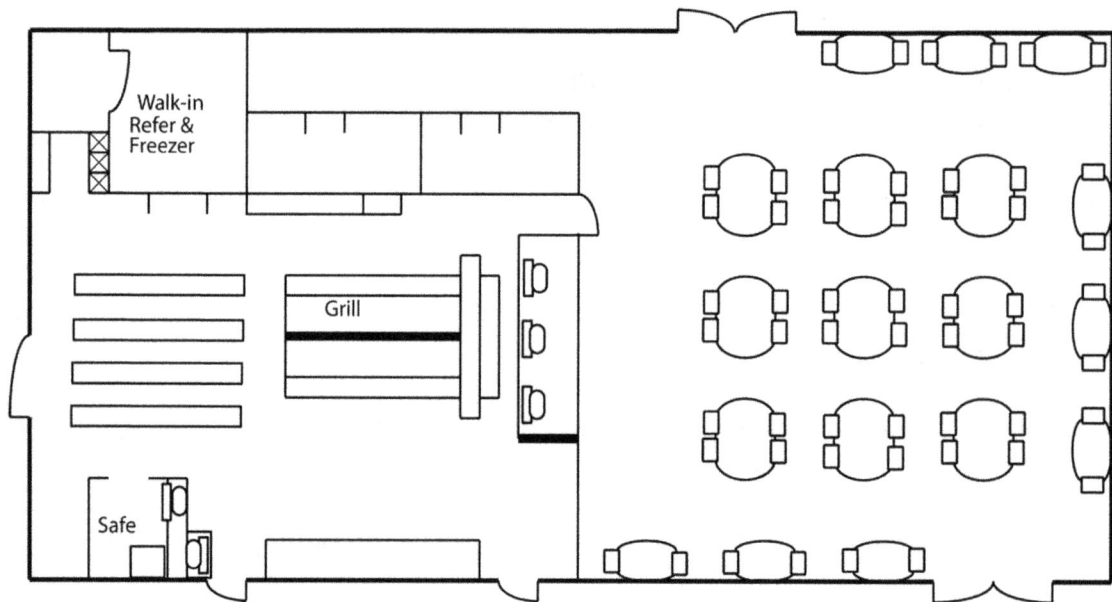

a drive through lane with the back window taking orders and payment with the front window handing out the food.

Sales at this location average $35 thousand per week and deposits are transported to the bank by an armored car company each day. The business is profitable as long as labor and food cost is kept under control.

The safe is in the manager's office. It is an electronic time lock model with an armored car drop compartment similar to the one on page 52. You will find that most security experts recommend the office location for most types of businesses that handle a lot of cash and need a private location to count drawers and prepare deposit drops into the armored car portion of the safe. Cash should not be counted in a public location.

Even restaurants in low crime environments should insure that the safe is located in an office where further burglary and theft protection can occur.   Bad cash procedures can result in exposure to robbery since individuals with inside information looking for an opportunity commit the vast majority of these crimes.

Each register should be equipped with an under counter drop safe where all large bills are deposited through out the day. The drop safes allow the managers to conduct register pulls from the box rather than having accumulated large bill currency stack up in the drawer, or worse, under the drawer. The drop safe should be large enough to accommodate a volume of currency without filling up too quickly.

Using the drop safe keeps the appearance of excessive cash in drawer to a minimum and reduces the occurrence of impulse crimes such as grab and run robberies when the drawer opens to complete a transaction.

Our next fictitious business where we will locate the safe is the convenience or "C" store that you can find on every street in America. Many of these institutions have an extensive history of robberies, theft and other crimes due to the availability in the past of lots of cash, low staffing levels and late night hours. The term for many of these businesses used by the police was "stop and rob".

Many companies have improved this exposure using a variety of cash handling innovations and increasing late night staff. Let's look at an improved profile.

Pete's Food and Beer:

Pete started his chain of C-stores five years ago from scratch and now has seven with average unit volume of thirty four thousand a week. Life is good since Pete doesn't have to pay royalties and an advertising percentage like his friends that own franchises. All of his stores are located on busy streets in suburban areas and have had a history of robberies until he got some good advice from his CPP security expert and installed the right safes and security equipment.

Pete also adopted good enforceable policies and procedures to control the cash and to make sure that it gets to the bank. His profit margin has improved by 20% by reducing shrinkage losses.

Among the innovations that Pete has adopted is the use of time delay change fund safes in the front counter locations in his stores. You simply can't get more than change for a twenty dollar bill at night unless you want to wait for the change system. Large bills fed into the cash system are automatically screened and counterfeit bills are rejected.

So far the bill reader has never been wrong and lots of phony bills have been rejected. The armored car truck picks up the deposits each day from his new safe where all currency fed into the safe is counted and stored in a cassette. The safe reports the total on a receipt and the armored car guard slides the cassette out and inserts a new one to be filled up each morning and also re-stocks the time delay change dispensers.

The cost of paying for this service is more but Pete figures that he is saving lots of money on management time since they no longer have to conduct drawer pulls, spend time counting money, preparing deposits and writing it all down on paper like they used to do. In fact Pete found that the reduced level of register theft alone, almost paid for the service last year. Like we said, life is good!

The only issues that Pete has to deal with now, is to make sure that the armored car company pick up does not interfere with his peak business hours during lunch.

The Armored car contract calls for cash accounting services provided by the companies' own money-counting operation. Reports are E-mailed to Pete daily allowing him to readily see that his deposits balance with sales numbers and any discrepancy can be quickly addressed.

Much of Pete's other losses were addressed by the other policies, procedures and equipment that Pete introduced into his business. When you own a business that has an average profit margin of 2% and it is typical to have 3% in shrinkage, it takes a lot of careful management to make a reasonable living.

Looking at waste and vendor fraud can also attack the 3% still sitting on the table.

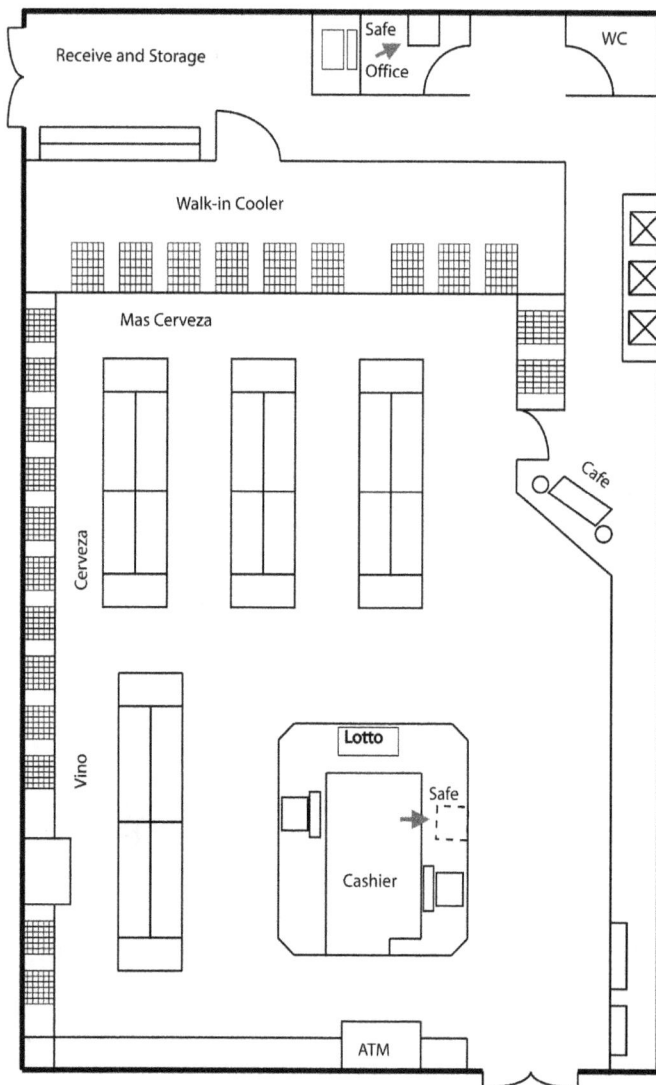

Cobb City Lock and Security Supply

The next fictional business floor plan is a parts distribution store. Cobb City Lock and Security Supply has a walk up counter and a large stock storage area. The sales department is located in a room next to the service counter and the shipping and receiving functions at the back door office. The majority of sales at Cobb City Lock are through telephone and outside sales orders.

While this type of store will do a large credit card and open book accounts sales percentage, and does not take in a large amount of cash, the business must still maintain a cash fund and provide storage for high value stock items that can come in as a received order for a customer such as precious metals.

The safe is located in the office and is a time lock electronic model that allows the cash drop safe to be opened between 8 - 11 each morning to allow for banking and the main safe door is programmed to deny access from 8 PM to 7 AM as a defense against armed robbery.

Our experience is that a warehouse district is typically isolated and can represent exposure to take over robberies as well as internal theft issues.

Lessons From Losses

The Business had an old Cincinnati Safe Company dial lock floor model weighing about 1000 pounds that was equipped with an internal dual lock drop compartment to protect deposits for armored car transport to the bank each day. The armored car company possessed one key and the store possessed the other. Both keys were required to open the lock during the armored car transfer. Deposit drops were made, witnessed and recorded on a log throughout the day

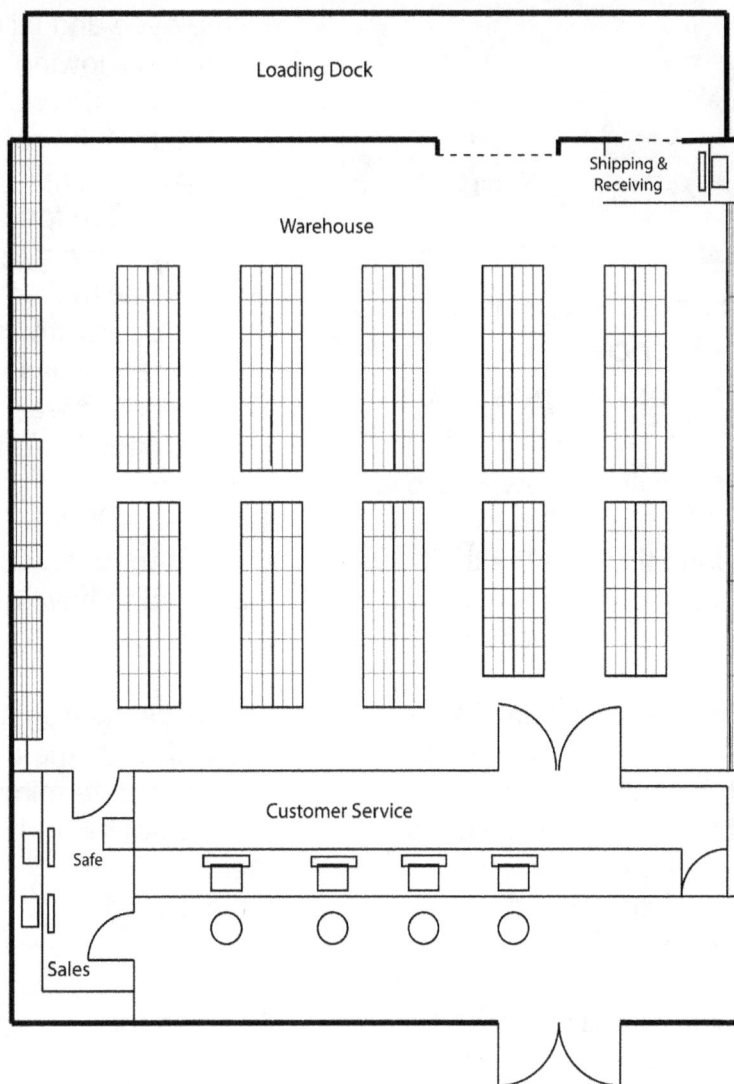

The longer key on the right is named the "Guard" or common key because it must be inserted and turned a quarter turn to the right before the "Security" key, on the left, can be rotated left a third of a turn to retract the latch to the open position. The lock is now in the open position with the Security key captured by the cylinder. In this Lesson From Losses, the armored car company retained the "Guard" key and the store the "Security" key allowing an opportunity for a dishonest employee to steal a large amount of money.

After the funds transfer is complete the lock mechanism is reset by turning the Security key a quarter turn back to the left and the key can then be removed from the cylinder. The "Guard

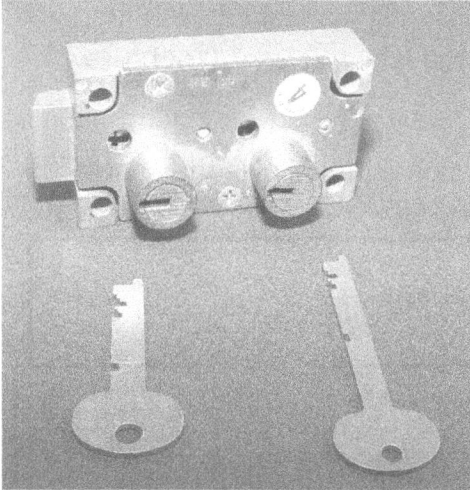

Drop safe compartment lock shown in the closed and locked position

Key" can be turned back to the door closed position after the door is opened at any time and be removed from the cylinder.

One day after the deposit transfer to armored car, the manager handed back the Guard key to the armed car employee and failed to turn the lock back into the closed position allowing open access to the drop safe contents for two shifts until the next scheduled deposit pick up found that the safe was empty of deposits.

Investigation found that the store managers often left the key in the cylinder due to lack of a sufficient number of keys for the lock. It was not readily noticed as being unlocked due to the fact that the compartment door was closed and unless you knelt down on the floor to pull the door open, it was not particularly noticeable that it was unsecured. In addition, the key could be turned partway in the cylinder toward the unlocked position.

During the time the theft could have occurred no fewer that eight managers and supervisors could have opened the safe but the loss had to have occurred after close on the night before the loss was discovered the next morning.

The case was finally solved during the police interrogation of the managers with a confession obtained. The theft it was found, occurred when the thief returned to the store in the middle of the night, opened the outer safe door and determined that his earlier afternoon discovery of an open armored car compartment had not been discovered by others. After cleaning out the money, the crook merely closed the compartment and turned the lock to the closed position before leaving.

Using an old safe with a single combination for multiple users is a disaster waiting to happen.

Today's electronic safes provide an audit trail of all users and operations conducted. Door latches automatically secure when the door closes for both inner and outside door usage. If your company still uses one of these old dinosaurs, please consider that the cost of

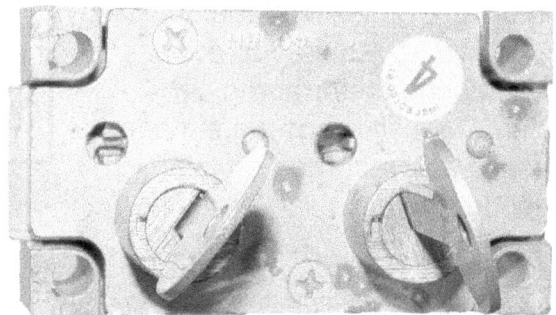

Drop safe compartment lock in the open position

replacement will often be less than the amount of even one deposit loss. When you factor in replacing the safe and whatever the contents were on top of business interruption and bad publicity, one serious burglary like the one just described could easily finance the replacement of all of the safes of a company with 10 operating units especially when you consider that the capital cost is spread over 6-8 years.

An Illustration of the compromised lock after the armored car guard removed his (guard) key with the security key still in the cylinder but turned partway.

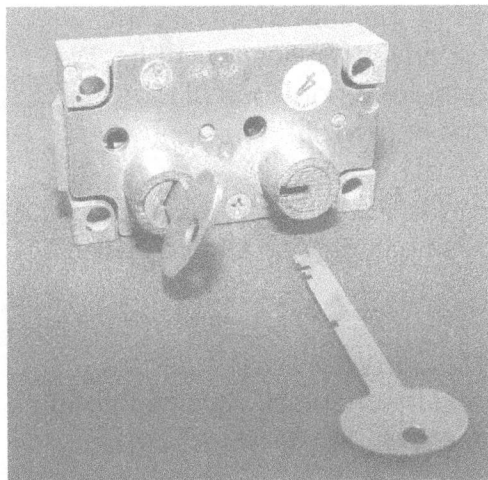

The security key cannot be removed from the cylinder without locking the door. However since it was common practice to leave the key in the lock, the lock was compromised and with the door closed, but in the unlocked position, it was not noticed.

If you still have an old style dial safe, you should know that crooks over the centuries have developed a number of ways to get into even the most apparently secure bank vaults let alone your little office safe. The methods burglars use range from manipulating the lock to blowing it up to other physical attacks such as using burning bars, cutting torches, grinding wheels and drilling.

Different procedures may be used to crack a safe, depending on its construction.

Lock manipulation

The most difficult way requiring the most practiced skill of cracking a safe is to manipulate the lock in order to obtain the combination required to open the safe without actually damaging the safe.

Some rotary combination locks can be manipulated by feel or sound in order to determine the combination required to open the safe. Manipulation often is the locksmith's preferred choice in lost-combination lockouts, since it requires no repairs or damage, but can be extremely time consuming due to lock improvements over the years, and is also a difficult art to master.

In the absence of any other information regarding the safe's combination, dialing every possible combination may open a combination lock. A reduction in solving time the experts tell us " might be obtained by trying all possible settings for the last wheel for a given setting of the first wheels before nudging the next-to-last wheel to its next meaningful setting, instead of zeroing the lock each time with a number of turns in one direction". We did not understand that either.

Guessing the combination

A safe may be compromised surprisingly often by guessing the combination. This results from the fact that manufactured safes often come with a manufacturer-set combination. This combination is designed to allow the owner initial access to the safe so that they may set their own new combination. In other words, the safe was delivered and set up but the factory combination was never changed. Sources exist which list manufacturers try-out combinations.

Combinations are also unwittingly compromised by the owner of the safe by having the lockset to easy-to-guess combinations such as a birth date or driver's license number. We know of a number of cases the safe combination was filed in the most obvious of places like in store phone directories under "safe" listings and even on the safe itself! These guys are equally predictable in how they protect their computer passwords.

Another known way to obtain the combination is to steal it. A safe is only as secure as the confidentiality of its combination.

Auto dialers have been developed by a number of companies. Sorry, this isn't a James Bond device that instantly opens safes, but rather is set up and mechanically cycles through possible combinations. The process can take some time were told.

Most safes are susceptible to compromise by drilling or other physical methods. Manufacturers publish drill-point diagrams for specific models of safe. Both the manufacturers and locksmithing professionals tightly guard these drilling templates. We have to tell you, however, if it's been published anywhere and it is of value to criminals, it is very likely to be available on the Internet.

Drilling is usually aimed at gaining access to the safe by observation or bypass of the locking mechanism. Drilling is the most common method used by locksmiths, and is the only method that can be used in cases of burglary attempts, malfunctioning locks or damaged locks.

All but the simplest safes are designed to protect against drilling attacks through the implementation of hard plate steel.   The use of hard plate ensures that conventional drilling is not successful when used against the safe. Drilling through hard plate requires the use of special-purpose diamond or tungsten-carbide drill-bits. Even then, this can be a time-consuming and difficult process with safes equipped with modern composite hard plates. We once observed a locksmith go through 80 expensive drill bits before he was able to crack one of our locked out safes after about 8 hours of grueling work.

Some high security safes use what is called a "re-locker". Most modern safes are fitted with re-lockers, which are triggered by excessive force and will then lock the safe semi-permanently (a safe whose re-locker has tripped must then be forced, the combination or key alone will no longer suffice). This is why a professional safe technician will use manipulation rather than brute force to open a safe so they do not risk releasing the re-locker.

Drilling is an attractive method of safecracking for locksmiths, as it is usually quicker than manipulation, and drilled safes can generally be repaired and returned to service. Punching, peeling and using a torch are other methods of compromising a safe.

Torches and can be used to burn through the metal on a safe. One burglar tried this in a safe we had in New York and managed to get in but also burned up all of the money.

Other methods of cracking a safe generally involve damaging the safe so that it is no longer functional. Several years ago, a gang of burglars working in Long Island broke into one of our stores and simply beat the hinges off with a sledgehammer to get at the contents.

If they really want what you have in your safe, they may just blow the door off with what the experts call a "jam shot"

Secured boxes have existed for centuries, but it wasn't until the late 18th century that use of cast iron became widespread and was used to create solid metal boxes. During the 19th century, safe-cracking techniques became widely used in bank burglaries. In the 20th century, improvements in steel production and a decreasing reliance on physical currency led to a decrease in the popularity of safe cracking.

You need to match your level of protection to the dollar value of what you are trying to protect. You also need to remember, that the safe is only one part of your plan to provide a barrier to the risk of cash losses.

With the right cutting disk, this thing cuts through safe hinges like butter!

"Obviously crime pays or
there'd be no crime"

G. Gordon Liddy
1960's Watergate Burglar

Example of a "Patented Keyway" cylinder lock

You have already rudely been made aware that your lack of a good key control system has provided an opportunity for the loss of a lot of your hard earned profits. It really is more that just good locks; it's about having written policies and procedures in place that allows you to know what keys are in the possession of a particular employee.

It provides for:

- A signature acknowledging the issuance of the key.
- When the key must be returned
- Reporting of lost or stolen keys.
- Prohibition on copy.
- Prohibition on lending.
- Statement of consequences if policies are not followed.
- Provision for periodic key audits and the name of the person responsible.

PLANNING A KEY CONTROL SYSTEM

Let's look at your lock set options starting with your existing locks that you have in your business.

If you have typical mechanical door locks, the minimum standard requires interchangeable cores using a patented keyway so that your keys cannot be duplicated by any locksmith other than your own security equipment service provider. If your current lock bodies do not lend themselves to a retrofit, then you must really consider a whole new hardware set for each of your doors. You need to include interior locks, as well, if your old uncontrolled keys will still open those doors. After all, you are securing your offices, computer systems and product storage locations. And yes, the locksets need to match as to purpose throughout your company properties.

ANSI American National Standards Institute testing includes operational performance for endurance, strength against vandalism, and cycle time for length of reliable operation.

Grade 1 Heavy Duty locks are built for high use, more physically demanding applications. Robust materials and assembly methods are typically found in Grade 1 Locks. A fair example of use of a Grade 1 lock set is a rest room in a retail food environment. Installing a Grade 1 lock on the rest room may cost up to several hundred dollars (including installation) but will likely last years versus a Grade 2 Commercial Duty or Grade 3 Light Commercial Duty that will likely last less than a year.

Grade 2 Locks are usually recommended for office doors, storage areas and doors typically not used my multiples of people daily.

Grade 3 Locks are usually recommended for residential applications and low use doors in light commercial environments.

Your security equipment service provider will demonstrate the difference, if you ask.

What Key Control System Works Best?

For companies with frequent employee turnover, especially those located in a mall or similar environment, a self-changing "restricted keyway" cylinder provides optimum speed of change. These cylinders may be "self-contained" where use of "coded keys" and or special tools and new keys are used to change the key combination without removing the lock from the door.

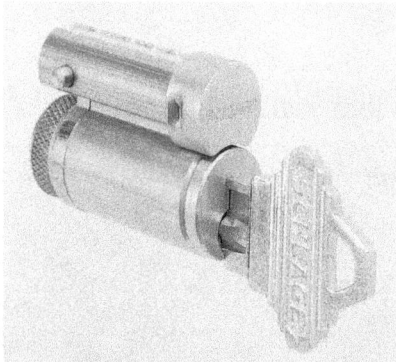

For companies with multiple types of applications within the premises such as door hardware, padlocks, file cabinets, electric gates, interchangeable removable cores may be the better option. "IC Cores" are removed by use of a control key and new cores are inserted within seconds.

For companies desiring the convenience of self-changing cylinders or interchangeable removable cores as described above but also desiring to prevent unauthorized duplication of keys, the recommended method is use of patented protected key control in either design.

For businesses seeking the optimum protection against drilling, picking, and unauthorized key duplication, a cylinder and patented key system meeting UL-437 high security is the recommended solution.

NOTE: **Any system employed without proper controls or poor management is a risk to security!**

Mechanical Versus Electronic Access Control.

Mechanical Patented Key Control or High Security Key and Lock systems allow the security in knowing keys issued may not be duplicated. This does not prevent lending, selling or misuse of the key. Remember what was said about written policies and procedures.

For many situations the ability to provide an audit trail identifying who accessed a door and when is critical information. The "who"

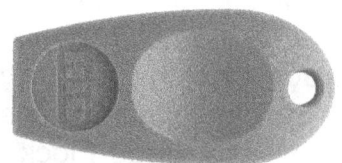

It's a Fob!

is identified by individually enrolled access cards or fobs. The ability to restrict entry via time schedules is also a benefit of electronic access control.

For commercial office building and many other restricted access settings, a number of really good multi-door electronic access control systems are on the market that are very affordable because the locking mechanism is a heavy-duty magnet attached to the door, which requires hundreds of pound of force to defeat, and no moving parts.

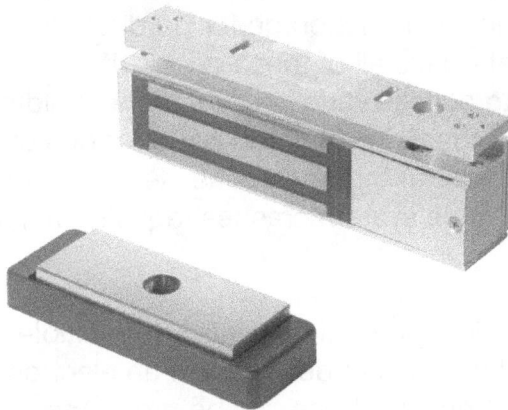

Access using a card/fob reader is quick and each entrance is recorded by user and time. Cancellation of access privilege is concluded with a few keystrokes in the software program. Doors can be programmed to automatically stay unlocked during a specified "open" time range and remain locked on the outside otherwise. Exit is automatic using an electronic sensor inside which requires that the door be pushed open and meets life safety codes.

Magnetic Lock Components

We have had these systems installed in a number of office buildings and there is no reason that they cannot be used in about any commercial environment. Back up power supplies keep the facility secure even during lengthy power outages.

A combination of mechanical and electronic security is really the optimum security recommendation. There are systems using "dual access credentials" offering patented key control, UL-437 and the convenience of interchangeable removable core with electronic access control allowing use of proximity, advanced iClass proximity or biometrics.

Another great replacement option for a business enterprise needing to control just a few doors is to install one of the new "stand alone" locks now available that have all of the security code information imbedded in the lock and can be easily rekeyed/recoded with new user information using the keypad or a PDA-digital assistant handheld device.

Note: any electronic access control system with a "mechanical over ride" is suspect if the override is accomplished with a traditional key system.

POLICIES AND PROCEDURES YOU NEED

The beginning of this chapter listed a number of critical

items that must be part of your key control policy. The list is not all-inclusive since your facility may be more complex than the typical retail establishment but the principle is the same when it comes to controls.

- **A signature acknowledging the issuance of the key.**

A primary rule is to know who has a key or card or proximity reader that accesses what is behind a particular door. It may be as simple as the average fast food restaurant that has two front doors, a back door, managers office and some secured storage for product. In this case, the manager key set needs to have a key that opens all of these doors. If your managers are carrying around 20 keys that they need to access various parts of the building, you need to rethink your keying strategy. It is important that keys that you issue for one of your locations do not fit others unless the authorized holder of that master key level is very high up on the food chain. Lose one of these and the whole system crashes requiring a huge re-keying expense.

Other businesses with a complex number of doors, multiple protection levels and multiple permission levels should be subjected to a cost benefit analysis to determine if an electronic system makes more sense. Relatively inexpensive electronic systems can be programmed at one PC to control dozens of doors in a facility that can specifically authorize a particular user to access the whole facility or as few areas as a lower echelon employee needs to go.

- **When the key must be returned.**

A written key return policy must be included with consequences for failure to return a key set when employment terminates or at any time that management demands the return of keys. Policies such as an agreement that the departing employee pay for any needed re-keying as a result of failure to return is not legal everywhere nor is withholding a last paycheck.   However the failure to account for all of the keys must trigger an immediate re-keying of the locks that the missing set had access to.

- **Reporting of lost or stolen keys.**

Lost or stolen keys must signal an immediate re-key of the doors compromised by the loss. Policy must emphasize that managers are required to exercise a high level of control and care when they are entrusted with your keys and that their loss be reported to senior management immediately.

- **Prohibition on copy.**

The use of a patented keyway was mentioned earlier and must be your standard for all of your mechanical locks. The alternative is the possibility of indiscriminate reproduction of your keys and you may never know that an extra set exists. If all of your key sets are accounted for and you experience a theft where keys are used, you will be inclined to blame someone currently employed rather than the ex-employee whom had an extra set made up before they were fired!

Patented keyways solve that problem because the blanks will not be available to the average lock shop. A further plus is that the authorized locksmith will reproduce your keys from the cutting code rather than copy an existing worn key (you know, like they do at your local Mom & Pop hardware store) that can fail.

- **Prohibition on lending.**

We can't over express our concern about lending and borrowing key sets. It is often the way that key sets get lost. The usual scenario is the overly busy manager hands a set of keys to an hourly employee so that they can retrieve a needed item for them. A number of subsequent consequences can result.

If what you are having the employee retrieving is important enough to be locked up with other important stuff, how do you know how many and how much of an item is really being taken from the storage area? You're busy, so you may not notice that the employee had time to go to his car or elsewhere and hide the important stuff he has just stolen from your storeroom.

You may want to seriously consider major sanctions if you discover that a manager has been lending their key set to an unauthorized employee.

- **Statement of consequences if policies are not followed.**

Okay, we need to talk about the consequences of broken rules resulting in the need to re-key your building. If you are the owner of the company that experienced the loss we described in Chapter One, than you have already lost a lot of cash and your safe and as a result have had to re-invent your whole security program. A brake-down in one component of your loss prevention program should not crash the whole system but it can have a ripple effect on other components. For instance, a burglar who gets into your building with a key will undoubtedly damage your camera system and other items while they are there so those items become a casualty of the failure of your key control system. In any case it is going to cost you a lot of money to fix the problem. You have to decide what consequences adequately motivate your managers to follow the rules and take the appropriate progressive disciplinary action with consistency and without favoritism.

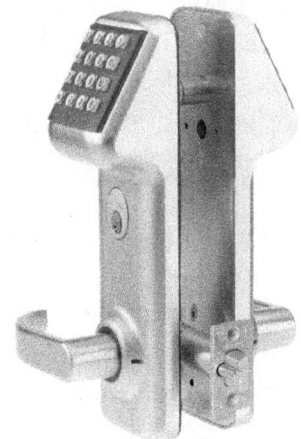

Stand Alone Electronic Lock

- **Provision for periodic key audits and the name of the person responsible.**

The last piece of your key control policy is to have a system in place to "inspect what you expect". A periodic audit of the system must be conducted in order to ensure compliance.

We recommend that this program be made a part of your standard internal financial audits that are normally conducted in most businesses.

By the way, all audits related to security systems, equipment and policy should be a normal part of your internal audit rather than being a separate audit that is not connected to the big picture and can be subject to falling through the cracks and simply forgotten.

KEY AND SAFE CONTROL

We have had a lot to say about key controls and systems and the need for all companies to adopt these controls. Some general precautions should become part of your business loss prevention culture and simply become a component of the way that you do business. While the following may seem repetitious, we cannot overstate the need to continuously remind your employees regarding the need to keep your assets secured.

All employees must be trained to never give keys to any person not authorized by senior management. Never give a Manager's cash register key to a cashier or other employee. Never give or loan keys to any other person without the knowledge and consent of the senior manager. Never leave keys setting unattended. Remember that there is an authorization and signature system in place that must be followed and no exceptions will be tolerated that violates the control of your keys and access to your business.

The store manager should be responsible for changing business locks, keys, alarm access codes and safe combination whenever a person possessing one or all transfers or terminates. Do not write the safe combination on anything that could be seen by or accessible to an employee (calendar, log, etc.). We once found the safe combination at one business on a Rolodex file of addresses and information in the manager's office filed under "Safe". This particular business did not have an electronic lock safe so the managers were all sharing the same combination.

Common sense practice dictates that the safe must be kept shut and locked at all times when unattended. An avoidable exposure is to allow your safe to be set on "day lock" which is an old fashioned term for an old style dial safe that allowed the safe door to be closed without actually throwing the bolt works. Such a practice should be prohibited if you have one of these old safes and considered it unlocked. Do not leave cash, checks or any other valuables out unattended. Place valuables in the safe and lock it.

Does the key you use to open the door to your business have hidden risks? The answer is yes!

Is the key you use every day to open the door to your business a "discreet" security device? How can you tell? Is there a Brand Name on the key such as Schlage, Yale, Sergeant or Best? Do you see any numbers on the head of the key such as 37545?

This information is very helpful to a knowledgeable criminal. A quick look at your key can provide a blueprint to a thief. The code or cuts can be read and be transferred to a key blank for a copy of your key without your knowledge.

Be certain you do not have a "direct digit key code" on your key. Your professional locksmith will know. Ask him or her if you are not sure. Loss prevention starts with the key to the doors of your business.

Do not be fooled by Do Not Duplicate or Neuter Bow keys. These substitute solutions provide a false sense of security. The "Do Not Duplicate" stamped or coined onto a key blank really amounts to a polite request, that is honored by few professional locksmiths and key-cutters. It is considered a weak attempt and alternative to patented key control. The bottom line is there is no legal protection in the event someone copies the typical key that bears this message.

The solution is to use a Patented Key Control System. Key Blanks are not available via key blank manufacturers, and are only made available from the original manufacturer typically through authorized contract professional locksmiths only. Manufacturers are forbidden under penalty of law from making key blanks available in the open market. This is excellent protection for you and your business. Key Holders will be unable to get a copy of the key. It is not impossible to get a duplicate, but at least very difficult and laws would have to be broken and contracts ignored to get a key made.

Neuter Bow keys are simply an attempt to confuse the local key cutter. The shape of the head of the key is changed from the original, and it is really a cosmetic change. This is another weak alternative to the patented key solution.

You should never stamp keys with words like MASTER KEY, Grand Master or put the address or building name on the key. A lost key amounts to an invitation to the wrong type of people.

You could have your locksmith stamp key with sequential numbers such as 1000, 1001, 1002 etc. making it easy to assign a key by number to a specific employee. In addition you could color code keys so that "blue" is the men's room, or green is the "accountant's office". In either case anyone finding the lost key will have no idea where these keys will work.

Managing Your Lock & Key System

Even if you are a small business, when you hire employees that will carry a key to open any door in your business, you absolutely should strongly consider implementing a Key Control System.

The psychology is relatively simple, when people are held accountable by policy, procedure and written signature they pay attention and are more responsible.

To review and maximize your efforts to control key duplication, your Key Control System should contain the following elements:

1.   A unique registered securely designed scalable system. Your professional locksmith will build a custom lock and key security solution in consideration of your people, operational and safety requirements. The key system plan should include room for expansion, eliminating

obsolescence and costly replacement.

2.   A "standard" Written Key Control Policy. Once you have a registered lock and key system, implementation is a critical key to maintaining a secure system. We provide a standard "template" which you may use or if you prefer, design your own. We highly recommend you issue the Company Key Control Policy when you issue new keys to every employee and you have each employee sign a key-holder agreement.

3.   Documented Patented Key Control Technology. Patented lock and key technology is assurance your investment will provide the highest rate of return. Patents protect you from unauthorized key duplication by preventing the manufacturing of key blanks. Professional locksmiths believe any "do not duplicate" or similar warning is simply not enough protection for your business or property.

4.   Record keeping & Capability of Audit. Professional Locksmiths recommend each registered system cut key has unique identification stamped on the bow, (numbers, letters, or symbols). In your "Key Log" records each key holder with the unique identification number found on the key. Each employee should sign for the key issued with the date noted for the record. Every key is identified as to each cylinder it will operate. This knowledge eliminates risk and when keys are found, it is easy to identify the key holder.

5.   Process for Retrieving Keys When People Leave the Business. Accounting for all the keys in the system eliminates the need and cost to re-key. By having people sign for the key when issued, and sign out upon return of the key, you are able to assess risk.

Professional locksmiths believe if you can account for all of the keys in the system you simply reissue an existing key to a new user. On the following page we have provided a sample Key Control Policy for your use.

Key Holder Policy

1.   EMPLOYEES ARE NOT ALLOWED TO SELL OR LOAN THEIR REGISTERED OPERATING KEY/CREDENTIAL TO ANYONE.
2.   EMPLOYEES ARE NOT ALLOWED TO HAVE DUPLICATE KEYS COPIED.
3.   EMPLOYEES MUST RETURN KEYS UPON LEAVING THE BUSINESS.
4.   EMPLOYEES MUST REPORT LOST OR STOLEN KEYS IMMEDIATELY.

FAILURE TO COMPLY MAY RESULT IN KEY HOLDERS BEARING THE COST TO RE-KEY THE FACILITY, TERMINATION OR BOTH

Each employee should sign an Individual Key Holder Agreement. You should maintain a confidential file for key holders so when locks are changed, people leave or are added you will have a transactional record of who had keys and when.

INDIVIDUAL KEY HOLDER AGREEMENT

You have been issued Key Number _____ for Store #_____

Located at _____, _____, __,

By signing for the key you agree to the following:

1.   You will not SELL or LOAN the key issued to you to anyone
2.   You will not COPY or DUPLICATE the key issued to you
3.   You MUST return this key upon leaving the business
4.   You MUST report lost or stolen keys immediately

Failure to comply may result in key-holders bearing the cost to re-key the facility, termination or both.

It is company policy to withhold your last paycheck until return of all Company Property has been completed upon your departure from the business, including the key issued to you.

I understand and agree this day _____,
                                       Day, Month, Year

Employee Number _____

Employee Name _____

Employee Signature _____

Manager_____

Date_____

Okay, you have managed to get the building secured and have adopted written key control policies and procedures.

You have new safes (bolted to the floor) that give you an audit trail and each manager has their own key and pin number for access. Your new written policy, signed by the managers, gives you control over loss exposure including frequent pin number changes, warnings to protect their key/pin, procedures for periodic audits and the beginnings of a company cash control program.

Let's look at some of the different hardware and lock types for each of our fictional businesses, where they belong and how it all fits together.

Starting with **Gordo's Fast Food** front doors, we can see that the two pairs of double doors need to be open during business hours and locked to the public during late night when only the drive through is open and of course when the business is closed for the night.

State fire codes usually require that anyone in an occupied building must be able to exit with <u>one motion</u> in case of emergency. That means you only need to push on the door to get out if the building is on fire or some other emergency requires immediate exit.

This also means that you cannot have a double dead-bolt lock requiring keys to exit the locked door. You also may not have a thumb-turn inside locking device for the same reason. Namely these devices take at least two actions to unlock and then to push the door open.

Double keyed deadbolt locks may not be used on exterior doors to secure an occupied building!

This means that your business would typically install an inside crash bar that when pushed over-rides the lock mechanism allowing exit with one motion. The door can remain locked on the outside during late night hours.

During open hours, the hardware can be locked into a fixed free opening position that does not require the latch mechanism to work every time the door opens and thus saves wear and tear on the lock set. Heavy-duty door closer hardware keeps the doors closed and should withstand moderate wind pressure.

The crash bar type hardware is also required on the back door for the same fire code reason. Other types of lock mechanisms such as barrel bolts are not allowed for use in an occupied building. While they are allowed when the business is closed, we do not recommend their use due to the likely-hood of the manager forgetting to disengage the lock when the business opens in the morning.

We recommend that the back door of your business does not have an outside cylinder or access since general security policy should prevent back door use for anything other than taking out the trash and bringing in deliveries during open hours. Armed robbers love to see businesses with uncontrolled back door usage since it adds to the element of surprise and allows quick entrance and exit.

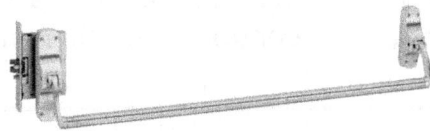

Your back door should be equipped with a bell or intercom to announce persons outside wishing to make a delivery or employees returning from a trash run and have a viewing device that allows your manager to visually inspect before opening the door.

Drive through windows need to be secured from the inside with no outside access to open. In our experience, all windows should be equipped with an auto open and closing device. These devices are activated either with a sensor or a bump bar that switches the motor on to open and closes the window when the operator moves away from the window.

We would like to add a special note about drive through windows during late night operations. Individuals gaining access to the restaurant through the open windows have robbed a number of restaurants. We recommend that the windows do not open more than 18" or so to prevent entry.

Door hardware accessing the manager's office should be heavy duty and should automatically lock when the door is closed. If you provide a dead-bolt lock that requires a key to open and to lock when the manager leaves, we can almost guarantee that the office door will be left unsecured the majority of time. Security measures that unnecessarily add extra steps will often be avoided rather than achieving compliance. A lot of confidential files and records are maintained in the managers office, so keep it simple and have the door lock automatically to keep unauthorized persons out.

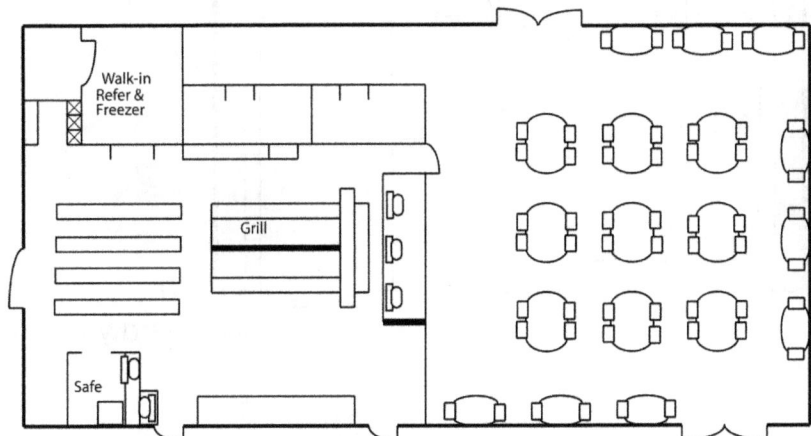

Cabinet locks and other secure storage areas all should be keyed depending on who you want to access these areas. If you intend to have a trusted employee have access to specific areas, the manager should issue a key for the duration of the task and maintain control when the storage area is secure.

Restroom door control can be a problem in fast food establishments where vandalism and unwanted vagrants can be an issue. You can install locks with a remote release button controlled by the manager when desired.

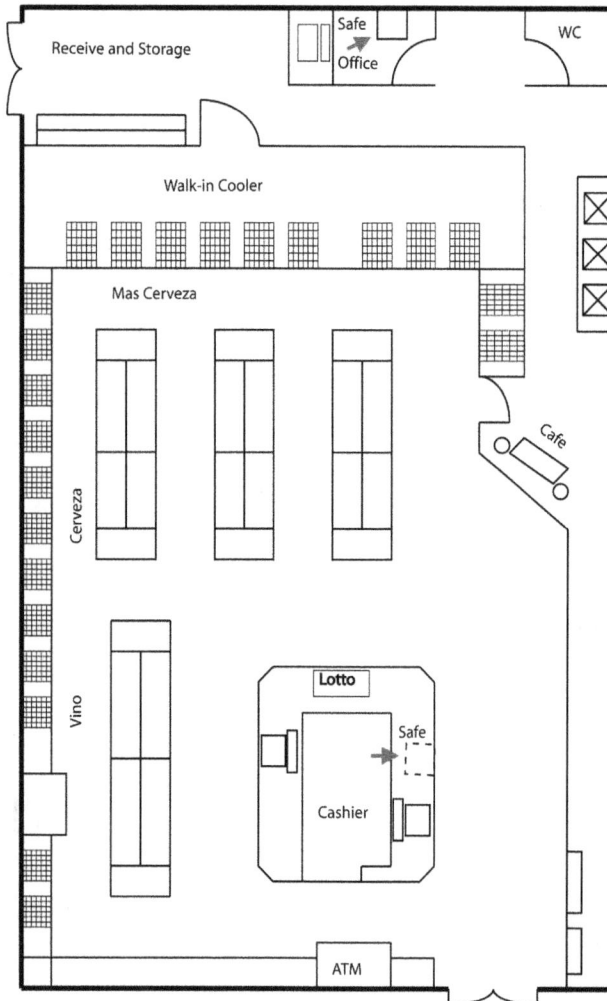

```
Receive and Storage       Safe      WC
                          Office

        Walk-in Cooler

        Mas Cerveza

  Cerveza                               Cafe

  Vino              Lotto
                            Safe

                    Cashier

                    ATM
```

Pete's Food and Beer somewhat resembles the restaurant as it has a front door and a back door in the employees only portion of the building.

Front door control should come in the form of a crash bar such as the one we illustrated on page 77. As with the restaurant model, the bar can be locked into the latch-retracted position allowing free entry and exit.

Heavy-duty door closer hardware keeps the door closed and should be able to withstand moderate wind pressure without being forced open.

The back doors are controlled by crash bar hardware and function in the same manner as the restaurant.

The managers office is equipped with the same type of interchangeable core (IC) cylinder as the front doors and will typically be key coded the same as the front doors.
Secure storage cages and rooms are also subject to the IC cylinder application.

Cobb City Lock and Security Supply have a number of different applications, as it is normally the type of enterprise that would be located in a commercial warehouse area. Unlike other commercial retail business locations that are in high traffic areas, the wholesalers tend to be in locations that have less police patrol protection and must rely on good night lighting, video systems, burglar alarms and steel doors.

The back access can be a combination of free standing and overhead rolling steel doors that provide maximum protection from burglary. After all, it doesn't make sense to under protect a door that a truck can back up to and burglars can empty your warehouse.

The business front door is a double aluminum door fitted with the usual crash bar hardware if there will be employees working in the building during hours closed to the public.

Since the back overhead steel doors are activated with a motorized switch from inside, a simple hasp and heavy-duty padlock arrangement can prevent forced entry attempts. In our back door example, the back dock has a smaller access door that can be utilized when a delivery is not in progress without requiring the large doors to be open.

If the dock access door is to be used as an entry option, it should be equipped with an IC cylinder lock and keyed the same as the front. All interior secure storage bins and cages should similarly be equipped with IC cylinder cabinet or padlocks to facilitate periodic key changes.

The sales office should be assumed to contain computer equipment as well as sales information that should be protected from unauthorized access and hard copy files should be stored in fire resistant file cabinets that are UL rated.

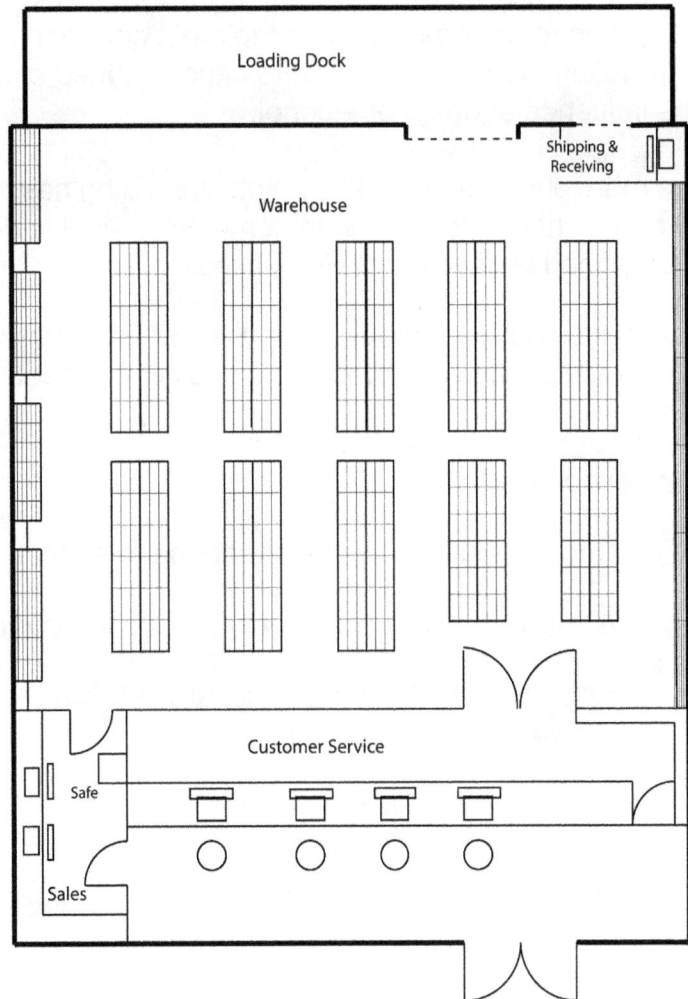

Loading Dock

Shipping & Receiving

Warehouse

Customer Service

Safe

Sales

Some facts about commercial burglaries are:

Commercial burglaries are more likely to be planned than residential burglaries and to involve a group rather than individuals.

Commercial premises are targeted because they are often large, vacant on weekends and after hours and situated in isolated non-residential areas, thereby limiting the amount of natural surveillance in the vicinity.

Larger retail outlets and manufacturing premises are the most commonly targeted in burglaries. Premises stocking goods that can be easily on-sold such as alcohol, tobacco and electronics, and premises that have large amounts of cash inside, are also more likely to be victimized

The vandalism costs associated with commercial burglary are generally higher than those for residential burglaries, and businesses can suffer considerable losses in time and resources while having to re-stock.

According to offender surveys, the most common motive for committing commercial burglary Is to obtain money. Other factors cited included excitement, opportunity, unemployment and The influence of drugs or alcohol.

The more entrance and exits points a building has, the more vulnerable it is to uninvited entry. All doors should be fitted with commercial quality dead latches. Using solid core doors with strong dead latches simply increases the amount of time needed to break in.

Doors and windows should be locked when the premises is unattended, obviously. We are amazed to periodically discover a business unsecured during mealtime and smoking breaks!

Glass doors should be made from burglar-resistant glass. Consider installing wire mesh or iron bars over all glass.

- Doors should not have exterior handles that can aid the use of pry bar tools.

- Along with solid core doors, be sure the door frames cannot easily be jimmied.

- Key systems for all commercial premises should be restricted and reproducible only by registered parties.

- Access to windows and the roof should be restricted.

**Interchangeable
core padlock**

Roller doors should be:

- Alarmed;
- Fitted to heavy gauge steel tracks;
- Locked, with a shackle protector and commercial quality casehardened padlock (internal fitting is preferable); and
- Operated by an electric motor to control access.

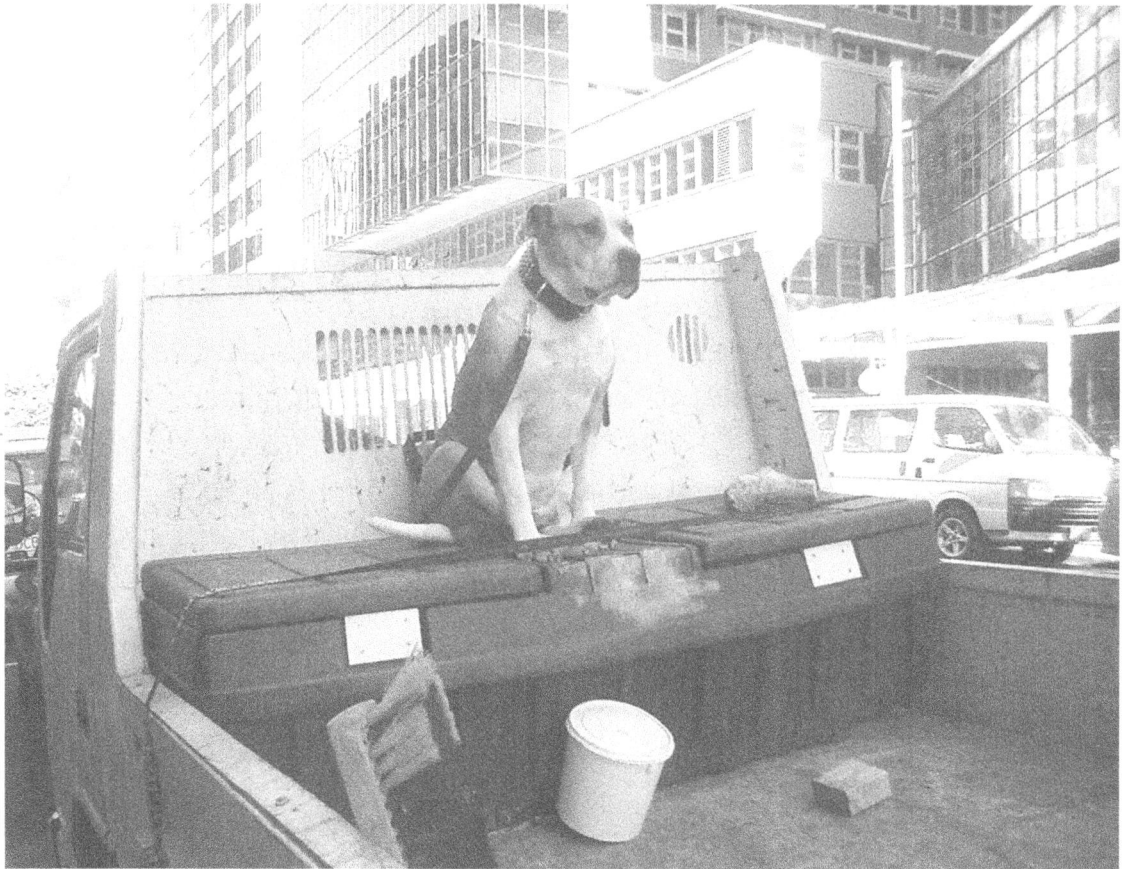

Locking up your tool box is important...
But not always necessary!

Chapter 5

Alarm
Systems

User error is the Number One
cause of all false alarms.

Statistically, 76% of all alarms
that you experience are caused
by your managers - or you!

Many business owners have a love/hate relationship with their alarm company. On one hand they provide the necessary burglary detection and prevention that you need and can be required by your liability insurer. On the other hand can be false alarms, alarms caused by managers forgetting their codes, after hours delivery people and repair vendors forgetting their codes, system breakdowns and did we mention middle of the night phone calls from the alarm company?

All of the problems you have heard about are true and also mostly avoidable.

But, remember, your not going to be dealing with some alarm company directly. The key is your relationship with your CPP loss prevention professional and the systems integrators that have installed and now maintain all of your security hardware. This is the company that you have identified as being capable of dealing with all of your integrated security systems issues. They will deal with the installation, set up central station monitoring, written response protocols, manager training, alarm code issuance and cancellation and take care of system repairs. Big companies hire Loss Prevention Directors to perform this important function. You can outsource and get the same results.

While the big company LP director has the expertise to know how to integrate the various components of a good loss prevention program, your outsource CPP consultant will do the same job but will need some input from you regarding how your business operates, what types of losses you have experienced and of course what policies and procedures you have in place.

Some alarm installation issues include what do you want the system to do? Will it be integrated with other security components such as a camera system? What do you want to happen if an alarm is set off in the middle of the night? Will it be used to control the back and other remote doors during open hours?

An alarm system is comprised of a control panel, one or more keypads to turn it on or off and a variety of sensors to detect doors opening or motion within a defined area. A dialing mechanism or radio back up or IP device contacts a central station operator in the event of an alarm or system trouble.

It is absolutely imperative that the installer uses the correct wire gauge and obeys local electrical codes. Many jurisdictions may require a licensed electrician to perform this task. All protection starts at the point of greatest potential loss and radiates outward. You would usually start where you keep money and other valuables.

Among the things that should occur in the event of a burglary, is that a loud horn or siren should sound at the point of entry. This effect may require more than one device. The purpose here is to disorient the burglar with a loud noise. To achieve this effect, you should install motion detectors in all areas of your business and don't forget to put one in the office where the safe is located.

At the same time that this event is occurring, the control panel should be notifying a central station that a break in has occurred at a specific alarm zone at your business location. This is a critical function of the system. If notification does not occur, the police will not be called. While this sounds obvious, many professional burglars will first cut your phone lines, often at the pole, before breaking in. You can defeat this burglar by having a back up radio dialer installed. The cost impact is approximately $10 to $20 a month above the cost of central station monitoring.

All doors and windows should have contact switches. Open and the alarm goes off.

The keypad arms/disarms the system and should be in a convenient location when entering or leaving.

The strobe light is located in the front sales floor area and flashes an intense light to alert Police or passersby that an alarm has been set off.

Passive infrared sensors detect movement. They should be on the front sales/backroom and in the office.

Wall mount Or...

Hold up buttons can be located in a variety of places not obvious to robbers.

Ceiling mount

The other route to monitoring is to have the system notify the central station using the Internet via broadband DSL or cable. Your CPP can advise you regarding the variable types of notification methods available in your area. It is important that all of your business locations have the same system and notification methodology if at all possible.

Hold up alarm buttons should be included in your system if your business handles cash or other disposable valuables. The buttons should not be placed next to the registers because you want your employees to follow your written policy for what to do in case of a robbery. An exception would be the small convenience store operation, which may have few employees working during late night operations and may even be placed inside bandit barriers or protected locations in the store. Read more on this topic in the policy chapter.

The use of alarm features while the business is open is the next consideration. You can set up your system back door alarm to function as a local alert to the manager if unauthorized use of the back door occurs. That is, a quieter local alarm separate from the main siren sounds requiring the manager's response. We recommend that this function be set to not allow managers to use a bypass code to circumvent the need to respond. An amazing amount of your merchandise or supplies can flow out of the back door if you do not maintain control.

Businesses such as fast food restaurants can program the system to allow a late night business mode where the dining room is closed and the doors alarmed in "stay" mode but use of the drive through window is allowed and employees can move around the interior.

Your alarm system should be programmed to allow a reasonable amount of time for your arriving and closing managers to set the system and depart without setting off the system unnecessarily.

When the system is installed and tested, you need to decide what will happen in the event of an alarm. When the central station operator receives your alarm notification on the computer screen, they are prompted to follow your protocols. Some of the following may apply:

POLICIES THAT YOU NEED

Should the police be called automatically or should the operator attempt to call your business first to determine if the alarm is an inadvertent event caused by your manager? This happens a lot. The alarm monitoring company has a list of your authorized users and you can arrange for each of them to have a code word that will allow cancellation of the alarm without police notification. This can cut false alarms and unnecessary police response when mistakes occur. And they will occur!

If the police are dispatched who should be called first to respond to the business? Who should be next? Somebody has to go and meet the responding police.

For those who do not particularly welcome middle of the night phone calls from the central station that an alarm is occurring at your business, you can consider a number of available services that are in the business of verifying alarms.

One of the best solutions is to hire an outsource company that uses a system that involves dialing into your business CCTV system to check for intruders. Should an intrusion be observed, the verification company operator can call the police and you. A properly installed alarm system will not have that many false alarms, so if an alarm does occur you need to take it seriously.

So, let's review a few issues related to your alarm system to remove it's presence as a contributor of stress in your life.

- The alarm system maintenance and operation is the contractual responsibility of your alarm system service provider relationship. Use your CPP loss prevention professional to help you manage the process.

- Your alarm operation procedures should be consistent for each of your business sites so that you can uniformly enforce policy. Policy must be in writing and all authorized users must sign off as having been trained. Enforce the policy!

- Each manager must have their own alarm code and neither borrow or share their code with anyone. Care must be taken to protect code usage from the view of unauthorized persons. Codes must be cancelled immediately if an authorized user leaves your employment or is transferred to a new site. New authorized users must be issued their new code and be trained before their first shift in responsible charge.

- Persons designated to be on the central station call list in the event of a police dispatch must respond to the business to meet the police. An outsourced alarm response contract is preferable. Don't even think of putting your secretaries name at the top of the call list (we have seen this happen!). Not only will she not respond in the middle of the night, but you will need a new administrative assistant not long after her second 2:00 AM call from the central station.

- Test the system regularly. Make it a contractual obligation of the installer to certify the system integrity on a regular basis.

Now is a good time to discuss the placement of the various types of alarm components in our fictional business establishments. We want to explain how each sensor type works and where it belongs.

Gordo's Fast Food has been equipped with burglary protection and a hold up alarm. Let's walk through the placement of the sensors and other hardware.

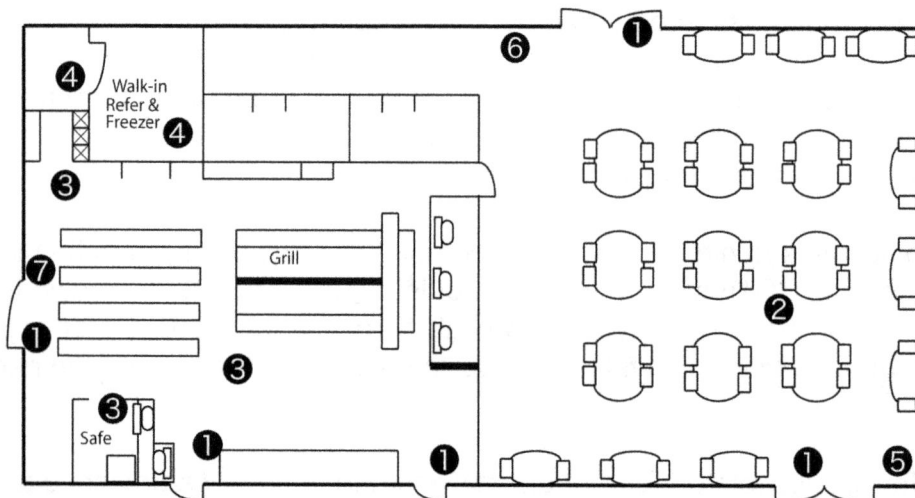

1.   Door and window contact switches - Open doors or windows and alarm sounds. The store perimeter doors and windows all have contact switches. The system allows the manager to set the system in "stay" mode for late night business that arms the doors but bypasses the drive through windows and motion sensors.

2.   Strobe light - Strobe pulses when alarm is set off to alert police and others with a bright pulsing light.

3.   Passive infrared sensors - Sense heat and movement and alarm sounds. By requiring both heat and motion to activate, false alarms are reduced.

4.   Hold up alarm switches - Press or pull and silent alarm is activated.   Our experience with restaurant robberies shows that many times robbers force employees into the walk in before making their escape. During the robbery, employees are often told to stay in the walk-in and sometimes the employees are tied up or otherwise restrained. For this reason, hold up alarm switches should be located no more than 12-18 inches off the floor.

Note: **We do not recommend that hold up buttons be placed near registers or the safe in the manager's office as this may provide a temptation to hit the alarm button rather than following your policy to give the robbers the demanded money. Remember that managers or employees attempting to resist may result in the robber escalating the level of violence and possibly injuring or killing one of your employees.**

5.   Key Pad - Turns the system on and off.   We recommend that where possible the key pad should be located reasonably close to the entrance/exit of the store and also have direct line of sight of the back door to allow manager control of the back door alarm function. If this is not possible, it is relatively inexpensive to install a second keypad near the back door.

6.   Siren/Horn - A loud siren or horn sounds when system is activated. This high decibel noise is installed to disorient a burglar. Place it in a location to maximize the sound effect throughout the restaurant.

7.   Local alarm/Chime - Sounds a noticeably loud chime or buzz when the back door is opened. The purpose of the back door alarm is to alert the manager that someone has opened the back door. The back door should always be under the managers control due to the likelihood of large amounts of food and other supplies "walking out the door" if it is uncontrolled.

Note: To ensure that the door is controlled by the manager, the back door local alarm can be set up to be always armed. That means that it will sound when opened and require a manager's code to silence it. When the door is again closed the system re-arms automatically. During open hours, the central station is not notified.

If you use a wireless installation, you can opt for a portable remote control!

We recommend that managers not have the ability to by-pass the back door alarm as what we found is that the majority of managers will simply come in at open, turn off the burglar alarm, key in the back door bypass code and leave it off all day. They will never notice the dishonest employee hauling your merchandise out of the door.

Thieves and armed robbers love uncontrolled back door access!

Your fire alarm system is mandated by local and state ordinances and is part of your system alarm panel function. You do not need a separate panel, just one that has enough zones to accommodate the fire sensors (unless the fire marshal says otherwise).

Pete's Food and Beer has been equipped with a burglar alarm and hold up switches.

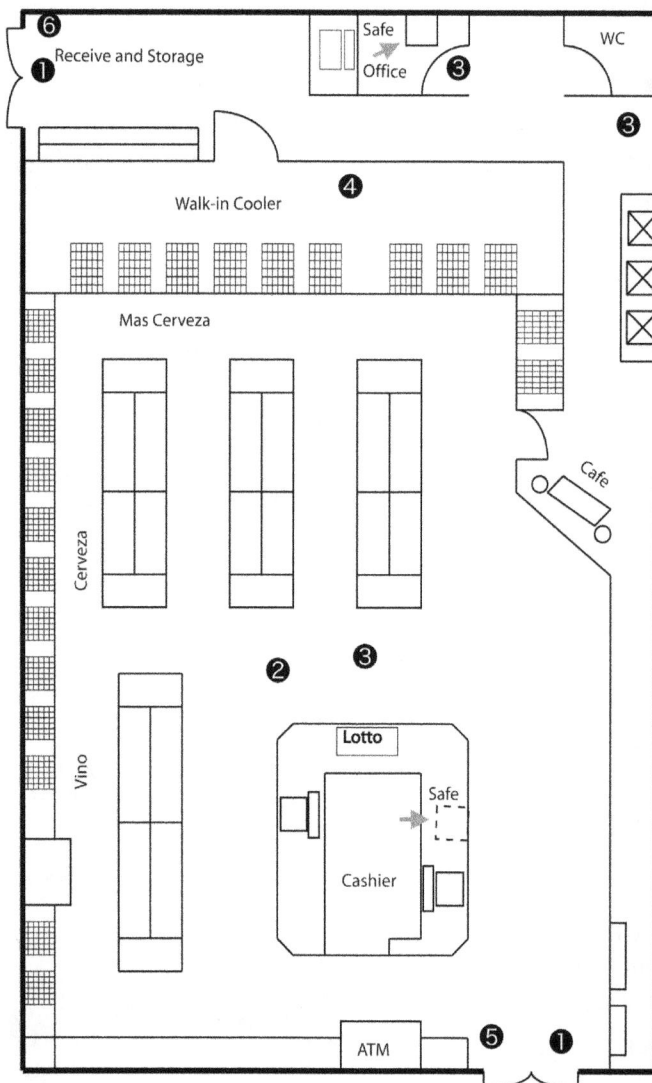

Alarm components include:

1. Door contact switches. Since there is only a front and a back door to protect, only two are installed to activate the system when doors are opened.

2. A strobe light is installed to alert police.

3. Passive infrared sensors (PIR) are installed to each cover a 360-degree area.

They are installed to cover the back hall areas and the front of the store to alert if the front windows are broken. A unit also covers the office interior since in our experience burglars have cut a hole in the roof or removed HVAC vents to drop into the office and access the safe. In a C-store it's all about protecting the beer, cigarettes and the money.

4. The hold up button.

We have placed the button in the walk in cooler for the same reason we put it there in the restaurant. Take over robberies often involve the manager and employees being forced into the cooler and phones may also be disabled.

We have a few other surprises in store that we will discuss when we install cameras in Pete's stores!

5.   Key pad.

We have placed the pad by the front door in order to facilitate turning the system on and off. As with the restaurant, great concern needs to be directed at controlling the back door to keep the stock from walking away and robbers from finding an easy way in.

6.   Back door alarm

The alarm needs to be loud enough to get the managers attention if an unauthorized exit occurs. We have observed systems that alert when the door opens and silence when the door closes. We noticed that after a while, the manager no longer hears it and does not respond to the alarm. You now have, for all practical purposes, an uncontrolled door.

The restaurant model of requiring a manager's code to silence the door alarm is the only way to insure monitored back door use unless, of course, the manager gives their code away to the employees using the door.

You can however, also enforce monitored back door usage as a condition of continuing employment. It works like this. Employees who open the back door without the manager's permission get one warning.   Disobey the rule twice and they will be terminated. You can also take the warning clause away for violations occurring after dark when the store is the most vulnerable to robbery. Managers must also follow the after dark prohibition.

We know of one company that laid down the law for all employees regarding use of the back door and experienced a substantial reduction of theft and armed robberies. They told us that at first it required the very painful termination of two employees before everyone understood that the rules would be taken seriously.

Cobb City Lock and Supply has been equipped with a system typical for a wholesale warehouse environment. Cobb City Lock hardware includes:

1.   Door contacts. The front door, the access door from the dock and the large roll-down door are protected and will set off the alarm if they are opened.

2.   Strobe lights.

These have been installed in the front counter area in view of the front entrance and on the back loading dock to signal that the alarm has been activated. Since our warehouse distribution center is located in a commercial area, both front and back entrances have wide road access to accommodate trucks and receive periodic police patrols at night.

3.   Passive Infrared detectors (PIR)

The business hours which are mostly 8-5 PM Monday through Friday and a half day on Saturday. Crime exposure is mostly after dark and a history of burglary dictates that protection levels address the exposure. The PIR's have been placed to cover doors and the warehouse interior space. Additional units are placed in the front customer service area and the Sales room area where the safe is located.

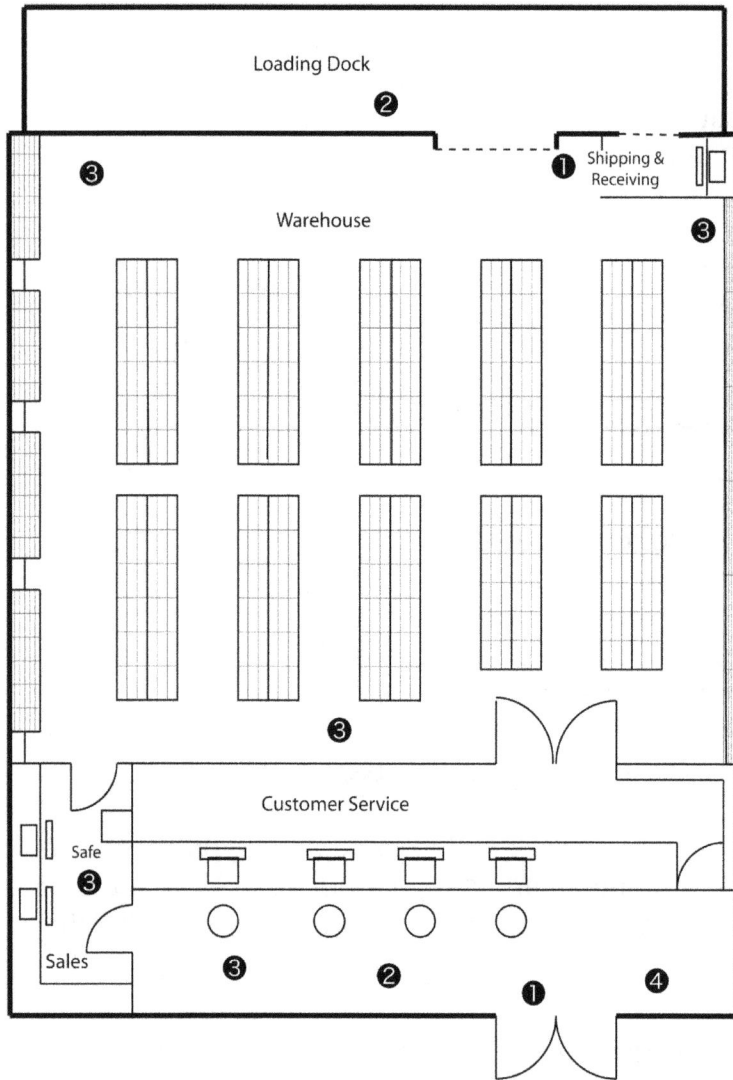

4. Key pad.

The manager arriving in the morning turns off the system. The employees at our fictional business all leave at about the same time each day with the manager setting the system. We have not added a keypad for the back dock door, as it is open all day to accommodate delivery drivers. The area is also controlled by a shipping and receiving person during all open hours.

The overhead freight door cannot be powered open without the receiver's key and all controls are located in area where redundant alarm sensors will detect an intruder.

We have not installed hold up buttons at this location due to the lack of any area history that would indicate that a robbery threat exists. However, should the concern arise, it is a very easy addition.

The real threat to a wholesaler is burglary and fire. The fire alarm system has been integrated with the burglary protection and a commercial sprinkler system has been installed throughout the building.

Fire pull stations need special wiring and sometimes a separate alarm panel depending on your state fire codes.

Our 2 cents on alarm systems priorities

1. Fire and Burglar alarms that do what they are supposed to do should be the FIRST priority. They need to detect what they are designed to detect, annunciate the event locally as programmed, and communicate correctly in a timely manner.

2. Using quality equipment, and installing it correctly is the next priority. That means the use of UL rated equipment with the correct wiring type.

3. Designing systems to be user friendly, easy to operate, and making sure the business management and all potential users are instructed on the correct operation and how to cancel false alarms should be the next priority. This includes a customer service phone number to call a live person in case the user is new, confused or having a problem with the system.

4. Cross or redundant zoning of sensors should be a high priority, combined with customer call list notification only on single and Police Department or Guard dispatch on multiple trips zones procedure to match. That advice is from the many experts in the alarm field that we know and our own personal experience based on ours and their review of years of alarm history, which concluded that over 95% of all dispatches would have been eliminated by this procedure.

5. Some form of dual call verification is a priority. Other forms of video and audio verification are good, but if comprehensive, can be expensive. Audio verification alone is unacceptable due to high false alarms due to noise generation from traffic to wind and weather.

6. Guard response should be considered instead of Police Department on outdoor systems, systems with unstable installation environments, or user activity that creates high risk. That means that you do not want to be sending one of your managers to your business location at 3 AM to verify an alarm because they will not be able to respond to a crime in progress and risk being injured or killed by the criminals.

False alarms are a problem, and your goal as a company is to balance elimination of false alarms, while still detecting VALID alarms, and then react to them correctly. That includes your responsibility to make sure that all of your users are trained and know how to deal with the alarm system.

Your alarm contract needs to specify exactly what response the alarm company will ensure that they will provide to inspect, test, repair and provide your people with good training. Do your part or plan on writing checks for false alarms!

TEST <u>YOUR</u> ALARM SYSTEM!

It is important to ensure that your security system is communicating properly at all times, especially if your system does NOT have Radio or Cellular backup. Regular testing of your security system will help insure its proper operation at the time of an emergency, and help prevent false alarms.

WHEN TO TEST
We recommend that your company test their system at least monthly or:

- When there are changes in your telephone service (DSL, call waiting and call notes, new jacks, etc.).

- When you experience telephone problems.

- When you suspect there is an equipment malfunction.

- When you have a power failure or lightening damage.

HOW TO TEST:
- Contact the central station before you do anything. You should have with you a card that includes your monitoring account number and the telephone number to call.

- You must notify the monitoring company when you are testing your system to prevent them from dispatching authorities on your alarm signals, thereby avoiding false alarms.

- Tell the central station to put your alarm account "On test" for a specific time period. Arm your system and then activate it and let the siren sound for at least 1 minute.

- Disarm the system and restore system to normal. Call the central station again and see if alarm signals were received.

- If signals were received, advise central station to take the system Off test.

Note!
Many municipalities require that business owners
license and register their alarm systems with the
police and fire departments and maintain call lists of
company contacts.

"Suppose ... burglars had made entry into this ... library. Picture them seated here on this floor, pouring the light of their dark-lanterns over some books they found, and thus absorbing moral truths and getting moral uplift. The whole course of their lives would have been changed. As it was, they kept straight on in their immoral way and were sent to jail. For all I know, they may next be sent to Congress."

- Mark Twain (1835-1910)
Pen name for Samuel Langhorne Clemens US writer, humorist, lecturer, river pilot.

**Camera systems can be simple
or complex...**

Chapter 6

Camera Systems

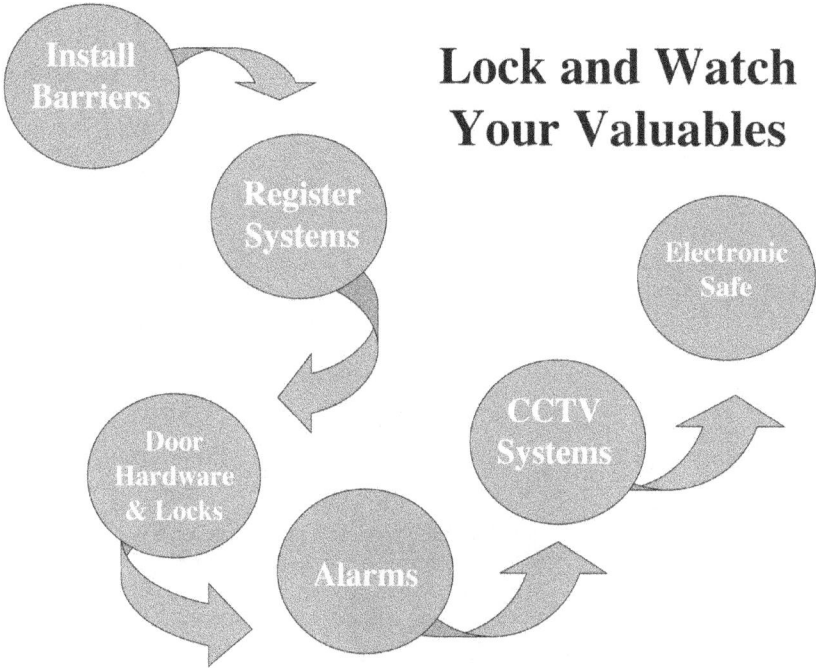

Lock and Watch Your Valuables

Install Barriers

Register Systems

Door Hardware & Locks

Alarms

CCTV Systems

Electronic Safe

This chapter deals with the need for a business owner or multi-unit operator to have the ability of being able to determine what is happening in the business when they are not present. We have to share with you that many people that you designate as managers are task oriented, performing functions in their task comfort zone and can be oblivious to operations around them or at least what the employees are doing out of their line-of-sight. Professional Managers, on the other hand, step back and observe what is happening through out the operation and only jump into the "task" arena when something is going wrong. Sometimes the business owner needs to see what is going on.

PLANNING YOUR CCTV INSTALLATION

All of us in general are aware that we are trading some of our freedoms for security. In spite of the Benjamin Franklin admonition that those that do have neither, the use of this technology is clearly becoming a normal part of our public life and in many cases becoming a tool we use for our home security as well.

According to a recent news poll from ABC News and the Washington Post, Americans are largely accepting about being watched by video surveillance.

The two news organizations jointly conducted a small telephone poll of Americans in 2007, to assess current opinions on public surveillance. Perhaps not surprisingly, considering that city surveillance projects seem to be proliferating every day, some 71 percent of Americans said they were in support of increasing use of surveillance cameras.

The support was stronger in women than men, and among those with a college degree as opposed to those who had a high school education or less. Strongest support was found among seniors over the age of 80, while younger counterparts from Generation Y are not quite as warm to the idea of more cameras.

The events of the Oklahoma City bombing and the 9/11 attacks may have helped sway public opinion to be more supportive of wide surveillance camera networks, this spread of cameras isn't limited solely to the U.S., it's an international phenomenon that limits to police and security manpower are forcing municipalities to turn to the use of surveillance cameras. The image quality of the latest camera technologies, from image stabilization to camera intelligence

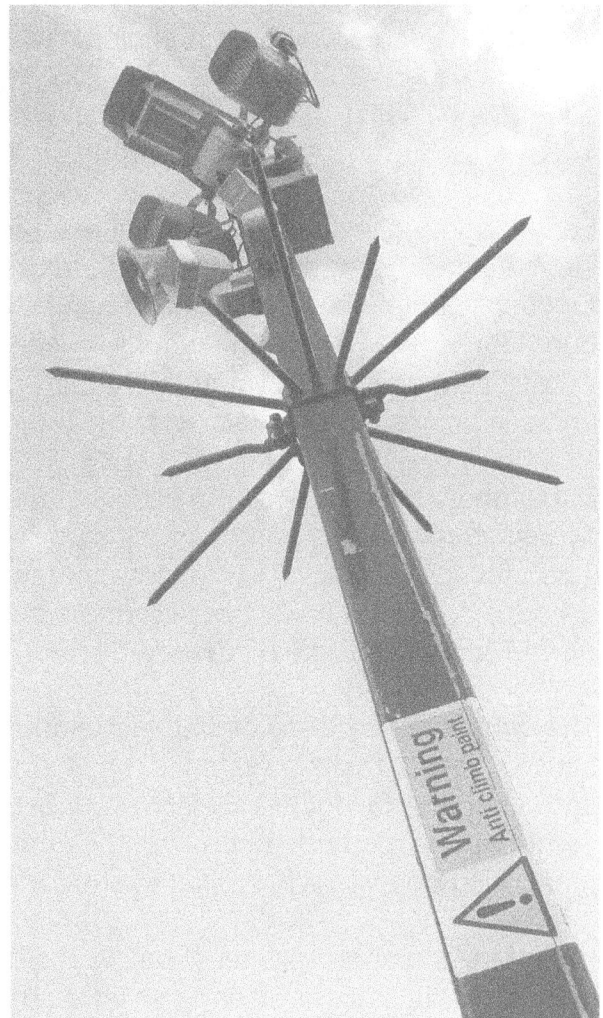

and greater image range, are central to increases in adoption.

While the UK has consistently been recognized as the international leader in surveillance cameras per capita, there are many other countries that are expanding their use of cameras. It has been said that the average Londoner is observed and recorded by 300 cameras a day.

A good CCTV system would have recorded the burglary that occurred in Chapter One when you lost some big bucks! It might have been prevented completely since the insiders that were most likely responsible, would know that they might be recognized and possibly even recorded off property at a remote location. The very clear trend is the movement toward the use of Internet Protocol or IP cameras, connected to a remote storage and surveillance facility that is located off site.

In much the same way as companies have used similar solutions to monitoring burglar and fire alarms, central stations are also evolving into systems that were primarily receiving alerts over phone lines to systems that are monitoring their client locations via DSL and cable Internet.

Early forms of the convergence of these two previously separate functions are evolving into services that handle the monitoring of all of a businesses burglary and fire protection functions along with the storage of a significant amount of recallable video of the business operations. That means that your service provider can receive an intrusion alarm signal, access your site video system and after verification call the police with a description of the crime in progress. The entire event is then available for the prosecution of the criminal.

Subscribers to these systems can use their PC from virtually any location that has Internet access to review any portion of the stored digital video records at any time. For instance, video found showing a theft or other criminal act, can be recorded on the PC and copied for use as evidence in a number of formats that can be viewed by any other PC or Mac that can play MPEG or Quicktime movies.

The purpose of a closed circuit television system is to not only detect and deter criminal activity. In fact there is evidence that the main purpose is not to prevent but to record criminal and other activity not beneficial to your business. Believe it or not, some of your employees will forget the camera is there and the criminals will ignore it. Cameras are great tools for monitoring good as well as bad customer contact skills performed by your employees.

Camera systems rapidly de-value in benefit unless you regularly monitor recorded activities during your business day and use your observations to catch thieves or others whose behaviors are negatively impacting your business and taking appropriate immediate action. But the most successful use is to catch people doing the right things and publicly reward the behavior that you tell them you saw on the 24/7 recorded video. Just think of the benefits of using the positive behavioral reinforcement of good employees to let any bad apples know that you are watching!

Recommended systems include the use of digital cameras and recorders if you have opted not to use off site IP service. Systems utilizing videotape are discouraged due to the breakdown of quality over time and the need to change and replace tapes regularly.

The current standard is to use at least digital video recorders as noted above. If, in addition, it is common and cost effective in your industry to utilize off site monitoring vial DSL or cable Internet connection, seek the advise of a your CPP security professional for options available to your business in your geographical area.

Digital Video Recorders (DVR) are sold in a number of configurations and the business owner needs to assess the value of a number of features currently available.

DVR's are essentially a large computer hard drive that has software installed that controls the recording of one or more cameras. They allow activity occurring in your place of business to be viewed at any connected video monitor screen or from a remote location by dialing into the system using a modem to access the current activity or previous recorded activity. Recorded activity is stored on the hard drive until it is full and then begins to record over the oldest recorded data. The process is governed by the size of the hard drive, the number of cameras attached and the quality of the image being recorded.

Each DVR has either 4, 8, 12 or 16 inputs to plug in your cameras. Each camera image is recorded on a separate portion of the hard drive and a significant number of days can be recorded and subsequently replayed. For instance, a DVR with 760 MB of memory can record 16 cameras simultaneously at 8-10 frames per second with high quality resolution for 40 to 60 days. The system is able to do this because digital recording can be set to only record when some movement is occurring in the view of the camera.

This means that if you are viewing and recording your loading dock, nothing records during the elapsed time between events where motion disturbs or interrupts the digital pixels being viewed causing the software to record the event of the changed picture. So cameras that are viewing a location where constant movement occurs are always recording the activity and cameras viewing intermittent activity are recording less often.

Digital Video Recorder

This is important to know because some security requirements may dictate that the cameras be constantly recording whether anything is happening or not on a 24-7 basis. This will allow you to prove that no event occurred during the time frame in question and that the system did not just fail to record.

During playback, it is important to understand that the user can select a particular time frame and range lock or protect the data for some or all of the cameras recording to preserve the image thus preventing that portion of the hard drive from being recorded over.

Captured images can also be down loaded onto a CD and be replayed at a later time. Be sure that the captured video is formatted on your system to replay using the common format MPEG4 or later on your computer. This important if you wish to record evidence of criminal activity and need to preserve the CD for police use.

Camera coverage should include sales floor or front areas such as entrances and dining rooms, cash registers, back door and storage areas and in some instances where security needs dictate, the managers office and particularly the area facing the safe. Other areas for consideration are parking lots and drive through lanes. Cameras should never be placed in any area where an expectation of privacy exists such as a rest room or employee locker room.

Audio recording is discouraged due to the prohibition in many states as well as the requirement to notify all parties being recorded. We recommend that you never audio record anything because of the legal pitfalls of doing so.

A primary concern related to camera system installation is making sure that the video is recording what you need to replay later. For instance, a long shot of your parking lot will allow you to see cars entering or leaving but will not be focused enough for you to read license plate numbers or see peoples faces. If you need to see faces, cameras should be placed so that you can identify the person eye to eye, so to speak, rather than from above the subject where a hat can hide facial features. New high definition digital cameras have been developed that allow you to zoom in and read license plate numbers and record recognizable facial detail from a significant distance away from the action.

An additional consideration is that unless you use an ultra low light camera, they cannot see in the dark. The good news is that low light cameras are very affordable and can work well in dark locations with the aid of infrared light sources.

Protective housing

A number of POS manufacturers and at least one after market company we know can provide systems that integrate your video with your POS register system. This allows a view of the transaction with an image of the register receipt imposed on the monitor view, so that you can capture an image of your register operator under ringing sales or other prohibited activities to back up termination and prosecution.

The latest digital equipment using Internet

protocols is a system that is designed to send all of your video over the Internet via broadband access to be recorded and observed off site at a remove location. Careful consideration should be given to these systems as being the direction toward where technology is taking us next. Why have recorders on site when you have the ability to access your video any time you want it at any location on your laptop computer by user name and pin number with your surveillance subscription. That means that you buy and maintain less equipment even though the monthly cost might be a little more when you consider the need for broadband service at all of your locations and have to pay for subscription and other fees.

POLICIES THAT YOU NEED

- You written policy regarding the use of the camera systems must include some mandatory targeted observation time for all of your managers and the observation time should be documented.

- Camera systems do require preventative maintenance or they can be susceptible to failure at inopportune times. Some environments are worse than others and a good "PM" program can save a lot of money paid in emergency repairs. Be sure to use a camera housing to protect the equipment in dirty or smoky environments and to protect the equipment from tampering by your employees.

- Put your employees and your customers on notice that you are conducting video recording using appropriate signs.

- Your written policy should treat any attempts to disable or abuse the system as you would with any act of vandalism with disciplinary action up to and including employment termination. It should not be possible for managers or employees to turn off the DVR or manipulate or move camera focus. You can install tamper alarms on the camera housing.

- Make sure that all equipment problems are quickly repaired. Your system installer may be able to provide loaner equipment for critical components such as DVR's and monitors.

- Turn off video monitors when you close for the night. The system will still be recording and you will extend the life of the monitor significantly.

So what are some of the considerations related to the placement and use of camera systems?

Did you know that an agency of the federal government has issued a guideline that sets a performance standard how a camera system should be installed in a commercial business? That performance standards state where the cameras should go? What the quality of the image should be for playback? That the standard specifically references banks and convenience stores? That the agency in question is none other than the Forensic Science Division of the FBI? The Department Of Homeland Security.

If your company is looking into installing camera systems, you may want to take a few minutes to consider the following and if you are really turned on by such governmental elocution, you can obtain a copy of the standards at the Forensic Division website.

The standard is published in two parts and in Part 1 addresses system design, recording systems, cameras, media, system maintenance, retention of recordings and evidence handling.

The stated purpose of these requirements is to "increase the likelihood that images recovered from CCTV systems are sufficient to enable law enforcement officials to identify people and objects depicted therein".

Part 2 of the standard deals very specifically with the use and installation of cameras in banks and convenience store applications. Floor plans are included. This soup to nuts approach appears to be intended as a standard for all retail applications. As you can imagine, the government would like to see the days of crappy un-viewable video from crime scenes to be a thing of the past. The only way they see that dream becoming an eventual reality after viewing miles and miles of fuzzy bank robbery video, is to publish a clear document of standards stating how the system is supposed to work.

So why is this important to the installer of security equipment and the end user customer? Is it because of your potential liability exposure in the event that your company is sued following a crime loss or an event involving injury to one of your customers? Would you have some responsibility if the person suing your company proves in court that the equipment that you installed failed to perform it's state purpose resulting in injury to their client?

We don't know for sure because we are not lawyers. We are, however, experienced at getting sued for alleged inadequate security resulting in a claimed monetary loss/injury/death to a customer or invitee or employee on the premises of a former corporate employer. For the most part the suits were settled for fairly insignificant amounts or were dismissed. That was, however, before a number of published security standards began to emerge after 2001.

As a Regional Loss Prevention Manager for the Big Company (read deep pockets) getting sued, guess who had to go to the deposition and defend what security systems, policies and procedures were used and why? For the most part, since there were no published standards, only general industry practices for comparison, it was fairly simple to show that not only did the company provide reasonable care for the customer/plaintiffs safety but actually exceeded the level of protective systems that were provided in similar establishments in areas with similar crime history. Therefore our attorneys would argue, while extraordinary barriers could have been possibly able to prevent the event from occurring, the likelihood of such an injury event occurring was simply not foreseeable. Case dismissed!

Published standards, on the other hand, can give a plaintiffs attorney a potential blue print to follow to determine if a case might exist that could allow some money damages to be extracted from a company obliged to provide reasonable care of his client, "the victim".

The standards that get published can come from a number of directions that you need to know about. As mentioned above, the folks at Homeland Security are now in the business of publishing standards that may or may not be widely known even to the industry segment expected to follow them. The CCTV standard has been around since July 2004. It came to our attention when a lecture was attended in 2005 where an FBI Forensic Division agent explained the program with a PowerPoint presentation to a room full of law enforcement and loss prevention managers. Nobody there had heard of it before.

What all of this means to all of us is that the hardware that you buy must meet the performance standards that are published. Don't even think about buying cheap systems on your own or from a dealer who is not aware that published standards exist.

The first fictional business is **Gordo's Fast Food**, which we have already equipped with a good lock system and commercial burglary and fire alarm.

As you can see, our cameras have been placed as follows:

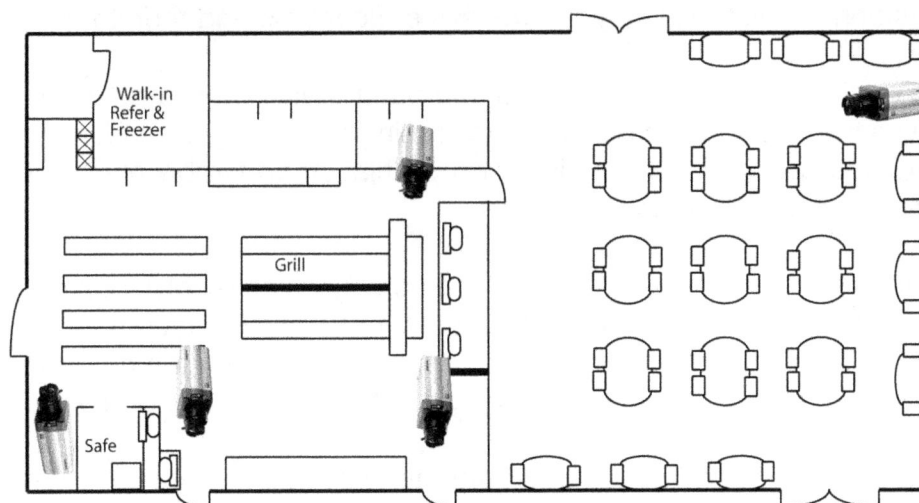

Note: We told you that you need to provide a bubble or housing to protect all cameras in the restaurant and as a general rule, all video monitoring should <u>not</u> include audio recording due to privacy laws in many states.

1.   Dining room:

The purpose of this camera is to observe the front counter from a far corner looking across the dining room. In our experience, this camera acts as a deterrent to pick pockets and unruly individuals.

2.   Front Counter.

The counter camera should have a good view of both your register operators and customers. You should be able to clearly see whether money is placed in the register during a transaction and the customers' facial features. You may need to install a second camera in the opposite direction if the first camera does not give you sufficient detail. You should avoid camera angles looking down on people's heads, as all a robber needs to avoid being filmed is a hat!

3.   Front (Food) Window:

This camera angle is used to view the transaction completion with food going out of the window. Since errors or order changes occur here, you need to be able to see the correction and also view the customer in the car.

4.   Back (Money) Window:

Since upward of 60-70% of business for many fast food restaurants is through the drive through, viewing the money transaction is very important. You are monitoring the cash transaction and the cars' occupants.

5.   Back Door:

Here is the opportunity to see what is happening at the back door when your not there, Is the manager monitoring and controlling the door? Is it trash going out or your food products? Is the door being used after dark?

The next consideration is the location of the system controls and monitors.

As we stated earlier, the DVR is really just a computer that is dedicated to recording your cameras versus the one you use for word processing or viewing spreadsheets. It should be kept in a protected dry environment with good ventilation preferably away from contaminating chemicals and especially restaurant grease.

The monitor that allows you to see the real time activity being recorded and the history of what already has been recorded is usually located in the manager's office. An additional consideration is to place a monitor on the front line showing only the counter so that customers can see that they are being observed. The purpose is robbery prevention.

Many fast food restaurants also install outdoor cameras to monitor the parking lot and the drive through lane. They have found that is helpful to the manager working on the line to be able to look at a monitor located above the food window to see the number of cars queued up in line. It is also helpful to observe night activity in the lot to be aware of and act on loitering and other undesirable activity.

Pretty much all of the basic digital cameras and recording equipment is capable of off-site monitoring and recording. Most business owners we know really like the ability to observe their business activity unannounced.

Having the ability to impose cash register transaction detail over the recorded image is also a desirable feature that we discussed earlier in this chapter.

Don't forget to use the information that you record to identify and reward good behaviors not just to catch people doing bad things.

Catch them doing something right and reward good behaviors!

Pete's Food and Beer has been equipped with an alarm system, key control and a high tech cash handling system. It has also been provided with an interactive camera and security system.

Cameras have been placed as follows:

1.   Front Door:
A good face view is recorded of everyone coming in the door.

2.   Service Counter:
Two cameras address the front registers in opposite directions. This allows for a clear view of register transactions as well as Lotto and ATM machine activity.

3.   Wine and Beer Coolers:
A camera is aimed from front to back to record activity at the coolers. Another camera addresses the back of the store.

4.   Back Door:
Back door activity is recorded that can be used to determine if policies and procedures are being followed.

5.   Office
It is where the money is stored and deposits change hands with the armored car company. You definitely want to record what happens when these guys show up and take your money away! It should also not be a comfortable place for managers and employees to hang out rather than be working out front.

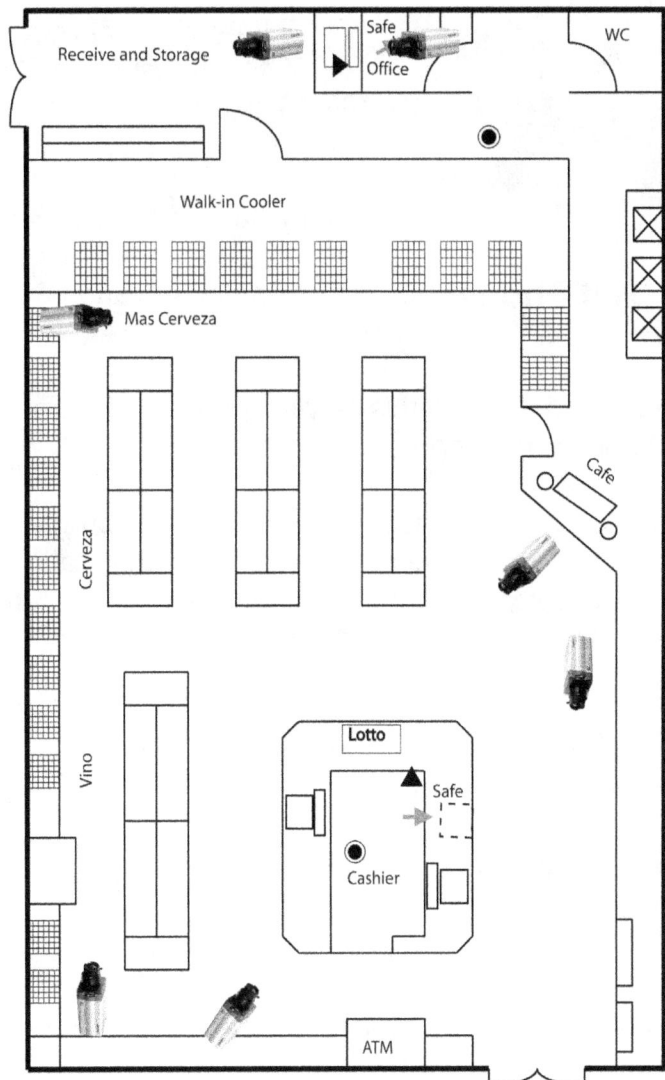

A number of companies offer interactive systems mostly for convenience stores and restaurants. They charge anywhere from $200-$400 per month and it works like this:

In addition to the cameras, DVR and monitors, the interactive company also provides a server to transmit video to a central station where remote operators can view your business when they are alerted to a problem or by prearranged random checks. Most contracts call for 2-3 random checks per day.

The interactive part is that the store is also equipped with audio equipment allowing conversation to occur between your manager and the monitoring operator. A call button and a special dedicated phone are also installed.

Hot Phone!

If you alert the central station regarding a problem such as a suspicious person in the store via the alert button or the direct-line phone, the operator called an "intervention specialist" comes on line to view the business and investigate the nature of the problem. If appropriate and it appears safe to do so, the operator will converse with the manager and announce verbally through speakers located through out the store that they are security and ask the person to leave.

The manager can also pick up the dedicated phone and talk to security personnel. Managers can routinely ask for services such as an on-line observation as they go safely to their cars at night at closing time.

In order to perform this service, parking lot cameras are usually also installed and good lighting is very important.

The interactive company also acts as the burglar alarm system during closed hours and if electronic motion sensors alert the central station, the operator can identify and verify the illegal activity and contact the police. This system virtually eliminates false alarm response since all alarms are verified before the police are contacted to respond.

You can find these specialized companies by consulting with your CPP loss prevention professional who can help you determine equipment and camera system placement that will be needed to ensure the proper coverage of the business.

Many large central station companies, including those that are Internet based are now providing expanded service programs.

Cobb City Lock and Supply has been equipped with a camera system suited to a warehouse environment.

Since a large amount of products are received and shipped, the system must have the ability to record the receiving process, verify that procedure is followed and be able to watch the shipment in the dock area until the contents are broken out and placed in stock.

The various camera positions shown are intended to represent the tasks each camera should perform. For example beginning at the front door, the first camera that we see will monitor the front counter sales area.

1. Front Counter:
Monitoring walk in ordering and payment collection procedures.

2. Sales Room:
Keeps an eye on the cash deposits and is the location where the system is recorded and the business activity can be monitored by the manager.

3. Warehouse:
Cameras on each corner of the warehouse are intended to show the monitoring of the open space where the stock is stored in boxes and bins. Coverage should include a clear view of each aisle and have no dead spots or blind areas that escape surveillance.

4. Receiving:
This location represents the monitoring of all receiving and shipping activity. This task may require more than one camera to ensure that the necessary angles are covered and no activity is missed.

5. Back Dock:
The two outside cameras represent the need to cover the dock from all angles in order to provide observation of arriving and departing deliveries. Camera views must also cover entry and egress out of the inset back door and activity at the freight-receiving window.

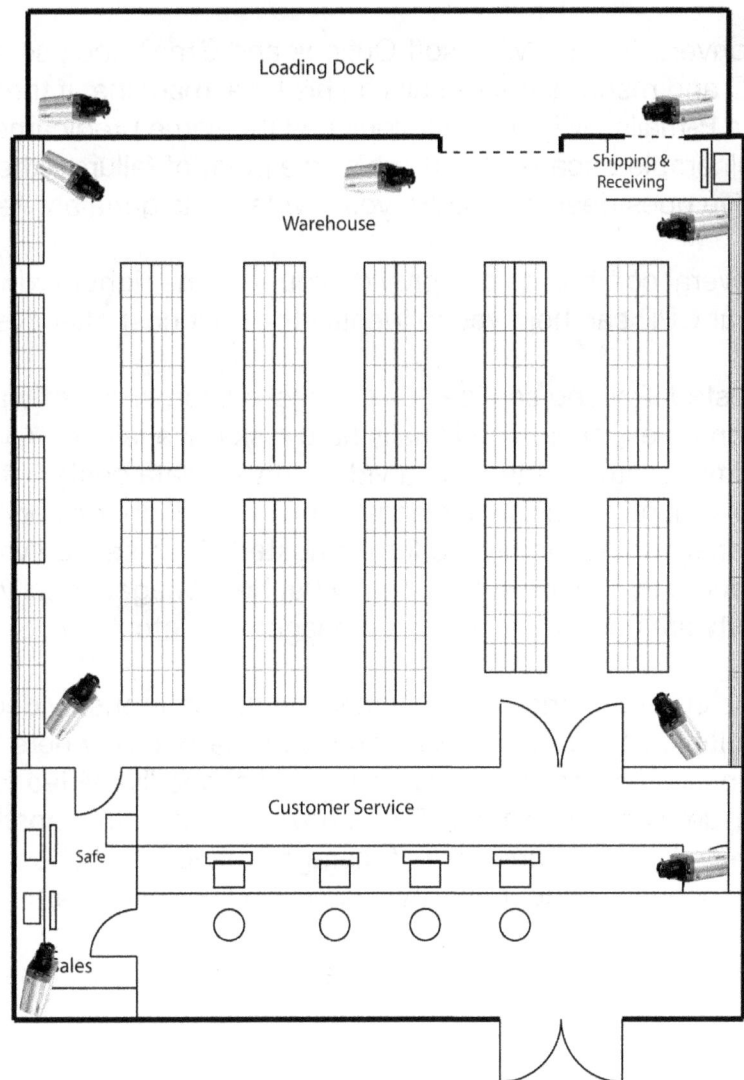

Loading Dock

Shipping & Receiving

Warehouse

Customer Service

Safe

Sales

The simple principle is to be able to watch and record everything that has the likelihood to disappear if you don't!

So What is the next big thing in video surveillance?

Hosted Video Solution. How and why?

Just as Google G-mail service is a hosted E-mail service that makes management of E-mails easy to use and easy to access: Hosted video solution allows management of live video views, recorded history and user accounts easy and simple to manage. The by-product of a hosted video service is no more software upgrades, no more worries about hard disk failure and no more management of switches and other network devices. The hosted video provider manages all the "back-end" work.

Conversely, with Microsoft Outlook and Gmail, the user must download all E-mails to his local PC and manage the E-mails on his local machine, if the hard drive crashes – there goes all the E-mails. Microsoft Outlook has the same predicament as a local DVR, where they are all vulnerable because there is a single point of failure – the Hard Disk Drive. When the hard disk drive goes dead on a DVR, your evidence is gone as well.

Several companies can provide you with the right hardware equipment for this application and your CPP can help you to identify the best cost effective alternatives.

Hosted IP video service rids the end-customer of software upgrades, network management, storage expansion and finally hard disk drive failure. All these things are done by the administrator at the hosted video service data center. It is a service the end-customer uses on a monthly basis. It is analogous to a cell phone service. The end-customer pays a small, manageable monthly fee for the hosted video service vs. paying a large sum up front for a video surveillance system that must be managed locally through a burdensome process of software upgrades, network management, etc.

The end-customer can now manage the enterprise video using a web-browser to manage multiple sites while drinking coffee at Starbucks, where Wi-Fi is available. With hosted video service, the end-customer can now manage live video feed, recorded history and user access, anytime and anywhere. This is now a reality with a hosted video account. Transparent to the user, all the management of storage, network switches, software upgrades are all done behind the scenes, without any involvement by the end user-customer.

This simplified and cost effective solution is *the* next step application. Your security alarm dealer and central station now can offer burglar alarms alone or bundle the burglar alarm with hosted video.

It's available now and getting more affordable!

Who needs a "fence" to dispose of goods stolen from your company!

Where's my stuff!

If you have ever experienced the theft of your merchandise and wondered where it went to be disposed of, we have some ideas for you.

Before the Internet, it used to be the local flea market where your stolen items would show up for sale at a discounted price and it still can be. But, with the explosion of merchandise auction web sites, it is beyond easy to dispose of the stolen swag and you will never know!

If you have been the victim of a recent theft, it pays to go to some of the sites and see if your stuff is there.

Here are some Warning Signs of Stolen Goods at an auction site.

Obviously these are not proof of stolen goods, but an auction that fits several of the following criteria may be worth further investigation.

- **Merchandise listed as NWT, or "new with tags"**

- **Price below wholesale**

- **Large lots (perhaps 50 or more of one kind of item, in various sizes)**

- **Multiple items offered by one seller**

- **Goods from a company's latest product line**

- **Items that are not yet available in stores**

- **Products that match the description of your goods recently stolen in quantity**

- **Sellers who have ZIP codes are in the same area as your recent thefts**

- **Gift cards, especially in large amounts and from various retailers**

- **Short auctions (because the seller may be trying to evade detection)**

- **Sellers who require money orders rather than easily traced PayPal or credit cards**

Check out the local auctions today! If you see your stuff, contact local law enforcement and get help. They may be able to do a "buy and bust" sting and you may be able to help them catch the culprits. Don't be surprised if you find out that there is a connection to a past or current employee!

"The ideas I stand for are not mine. I borrowed them from Socrates. I swiped them from Chesterfield. I stole them from Jesus. And I put them in a book. If you don't like their rules, whose would you use?"

Dale Carnegie
1888-1955

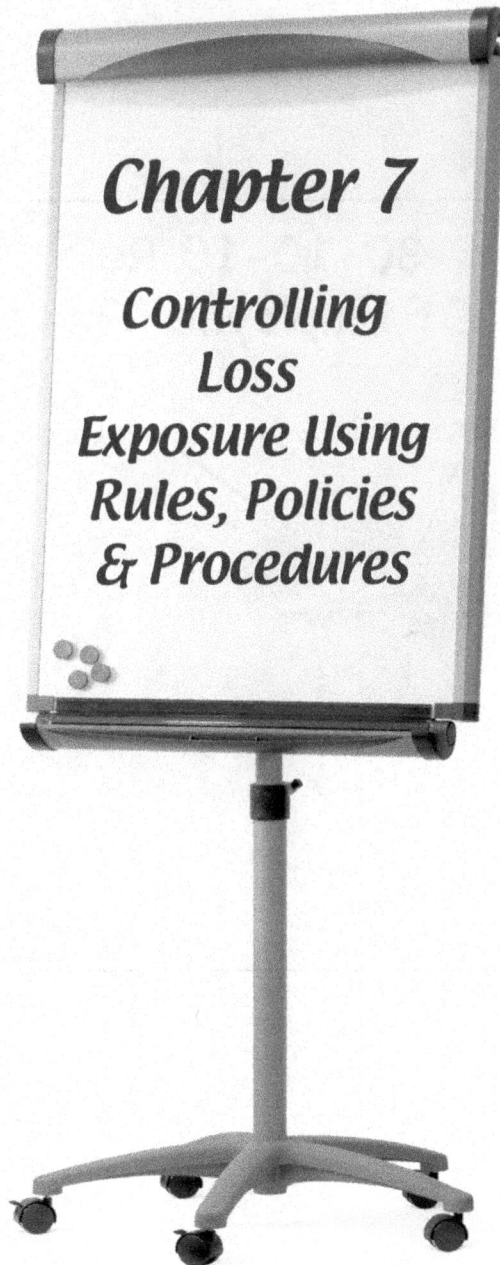

Chapter 7

Controlling
Loss
Exposure Using
Rules, Policies
& Procedures

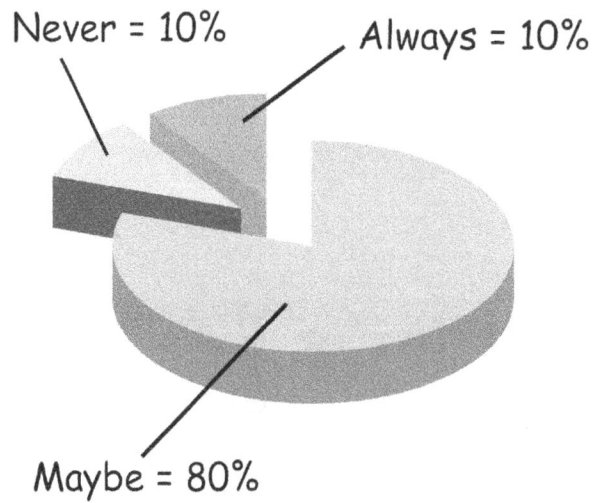

80-10-10 Rule
Of Employee Theft

Never = 10%   Always = 10%

Maybe = 80%

The purpose of rules and policies in any organization is to ensure the protection of assets and people. We need to start this chapter with a disclaimer that we are not attorneys nor are we human resource experts. We are loss prevention professionals that have had for many years the assignment of protecting our corporate employers from all of the hazards and exposures that are the cause of numerous business failures and bankruptcies annually. It is our desire that your company not join the ranks of those who failed to protect their profits.

We will advise you repeatedly, in this chapter, to have your employee policies and procedures reviewed by an attorney knowledgeable in labor laws.

It makes all the sense in the world to start your loss prevention program efforts by looking at how you go about hiring new employees. It makes a lot of sense to find and train the best people that you can. The following section contains some recommendations related to background investigations and hiring practices from a security management point of view.

Here we invoke our caveat that we are not HR professionals, but rather have many years of seeing the results of poor pre-employment planning and post employment human resource management.

EMPLOYEE SCREENING

When the hiring process, includes interviewing and a suitable screening of all applicants, it enables employers to create an efficient and more diverse workforce. The more thorough the planning process a company puts into these pre-hire initial employment steps, the greater the likelihood of finding good employees and the lower the possibility of future employment litigation.

All companies should provide applicants with standard employment applications, review resumes and conduct interviews. If you do no have your own human resource professionals and employment recruiters on staff, you really should look into outsourcing these valuable services and use personnel trained in conducting pre-employment interviews. It is their core competency and probably not yours.

Lessons From Losses

John was hired as an assistant manager by a Virginia based restaurant chain. Due diligence in the form of a background check was conducted by the companies HR manger and a third party company who conducted the check did not find any significant problems. John had stated on his application that he had worked for a dozen years most recently for a local restaurant company now out of business. Contacts to the listed numbers were not answered. However since John interviewed well and demonstrated very good knowledge of the restaurant business he was hired.

John's VA Mugshot

The company training period was 7 weeks and included positional and management training all of which was completed satisfactorily. On his first weekend out of training assigned as an assistant manager at one of the company restaurants, John was scheduled to close Friday night, open Saturday, open Sunday and open Monday.

Normal duties of the manager included preparing deposits, which were taken to the bank by the manager in charge twice a day once in the morning before opening with the deposit from the previous night and once in the afternoon with the days' shift deposit. On Monday morning, before the scheduled opening, John told the employees that he was going to the bank. When John failed to return to open for business, the employees became concerned that John had been a victim of an accident or something worse and contacted the store manager.

The store manager and subsequently the police were unable to locate John who had apparently vanished along with the store deposits from Friday night, Saturday day shift and night shift, Sunday dayshift and night shift. The weekend total was about $15,000 – vanished!

As further investigation occurred, it was determined that the background investigation had only included a local police records check. The statewide check revealed that John had an arrest warrant outstanding for a similar crime in Northern Virginia, and was also wanted for a probation violation. Another arrest warrant was issued for the apprehension of the now long gone John McKinley who by every ones judgment ran a very good shift!

John was finally arrested in Mississippi after committing another restaurant deposit theft and in my last conversation with the county sheriff the now incarcerated John was working roadside cleanup with a group of other inmates on a stretch of US Route 15 with an opportunity for parole in 5 years.

Background investigations must not rely on only local checks, as many court jurisdictions may not be tied into state record systems automatically. While it may have changed, as of the year 2000, criminal records in New York City must be conducted separately for all 5 boroughs to obtain a citywide record check on an applicant.

Employment records with gaps of time that cannot be verified should result in a huge red flag for hiring managers and must be resolved before you invest your time and money with a new employee.

Unfortunately, many businesses rely on inadequate practices for background screening of potential employees. Employers without a plan who choose to "wing" their way through, end up all too often making quick hiring decisions to fill a position and end up repenting at leisure when all sorts of personality and productivity problems surface. A false sense of security causes them to make common mistakes that can leave them exposed to even some costly litigation exposure:

Should you rely on the applicant's statements?

While your applicant may not tell you outright fabrications, important information about his or her background may get left out. If you fail to ask specific direct questions about the information on the application and in interviews, some may feel vague answers or omissions are acceptable.

If you just asked a question that requires a "yes or no" answer and the applicant rambles off in another direction, there is a red flag on the play!

Some unethical individuals will have few misgivings about misrepresenting the truth if they are desperate enough to get hired. Relying on the applicant to provide comprehensive, accurate information may leave you without the information that you need to make an intelligent decision.

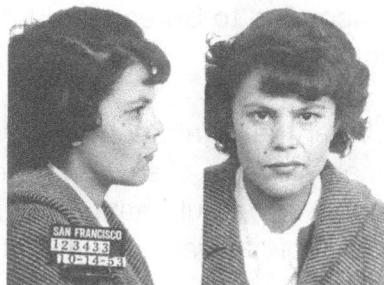

Who is that new employee really?

Should you rely on what the recruiter tells you?

Because independent or even in-house recruiters perform a number of valuable services, it may be easy for the boss to step away from responsibilities in the hiring process and let the recruiter do the work and make the hard decisions. But remember recruiters; especially independent service companies are in the business of placement, not research.

While they may perform some background activities such as confirming academic degrees or past employment, recruiters don't offer the comprehensive background checks that can insulate your business from potential liability. In fact, standard language in the agreement that you signed with them will likely absolve them of any future liability.

How about relying on the consensus of interviewers?

Some companies have adopted the practice of making hiring decisions by committee.   If a candidate looks good on paper, interviews well, and is viewed positively by the interviewing team, a vote settles the matter. While personality and interview presentation skills matter, you should remember that every person that you hire could eventually impact your entire operation. Your team of interviewers can confirm that the applicant has the appropriate skills and traits for the position, professionally conducted background checks offer a critical verification that the judgment to select the candidate is the right one.

Did you know that statistics overwhelmingly demonstrate that any company could be at risk for making bad hiring decisions, and case law combined with jury awards support the argument that you simply cannot afford to ignore the risk?

According to some recent studies we found:

"Research conducted by the Society for Human Resource Management shows that 50 percent of all resumes and applications contain fabrications."

"The U.S. Department of Commerce estimates that employee theft causes 33 percent of all business failures."

"According to Bureau of Justice statistics, workplace violence accounts for 18 percent of all violent crimes."

"Under the legal doctrine of negligent hiring or retention, an employer has the duty to protect Its employees, clients and the public from injuries caused by employees whom the employer knows or "should have known" pose a risk of harm to others. Likewise, an employer may "be held liable for failing to investigate," discharge or reassign an employee."

"Overall, 66 percent of negligent hiring trial cases result in jury awards averaging $600,000 in damages. And, the Workplace Violence Research Institute reports that the average jury award for civil suits on behalf of the injured is $3 million."

6 More Reasons to do it right

Beyond the many good reasons to screen out potentially bad employees, employers with comprehensive background screening programs also enjoy many other benefits. We think the following list is very compelling

1. Do you need to comply with federal regulations?

For instance for those engaged in transportation and interstate commerce, the Department of Transportation (DOT) oversees drug and alcohol testing programs on mandated employees.

The DOT requires employers to conduct a pre-employment drug test and obtain a two-year drug/alcohol test history. Additional regulations set forth by the DOT require employers to monitor their employees on an ongoing basis. DOT employers who fail to conduct this screening are subject to penalty fines. Fines if assessed, record-keeping fines can begin at $500 per day, and the fine for knowingly falsifying records can be $5,000.

2. Better attendance and lower turnover

A number of studies have been published that conclude that employers who conduct thorough background screening, including reference checking, experience better employee attendance rates and lower turnover. In addition, employers may see reduced healthcare and workers' compensation costs.

Costs associated with healthcare benefits, job-related accident frequency and resulting workers' compensation claims, have been shown to be directly related to background screening. There is a correlation between your claim frequency and hiring the best overall employees because it makes a difference in terms of attitude, safety and performance. When a drug free workplace program is also in place, you may be able to experience even greater cost savings.

Some safety experts recommend that employers should conduct a post-conditional job offer workers' compensation search on applicants for jobs that require manual labor, standing for long periods of time or performing other duties that can lead to stress injuries such as chronic back pain. Your workers compensation insurer can also index the employees name and view prior claims in the event any new injury claim is filed while in your employ.

Fraud associated with Workers' Compensation claims, especially in regards to back, repetitive motion and other chronic pain complaints that are difficult to measure, is well documented.

3. Less theft

Overall, employers who conduct background screening experience fewer incidents of employee theft, fraud, embezzlement and shrinkage. London House, a company specializing in conducting psychological testing for employee honesty, determined a number of years ago that screening may reveal past theft or other criminal behavior, possibly preventing a bad hire. But also, having a solid background-screening program sends a message to potential employees. It demonstrates that an employer is concerned about who has access to financial or material assets and that the company will take appropriate action if necessary.

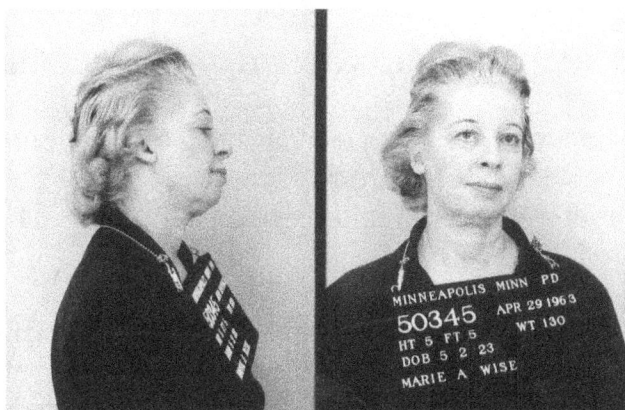

A crook who steals all of your money can look just like some ones grandmother!

Honest people want to work with other honest people!

4. Less litigation

Background screening enables an employer not to hire a potentially bad employee, reducing the risk of accidents, criminal activity and violence—all of which may result in litigation. This is important if you ever have to defend yourself from a negligent hiring litigation. This can occur when someone claims that one of your employees through either direct action or negligence was the proximate cause of some injury to them. You'll find your self saying: "If I just knew then what I know now, I wouldn't have ever hired him"!

Your screening program can help to demonstrate that you took reasonable measures to investigate the employee's background pre-hire. Consequently, exposure to a courtroom trial, bad publicity and hefty penalties is greatly reduced. It is called reasonable care.

5. Confirm an applicant is whom he or she claims to be

Now as never before, identity theft is a common problem. Employers must ensure that a potential employee is who they claim to be. Confirm an applicant's social security number by running a check on whether or not the number is valid by the screening company. In addition, a critical post-hire check is the I-9 verification, which must be conducted within three days of an employee starting his or her job. This search allows an employer to know whether or not a person can legitimately work in the United States.

A number of new programs have surfaced allowing employers to verify identity by calling INS and providing the persons name and social security number. A number of private companies can also allow you to conduct an outsourced check on all of your current employees for eligibility.

6. More productive and better-qualified employees

The more you do to evaluate and qualify your job applicants through interviews, reference checking or background screening, the better its overall workforce will be. And, the greater the depth and "bench strength" you have, the better your overall productivity and performance can be.

When you screen your applicants, you're more likely to find qualified employees for your open positions. Previous employment, education and professional verifications are just the beginning when determining whether an applicant will appropriately fit your needs.

You must protect everyone you employ by checking the criminal histories of applicants. If you knowingly hire ex-offenders with violent backgrounds or participate in work release programs to fill positions, don't be surprised when a lot of other good employees leave. Think about it. Would you want to work at a company who hires felons? Would you want your kids to work there?

Employers who fail to exercise due diligence in their hiring practices risk hiring criminals at the very worst and unqualified workers at the least. They also risk workplace violence, theft and litigation.

Companies that experience an incident of workplace violence are exposed to several potential legal issues, including inadequate security, negligent hiring, negligent retention, and negligent supervision. Companies can take two basic steps to mitigate these risks: implementing an applicant screening process and a prevention program. The applicant screening process should aim to identify and weed out potential problems. All job applicants should be required to take a drug test, and they should also be subjected to criminal background checks, credit checks, public-filing checks, driver's license checks, educational background checks, verification of previous employment, and reference checks. Any applicant who misrepresents or lies about his qualifications should raise a red flag. Did you know that only 35% of employers do a background check?

Your company should consult with an attorney to make sure they have covered all the bases during this process. The prevention program should emphasize periodic employee training about the company's workplace violence policies and rules. A zero-tolerance policy for threats and intimidation and a clear and unambiguous definition of unacceptable behavior are essential.

Ensure all applicants complete the prior criminal conviction section on the employment application. If the applicant checks "yes" to the question of prior criminal conviction on their application, instruct your managers to contact a superior or the owner for direction on whether to hire or not hire this applicant. Do not hire applicants that are participating in a criminal work release program, drug halfway house or any similar program.

The background investigation should include criminal history and prior employment verification. Background investigations should be conducted by a reputable outside agency. Get their references and check them out before you hire the service.

Lessons From Losses – Background checks

According to a recent study, half of all companies do not conduct background checks on people that they hire. Even people with major access to company assets can slip in without a check on who they are and what they have done at previous employers. Lots of bad guys know that if they have a good story and look good on paper, they are in.

Consider the story of Lena the former controller, in a recent news story, who was accused of stealing more than $200,000 from a Foster City, California flooring company and needed to make restitution to minimize the amount of prison time she faced. Lena took the money from her employer by forging the chief executive officer's signature on checks and authorizing a line of credit, according to the District Attorney's Office.

When the CEO noticed the missing money, Lena allegedly offered to pay back the stolen funds. Instead, authorities were alerted and prosecutors filed charges. Prosecutors quickly learned that in 1999 Lena was convicted of grand theft greater than $400 in Los Angeles County and sent to prison. The loss was much more than $400, of course, the charge as stated means that the theft was a felony crime.

The problem, according to prosecutors, is that Lena found the wrong way to repay her debt to her former employer— by ripping off a book company in nearby Berkeley that hired her just months after she was charged with the Foster City theft and out on bail.

Prosecutors in both of the cases, which are located in separate jurisdictions, offered her five years and possibly less if she made full restitution.

While Lena's new alleged crime in Berkeley did not add to her charges in Foster City, it did prevent her from making the restitution on which her plea bargain offer was predicated. The additional theft charge also makes it clear that Lena apparently had no desire to stop taking money. Not only was Lena on bail and awaiting a settlement in the Foster City case, she had already previously served one prison stint for grand theft in San Francisco.

So, at the time of her Berkeley arrest, she also had a pending case out of Foster City for which she was on bail. In the Berkeley case, she faced up to eight years because of the amount of money in question and the charge of committing a crime while on bail.

The book company in Berkeley found out that they had a problem in a novel way. An employee at the book company had picked up a copy of the local newspaper and had spotted the article about the Foster City embezzlement by a defendant named "Lena" – with the same last name as their Lena who was their new controller at his work place.

When confronted by management at the book company, Lena reportedly protested the article was about a different person. She claimed to be a victim of identity theft but conceded she never reported the crime.

The company management contacted the DA in the Foster City crime who thought it was a plausible enough explanation and offered to provide a Department of Motor Vehicles photo for comparison of the two supposed Lena's.
The Lena arrested in Foster City had never been booked into the jail so there was no photo with the Sheriff's Office.   So, the DA said he left the drivers license photo with his receptionist and never saw the woman from the book company who picked it up.

This is good…apparently the person picking up the photo from the DA's was none other than Lena who switches the photos so the Berkeley company gets "proof" that there is a different Lena involved in the Foster City embezzlement.   The switch was discovered during a follow up call by the book company CEO to the DA and a subsequent meeting and sharing of photos revealed the ruse.

An audit conducted the following week reportedly proved the book company's sinking suspicion. The Lena they hired was the same woman who now was about to face prison time in two counties. And a lot of money was missing.

An employee at the Berkeley Company said Lena was fired and prosecutors in Berkeley have filed new charges.

During Lena's tenure as the book company, an employee was quoted as saying that there were constant mistakes and corrections. "We all just assumed she was incompetent, but maybe not so much," he said
Lena ended up pleaded guilty to six felony charges of theft and forgery in Washington State. In return for the plea, faces just under 22 months in prison when she was sentenced.

However, before Lena can begin her sentence there, however, authorities in San Mateo and Alameda counties plan to bring her back to California, where she faces prosecution on three separate cases lodged before using a false identification in Everett, Wash. to gain employment and buy a SUV — a crime that tipped off local authorities to her whereabouts and which appears to have ended an ongoing crime spree.

Prosecutors in California could have waited until Lena finishes her sentence in Washington before pursuing their own cases but both county officials agreed to move forward.

Considering the very small cost of determining the background information on a prospective employee, it is totally astonishing to read about how easy it is for a con artist thief to dupe numerous companies into hiring her in to a position of trust.

A basic principle of loss prevention that most experts agree on is the fact that some of your employees are totally honest and others are totally dishonest. The majority are somewhere in the middle.

We call it the **80-10-10 Rule.** That means that 10% are honest, 10% are dishonest and the rest will fall into either camp depending on a number of circumstances. The model looks like this:

The purpose of your loss prevention program is to disrupt the elements that make your company attractive to the dishonest and those prone to dishonesty.

Embezzlers have always been around and often get caught!

Opportunity

Keeping your valuables in locked and otherwise hardens the target to thieves. Conduct frequent inventories and enforce all cash control procedures and policies.

Risk

Good controls on cash and valuables will make it easier to hold employees accountable. Make it well known that employees who violate policies will we disciplined and those caught stealing will be prosecuted.

Reward

Physical and written controls reduce the payback to the dishonest employees. Keep your assets trackable with an audit trail to reduce the exposure of a large dollar amount. When you button down your controls you are able to start realizing the Competitive Advantage you deserve because you will begin to take more of your profit dollars to the bottom line.

You will also send a message to the dishonest employees that they are better off working elsewhere. Your honest employees and the 80% on the fence will gladly appreciate the new work environment and will realize the increased job opportunities that develop in a profitable enterprise.

Risk

Reward

Loss Triangle

Opportunity

In order to keep the majority honest, it is necessary to set standards of behavior that all must be held accountable to. We have discussed some of the basics in earlier chapters.

1. **All rules and policies must be *Written.***

So called "unwritten rules" which assume that you want people to perform in a particular way is doomed to failure.

2. **Everyone affected by the rule or policy must have it explained to them.**

Having it in writing is not good enough. You must tell people why the rule exists in understandable terms.

3. **You must also tell them what will happen if they fail to comply with the rule or policy.**

A clear statement of consequences sets your expectations of how the behavior can affect continuing
employment.

4. **Everyone affected by the rule or policy must receive a written copy of it and sign a statement that they have received and understand the consequences of non-compliance.**

There should never be an "I didn't know" defense related to non-compliance of policy. The signed statement must be placed in the employees file and retained as a permanent record.

5. **The rule or policy must be enforced consistently.**

A key part of your progressive disciplinary policy is to enforce the rules impartially for all employees. A result of firing some employees for a rules violation and not others for the same offense can be an EEOC complaint or a visit from other labor regulatory agencies. The penalty for losing is often in part or combination, the payment of back wages, a penalty and reinstatement of the employee to their previous job.

Remember...Fire in haste, repent at leisure!

The document containing your rules and policies we will call your company Policies and Procedures Manual or Employee Handbook.

It can be ten pages or a hundred, depending on how complex the subject is in your type of business. Companies with a lot of governmental regulatory requirements will often list these requirements in the manual along with the specific employee role in compliance. A small chain of Convenience Stores, on the other hand may have a shorter version. Especially if cash and inventory automation reduces the number of tasks that are needed to protect the business assets.

All companies should have a business goal or "Mission" statement and a pledge of fair treatment in the first pages of the manual. In that statement the company three step progressive disciplinary process should be explained and the specific behaviors that will warrant immediate termination without written warnings.

These issues of gross misconduct should include the following examples:

1. **Theft or unauthorized possession of company, employee or customer property.**

This really requires that you adopt a realistic threshold. If you choose to adopt a "Zero" tolerance policy, you may be forced to fire a good worker over an incident or item of minuscule value that can be corrected by a closed door counseling session.

You really must be able to prove theft, not just suspect that it occurred. All theft should be reported to the police in order to ensure that a proper and legal investigation occurs. In fact, your insurance company may require a police investigation prior to the payment of any covered loss that you claim.

Everybody gets a copy of the Employee Manual!

In the event that the police establish probable cause to initiate a prosecution your policy should specifically support the prosecution and you should accept no offers of repayment from the suspect unless you have court ordered restitution as part of any plea agreement.

Accepting payment to make the criminal case go away is not a good option and sends the message that if you steal and get caught, the worst thing that can happen is that you have to pay the money back!

2. **Destruction or abuse of company property.**

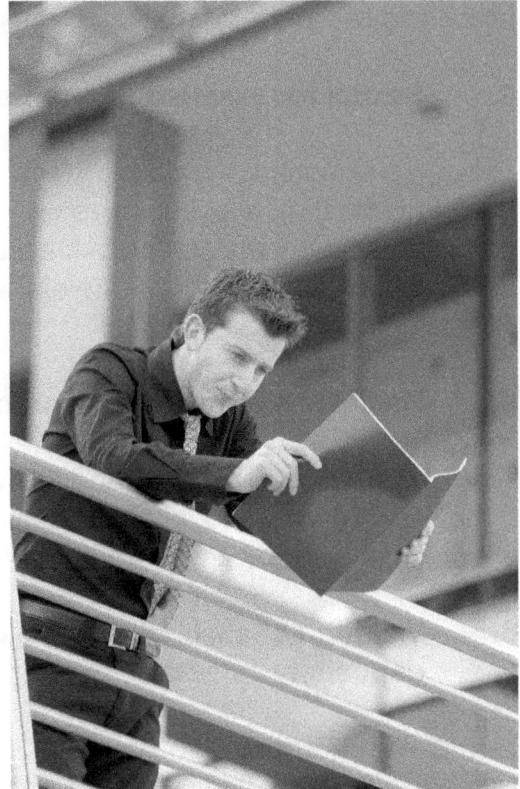

Having someone intentionally break or vandalize your property is really annoying and could certainly be symptomatic of a deeper problem. Today the offending employee may be damaging the wall but tomorrow the anger may be directed at another employee or yourself!

3.   Inappropriate behavior toward a customer.

Let's face it, rude behavior toward your customers is the last thing that you need. It demonstrates disrespect for their employer and themselves as well. In addition, in our experience, many incidents of customer abuse translate into lawsuits and complaints of perceived racial overtones.

4.   Sexual harassment of another employee, customer or others in the workplace.

This   issue is a huge problem in many workplaces and can cost you big bucks in "quid pro quo" (this for that) allegations as well as hostile work environment complaints. Many large companies have created specific sexual harassment seminars for managers and it is certainly advisable to adopt one of the many written programs available from human resource specialty companies.

5.   Racial harassment or discrimination.

Any form of discrimination in today's workplace is just plain wrong and simply unacceptable behavior. You must not allow an environment that is supportive of racially or ethnically based abusive behavior by any of your employees even in the form of supposed jokes.

6.   Violation of cash control policies resulting in a significant loss of cash or deposits.

Termination is appropriate for an individual who fails to discharge their duties and responsibilities resulting in a cash loss exceeding a significant amount. The word "significant" must be defined by your organization and must be consistently used as a benchmark requiring termination of employment.

This a tricky issue for most companies. Clearly a manager who fails to make required deposit of funds at the bank has demonstrated gross misconduct and can be prosecuted in many states. How about a manager who leaves a cash drawer on the desk in the office unattended and $300 is found to be missing when he returns? It is plainly a significant amount of money that has gone missing due to the manager's negligence.

We recommend that you establish your own disciplinary threshold, but keep in mind that you have to maintain the same standards for all no matter how much you like a particular employee. Your employees must understand that you will enforce all company rules related to cash controls.

7.   Use, possession, dispensing, selling or being under the influence of illegal drugs or alcohol while on company property.

This is a major concern of many companies and those who do business with the federal government usually have to maintain a drug free workplace and you should as well. Employees with substance abuse problems can cost you a lot of money due to higher incidence of work related injuries and resulting Workers Compensation claims.

What this means is that you should institute mandatory drug testing for all new hire employees and random checks ongoing if this practice is consistent in your industry *and meets the approval of legal counsel.*

The fact is that companies with out substance abuse programs have a bigger problem dealing with the issue and can only regulate behaviors that are observed by the manager. Some of the red flag behavior includes excessive absence, poor work performance and signs of obvious impairment.

8.   Possession of a firearm or other dangerous weapons on company property.

This rule is needed as an important effort to reduce your exposure to workplace violence. We recommend that you tell your employees that carrying or possessing dangerous weapons on company property is forbidden and will result in termination of their employment.

9.   Violation of safety policies or disorderly conduct or "horseplay" resulting in injury to other employee.

Our experience has been that allowing even minor physical horseplay at all tends to escalate into more negative behaviors such as fighting and inappropriate touching or sexual assault. Put an end to it before someone gets hurt and you have to fire all of those involved.

10.   Assault, using threatening, intimidating or abusive language to other employees or customers.

Abuse, intimidation or at it's extreme, assault and battery must be dealt with immediately and decisively when encountered by management. There simply is no justification for allowing the bullies of the world to be in charge of your business.

11.   Insubordination such as the refusal to follow work direction or assignment.

We are talking about the individual here who for whatever reason refuses to do the work that you or your manager has directed them to perform. We will assume, that you have provided your employees with a job description outlining their basic duties and have provided documented training for all tasks that you expect them to perform.

For instance, we would refuse to go out and wash

the windows unless we had adequate training and all the safety equipment was provided! (We would also ask for more money...)

12.   Falsification of company records or giving false information or explanations to company officials.

This rule addresses the unhappy circumstance when one of your managers decides to falsify inventory records rather than admit to an escalating shortage. They would rather cook the books than deal with the problem. It also addresses the instances of padding payroll records, expense reports and timecard fraud.

This rule can also cover the failure of an employee to participate in an investigation related to shortages or other policy violations and provides you with a false written statement relative to what happened and their involvement.

13.   Violation of security policies or procedures resulting in injury or crime loss.

There always exists the possibility that an employee will disregard a security policy allowing an opportunity to arise that is noticed and acted upon by a criminal. An example that we are aware of involved a restaurant manager who directed that the back door be used at night in violation of policy for safe trash removal. The pattern of opportunity is noticed and one night, an armed robber is waiting just outside to confront the employee and force them back in to rob the store.

The gross violation of policy, in this case, has risked the lives of all of the employees and must be dealt with as a proximate cause of the crime loss.

The example policies above are some of the things that can get you fired at most companies. You may have more!

The lesser included offenses and transgressions should include:

•   **Cash policy violations with a less than significant loss.**

Small periodic cash shortages must be addressed and corrected before they be come a large problem that you have to fix through termination. It makes little sense to keep issuing written warnings for the same uncorrected problem.

•   **Time and attendance violations.**

Being late affects everyone's workday so you need to decide how much is too much.

•   **Excessive phone calls of a personal nature.**

Now you have personal cell phones to contend with. You certainly must be specific about the use of company phones as well as the other electronic devices that can interrupt your business. Don't forget to include personal text messaging on company time as well.

- **Solicitation or collection of funds for non-approved purposes.**

Is the "March Madness" basketball pool allowed? How about other collections for charitable events or sick relatives? A good policy is to just say "No!" to all of it. Consider if you will the employees who are just making ends meet financially being constantly solicited for contributions for baby showers, birthdays, going away gifts etc.

- **Distribution or posting of pamphlets or other unauthorized materials in violation of the company "No Solicitation Policy".**

If you are a non-union business and want to stay that way, this is a good policy to enforce. This rule must also include any solicitation for political purposes or "good causes".

- **Leaving work or station without manager approval.**

This has to do with the wandering employee who can't seem to stay on station and/or otherwise on task. In an office environment, this wandering can escalate to the point where no one is ever at their desk to answer phones or can be found when needed. For years as a corporate employee, I was always astounded that some people who had desk jobs were virtually never at their desks and the voice mails left were seldom answered.

- **Misuse of company computer equipment.**

This topic has to do with controlling what happens as the result of improper use of company computer equipment.

The list can include:

* **How much surfing on the internet for no discernible company reason you are going to allow?**

* **What may be sent on company E-mail systems - enough with the jokes and chain letters!**

* **Password change requirements.**

* **Protection of sensitive company and customer information.**

* **Abuse of equipment like what happens if you leave a lap top in your car and it gets stolen.**

* **Your policy regarding supervision of use.**

- **Absence without notice. (AKA "No Call, No Show")**

Most companies allow either three occasions or three days in a row to qualify for the "early retirement" from their job program!

- **Violation of safety rules.**

You have to be careful with this one but given the cost of Workers Compensation coverage and claims charges, the employee who simply cannot work within the safety guidelines needs to either have their attitude adjusted or be shown the door.

Typically your progressive disciplinary process should provide for documented consequences that include written and final warnings before termination occurs.   Most companies have adopted the process of verbal, to written warning, to final written warning and termination.

The key to success is to be consistent anytime the rules are being enforced.

You should include statements that the contents of the Policy Manual is considered confidential and should in no way be construed as creating an express or implied contract of any sort nor any assurance of continuing employment contrary to the companies "at will" policy of employment. The idea here is not to allow your employees to think that they have an employment contract with you.

What are some other items that should be included in your employee handbook?

For some categories of employees you will need to address the issues of ethics and conflict of interest. We recommend that you analyze your list of best business practices and determine which of the items would cause your business harm to its good name if not followed.

You should want to address the issue of gifts, both received and given. What constitutes a good will gesture and what is considered a payment in kind? It is prudent to list acceptable values and items so that no need is required to determine if an ethical transaction has occurred. Keep it simple, but be specific what your expectations are regarding all ethical issues.

Your company may have proprietary information or processes that need to be protected from being divulged to unauthorized persons or competitors.

For some companies, a separate non-disclosure agreement may be needed and we recommend that you address the issue with an attorney to make sure that your intellectual property is protected. Your attorney can advise you regarding the requirements that you must enforce including any non-compete clauses that may need to be added in the event that an employee with valuable proprietary information leaves your employment.

If you do have the need to write employment contracts for specific individuals or outsource services, have your attorney assist you with the contract language. It is important that contract employees and services have their job or service responsibilities in writing before they become engaged in providing the service. We know one business owner that made the mistake of hiring a service provider who began providing professional service at the business location, which is a medical office without a letter of offer from the business owner and without a signed contract.

The story became a nightmare for the business owner when the service provider made a number of demands that they wanted in the contract language before they would sign that far exceeded the verbal agreement that the business owner thought was established. The lawsuit is still pending regarding issues that were still unresolved when the contract person was terminated.

Your handbook will need to address the topics of employee safety rules. Presenting the general company safety policy in brief form is needed from the first day of employment. You should address specific task related safety practices and equipment during positional or task training sessions. As always, each specific task should have a checklist of job safety requirements with written sign off that the training was received.

General safe behaviors must be discussed such as slip and fall prevention, proper footwear that you require, locations of emergency exits and fire extinguishers. Safety programs are addressed in depth in a later chapter.

Also needed during new hire orientation is the topic of security rules in your business. The rules should state what behaviors are risky and are therefore prohibited along with what to do if a crime such as robbery or disturbance occurs.

The manual should cover arriving at work, closing the business, robbery prevention, being alert to criminal activity on the property. A later chapter discusses security policies.

Lessons From Loss – Written Rules

This lesson is about Stacy, The former office manager of a local fire protection district in the mid-west who was charged with stealing more than $21,000 by using a work credit card for personal expenses. In her state, that's a Class C felony charge that was filed by the local district attorney in county court.

Stacy was the office manager when the fire district board learned of possible misuse of district funds during an audit and approached her for proof of reimbursement, said the district attorney. He said Stacy never returned to work after being informed of the allegations and the board fired her.

Authorities allege $22,236 was transferred to Stacy's credit card between June and January after she set up an automatic electronic transfer that allowed her to pay her district credit card with the district's bank account. Of that amount, an internal review showed Stacy charged

$21,257 for personal use.

Her attorney said Stacy broke no rules and reimbursed the district for her personal charges. He also said the disputed charges are "much, much less" than $21,257. First of all he said that she had permission. Second, her conduct was the practice of the fire protection district.

Though there was no written policy, board members said it was understood that district credit cards were to be used for personal use only if district employees had an emergency.

There are a lot of issues in this lesson that may well apply to many small business owners who have not adopted checks and balances to control disbursements to vendors.

The key missing element in the story is the failure of the board in charge of managing the department to implement standard accounting procedures. Depending on the amount of revenue flowing through the office, they probably got off easy.

First of all having the person in charge of receivables also being in charge of payables without having a dual control system for approving invoice documentation and payments is like having the fox be in charge of the henhouse. The system must go beyond just having someone else sign checks, since lacking an approval system opens up many opportunities for creating and paying inflated or false invoices and other fraudulent transactions.

Stacy obviously saw other employees using business credit cards for personal use with impunity and could well be just the tip of the iceberg because she was greedy, came to some ones notice and got caught!

In the event that you do allow company employees to use business credit accounts or cards for personal use, all authorized account users must sign a written policy stating under what circumstances personal use is authorized, who must approve the transaction and how repayment must be made.

There is no such thing as an "Unwritten or Understood" policy. If you plan on enforcing any rule or procedure it must be written and acknowledged in writing by all employees that are affected by it.

This case has not gone to trial yet, but I bet Stacy beats the charges especially if her attorney can show any good faith reimbursement of personal charges to the county occurred at any time during her tenure as office manager.

In fact, I'll bet she collects unemployment.

Inspect What You Expect!

The Story Of The Shiny Nickel And The Three Pennies...

The nickel in our story represents the five cents that the average retail store makes as profit for every one dollar of sales. It's your 5% profit margin!

The three pennies represent the amount of money that the average retail store loses to theft, waste, fraud and sloppy accounting practices for each dollar in sales.

Unless the business owner, adopts a proactive cash control and loss prevention program, the three pennies are left on the table and are written off as the owner walks away! Can the profit pennies be recovered? Yes, but you have to invest in effective loss prevention practices and programs.

You do the math...

Recovering just one penny through good cash control practices and loss prevention systems, increases your profit margin by 20%! Why? Because the pennies are <u>lost profit</u> and return to the bottom line as profit.

Basic Cash Tools

Register + Money!

It is vital for the owner/operator of any business to establish adequate accounting procedures needed to track how revenue flows through the business. This can be referred to as the "Audit Trail" and works like a road map to identify where the proceeds of a sales transaction can be located at any given time from the point of sale to your bank balance. "Critical Control Points" are located along the way that are, simply, each place that money changes hands.

The main reason to document critical control points is the increased ability to hold specific persons accountable. Having established accountability, it is necessary to enforce the procedural rules needed to prevent loss.

An example of a Critical Control Point is "who is in charge of the register?" If you allow more than one person at a time to ring in sales transactions using the same change drawer, you lose accountability. Who will you hold responsible for shortages that occur?

Losses featuring high inventory variance are very likely due to theft of money and by failure of the register operator to ring in all of the sales to cover drawer shortages. You will not be able to identify the reasons for inventory shrinkage until you get cash policies and procedures in compliance.

Written policy should state that the person in charge of cash for the shift is designated the "Cash Manager". The Cash Manager is the starting point of the audit trail when at the start of the day the store bank is verified and the deposit prepared for transport to the bank. Each stop along the "trail" must be observed or the possibility of loss increases.

For the same reason that you have only one person at a time on a cash drawer, only one manager should handle cash transactions during a shift.

Providing a complete description of the Cash Managers responsibilities in your policy and procedures manual increases accountability.

- Every counting transaction is a Critical Control Point that represents the potential for a loss to occur if not followed.

- The audit trail is only valid as a tool if it can be verified by dual controls at all critical points.

- Dual control means that the manager and register operator have agreed on the amount and the verification is recorded in some manner such as card swipes using the POS system reader locate at each cash station.

- The rule is that whenever the manager's key card is used to perform a register manager function, the system should prompt the required action steps. For instance a cash pull function may prompt the manager to direct the register operator to swipe their register card signifying that the event took place.

PLANNING YOUR CASH CONTROL SYSTEM

A good start is an organizational statement of who exactly is in charge of the money during a manager shift. In our retail business assumption below, we will make the title of the person in charge of the business unit the "General Manager". We will have that person report to a "District Manager" who is in charge of the operation of multiple units in your organization. The titles, of course, may vary by organization.

Follow the money!

We will also assume that the business has a suitable POS register system that uses a key card reader, a pin number and connects to a managers work station with sales data polled nightly into the business' central office computer. The control and report features vary widely depending on age and brand so we will save the discussion of selecting the POS system for another time.

In a high cash flow business, we are also advocates of using small drop safes next to each register to accumulate large bills.   Minimizing the appearance of large amounts of cash in the drawer reduces the exposure to impulse robbery (grab the money and run) and reduces the temptation for the register operator to share in the sales proceeds.

MANAGEMENT RESPONSIBILITY FOR CASH CONTROL POLICIES:

*   The General Manager is ultimately responsible to see that all aspects of cash control are followed on all shifts.

*   The General Manager is accountable for identifying and correcting control weaknesses, violations and irregularities and communicating to the District Manager any issues or actions taken.

*   Only one manager on each shift will be accountable for cash.
    This manager will be called the Cash Manager.

*   Only General Managers, Assistant Managers and Shift Supervisors can be Cash Managers.

The Cash Manager is the only one permitted to perform these tasks:

*   Handling voids.

*   Ringing in employee purchases.

*   Relieving register operators for emergencies.

• Only Cash Managers may bank registers, pull cash and prepare deposits.

VERIFYING THE STORE CHANGE BANK

A number of other opening cash manager functions might include functions or activities that clearly establish the audit trail of cash moving through the operation. Any failure to follow policy becomes actionable and the reason for a loss occurrence can be determined. This does not identify anyone who actually took the money, but you get to find out why it happened and quickly fix the loss exposure to prevent future occurrence. The following list identifies a few activities for your written policy that you will want your managers to follow:

• Count and verify the store bank.
• Count and verify deposits left in the safe overnight unless armored car deposit transport is used.
• Count cash pulls from prior day and prepare yesterday's final deposit.

In other word, count all of the money that is available in the safe.

These three activities are needed to ensure that the starting change bank is correct. Deposit verification is, as we noted, for those businesses that carry deposits to the bank and do not use armored car.

CASH PULLS

 - The cash manager must pull cash from the drop safes hourly.

 - Register operators must verify the cash pull amount.

 - Cash pulls should be immediately placed in the safe.

 - Cash pulls should NEVER be placed into a pocket.

Any business with a high cash flow needs to have a system in place to reduce cash in the drawer. You need to do this on a scheduled basis when cash in drawer exceeds a threshold that you identify. If you are using the drop safes that we recommend, you can conduct fewer pulls and still keep the drawer cash level under control. To restate the obvious, less visible cash in the drawer equals less temptation for impulse drawer robberies and other register theft opportunities.

In a high cash flow business, the fewer disruptions to operations, the better. And cash pulls can be a disruption to customer service.

Keep it in a safer Place!

Your POS system can help with the problem. Many systems

allow the programming of pop up messages on screen to remind the operator to drop large bills and when to alert the manager that it is time to conduct a drawer pull based on cash in drawer totals.

Operators must verify the amount taken from the register. If the operator has not verified the beginning drawer and subsequent pulls are not witnessed, you cannot hold the operator accountable for shortages!

Cash pulled from registers must get to the safe as quickly as possible. The currency should be placed in a specific place in the safe. If the business uses armored car, we highly recommend that you use a tamper-evident plastic bag at the register, seal it and both initial the bag. This process adds the ability to hold the manager accountable if the bag is determined to be short when the contents are counted at the bank. The pull is dropped into the armored car drop slot on your safe and need not be counted again until it is opened and counted by the bank teller at the facility counting your deposit.

If you choose not to use this system, the currency must be counted again when the deposit drop is conducted at the end of the manager's shift. Remember that it takes longer to prepare the deposit if all the currency must be recounted and management time can be better spent dealing with customers.

The last part about putting cash pulls into a manager's pocket is obvious. It just looks bad if your customers see the manager pulling cash and putting it in their pocket. Some will think that a dishonest act has occurred.

BANKING REGISTERS

The cash manager must perform a number of other functions designed to establish the audit trail. The functions listed can be either manual or automatic depending on whether your POS can be programmed to perform them.

- **Bank register operators on.**

- **Assure register operator verifies beginning bank.**

- **Bank register operators off.**

- **Assure register operator verifies ending cash.**

- **Assure register operator verifies +/- on bank off report.**

- **Cash manager must review cash over/shorts, register operator voids, other balance.**

 The point to remember is that a POS electronic report is just as adequate as a written report that requires management time to process and have a place for the paperwork to be retained and having to have a retention policy and having to audit whether it has been retained.

SHIFT CHANGE BANKING

- The off-going cash manager must bank all registers and the store bank.

- The oncoming cash manager must verify the banking of the store and sign on to the system using their card and pin number.

These important functions must occur to ensure that the off going and on-coming cash manager's balance and a clear passing of cash responsibility occurs. Your POS system should be able to record the shift change event but managers must still personally insure that the deposit and store bank is correct.

END OF DAY BANKING

The closing cash manager must:

- Bank all registers.

- Determine final deposit.

- Verify closing store bank.

- Sign off the system-using card and pin number.

The idea once again, is that the purpose of these functions are to create an audit trail to track cash from the start of day safe balance to the register operator drawer bank with sales proceeds being collected and returning to the managers control and into the safe.

REGISTER OPERATOR POLICIES:

In order to hold register operators accountable, there needs to be a policy describing what tasks each shall perform. Some sample activities follow and suggest a pattern of activity.

Your activity pattern for a register operator will depend upon the sophistication of your POS system and how you have programmed the control and verification functions. The purpose of a required task or actions policy is to identify reasons why a shortage or loss occurs so that immediate correction can occur.

For instance a drawer shortage can be investigated by determining if the register operator had exclusive control of the drawer. If it can be established that the register operator failed to follow required actions/policies, you have established the probable reason that the loss occurred.

Register operators need very specific training about how you want them to handle money in your business. Remember there are no "Unwritten Policies".

 - Bank on to the register using card swipes and pin numbers assigned.

- Verify cash pulls by using card swipes and pin number.

- Bank off of the register.

- Place customers currency on ledge of register or on till tray until change is made.

- Place all currency face down the same direction in the cash till.

- All $20 bills and larger should be placed in the drop safe immediately.

- All $50 and $100 must only be accepted by a manager. - Drop excess $10's in the drop safe frequently.

- Not permit anyone except the manager to operate the register until banked off.

- Not use manager's register key card or pin number.

- Notify a manager immediately when a manager void is required.

- Initial or card swipe all manager void transactions.

- Not void an order to zero without manager approval. - Not use open coupon function as a method to void.

- Close cash drawer after each transaction.

- Obtain manager approval to accept any bill larger than $20. - Have manager handle any discrepancies with a customer.

- Assure only cash manager ring in employee purchases.

- Ring in all sales.

- Not give unauthorized discounts.

- Not give any free merchandise.

Any issues with register operator cash, excess voids or other activities needing correction or explanation must be addressed at time of bank off. Counseling of register operators for repeated variances must be arranged and noted to their personnel file.

You need to establish your operational standards regarding cash and negative sales activity variance. You have to have specific goals that you can manage to.

For instance, cash shortage needs to have an over/short standard to manage. You have to determine a threshold after which action must be taken regarding employee performance. So how much do you want to lose before you take disciplinary action? How much are you going to accept before you terminate employment for an excessive loss?

Let's do the math. If your business location has four cash registers and runs two cashier shifts per day seven days per week that is eight cashiers per day, 56 shifts per week and with 52 weeks per year that is 2,912 shifts.

If you allow a drawer cash shortage to be a mere $2 per shift, that extends to a potential of $112 a week or $5,824 per year. For each location.

Needless to say, you really need to have all loss thresholds included in your written policies and you must ensure that they are uniformly enforced. You can lose a ton more of money if you don't pay attention to other activities such as voids and returns.

Your list of sales deduct items to establish upper limits on needs to mirror your company financial profit goals. Variance goals should not be designed to give permission for your employees to routinely hit the upper limits. That is the same as telling a thief that they can steal up to a particular amount before the loss gets your attention!

Weighing the cash versus hand counting is faster and more accurate for most cash handlers

Making your register operators aware of the goals is crucial and as your focus increases and the voids and shortages are reduced, don't forget to also reduce the allowed upper limits. You may well find that the tolerance level has been set too high and you can recover more of your missing profits.

We think the key is to start with modest achievable goals and gradually decrease the allowable shortage as you train operators to reduce errors. Rewarding good behaviors when you observe operator improvement is a must.

Consideration should be given to simplification and automation wherever possible. In our experience, the more physical tasks are required to be conducted to make a system work, the more likely that they will be bypassed or ignored even to the peril of the manager running the shift. So money turns up missing due to cash policy violations on the part of the shift manager and another employee gets fired.

I want to share with you the experience of one restaurant company regional division that on average fired 25 managers a year for cash violations resulting in significant and even substantial cash losses. An additional 40 managers a year received written warnings for similar but less egregious violations resulting in lesser amounts. Yes, in a number of cases, they took the money and some were prosecuted but not always. Pretty crazy when you consider the cost of hiring and replacing managers from intake through the completion of training was at the time something like $4,000 each!

Automation considerations include some really slick systems developed by Brinks, Guarda and other armored cash system companies. We are longtime fans of automating cash functions in retail operations.

The system utilizes special safes that are installed next to each cash station and become the depository of all currency received at the station. That is, while maintaining a drawer bank of the appropriate amount, all bills get fed into the mechanism by the operator.

Drawer bankdown now merely includes the operator and manager verifying the drawer bank to the standard amount and obtaining a report from the register stating sales totals and the safe report that states the amount fed into the device. The two tickets must match for the drawer to balance.

On a daily basis, the armored car company comes to the location, opens the safe and extracts a sealed cassette containing all of the money fed into the safe since the last pick up. A ticket is issued to the manager and a new cassette is installed.

The armored car takes the cassettes to their money room usually controlled by the armored car company at their depot facility and the currency is fine counted to verify contents and your account is instantly credited with the amount.

The saving occurs because nobody is expending time and energy counting masses of cash each day, shortages are apparent at the time of each drawer bankdown and fewer people get fired because of ignoring cash procedure. All they have to remember is to make change properly and feed all currency into the machine.

You might want to have a chat with these guys. Especially if you are already using armored car service for deposit transport. **Read more about this in Chapter 9.**

Data Mining Using Exception Based Reporting

Managing your company cash sales can be very labor intensive. We have already warned you to never require a manual verification to be required when all you need is the user name/card swipe along with the pin number of the operator of the register and the on duty manager to get dual controls of your audit trail.

I have to tell you again that if the rules are too detailed, your managers will **not** consistently follow the policies. They are too overwhelmed by all of the operations related functions to all of a sudden become auditors of manually filled in reports and logs. You will simply not be able to convince them of the value of manual reports other than it is something that you want them to do and is merely busy work for them.   It will not happen even when you threaten to fire them. Furthermore, the moment that you fail to follow up on their missing manual reports, they will assume that you feel that it is no longer important and stop completing it. It is just too difficult for today's' managers to multi-task at that level and you will find yourself in the cash violation/write-up/termination rut that we spoke about before.

We recommend that all but the most basic controls be automated and controlled with exception based auditing systems as an accounting function and not be an operations based function.

That means the key requirement is to insure that every one of your management people understand the basic controls philosophy of your organization and agree that they will consistently support the audit trail functions of operations management including:

1.   Manager store bank on using cash system POS equipment.
2.   Drawer assignments to specific banked on operator to POS.
3.   POS bank down of the responsible operator.
4.   Manager shift change accountability for deposits.
5.   Shift change and store close using system POS functions including report generation to the office.

All other controls functions can be monitored using exception reports generated by the POS system for small operators. The exceptions are based on your established and written acceptable cash over/short policies and other sales deduct ceilings such as those for returns, deletes, item and total voids and other key strokes that deduct from sales totals and are susceptible to abuse and theft given the type of business that you operate.   As long as you are able to separate the red flagged exceptions by operator, shift and manager on duty, you can enforce the cash policy with a minimum of manual reports and busy work.

A daily review of the exception reports, at a minimum, will flag operators that exceed the ceiling for the excepted item allowing you to immediately ask for an explanation from the employee. The best timing for fixing violations is at the time that the register is banked down at shift end.

The nice thing about exception based reporting is that the managers and register operators can be set up to show accumulated variance from exception ceiling amounts. That means that you can establish averages for the control items such as cash over/short and reward improved behaviors for those who run toward or exceed the outlier boundaries. That's right, you can spend your time to concentrate on rewarding good behaviors instead of punishing people for the failure to fill out forms!

The answer for larger companies is to obtain Exception Based Reporting software from one of the many suppliers or to outsource register report analysis to one of the companies that can provide the service if you do not have an accounting department with analysts assigned to audit your cash reports on a daily basis.

These guys will tell you that every hour of every day that you don't have an integrated comprehensive loss prevention solution, you could be losing thousands of dollars of revenue. The preliminary results from the Annual Retail Security Survey conducted by the University of Florida indicates that 44.5% of shrink is now caused by employee theft and fraud. Employee theft has increased from 41% in the 1997 survey and from 38% in the 1996 survey.

Exception based reporting solutions are aimed at this 44.5%. Personally, I think that this number is low since it is based on the surveyed results of Big Box Companies that spend on average .6% of total revenue on loss prevention programs, people and equipment to keep their loss percentages to a claimed 1.6% of sales. In the real world of small and mid-size company retail, the number is closer to 3% shrink on average.

Providing data for this client is a server, such as an IBM RS6000 or Sun server, an AS/400, or an IBM mainframe. A database on the server contains sales data collected regularly from the main retail system. The program essentially crunches your downloaded sales date reports to find the high-risk transactions that cause you to lose profits.

The software system is, in some respects, an Expert System: it incorporates the rules of thumb and statistical methods used by loss prevention specialists for many years, but is capable of applying these to large volumes of data in a timely manner, the manufacturer states.

The basic approach of the system is that certain activities are high risk. These activities in themselves do not necessarily indicate fraud, but an employee who performs more than the usual amount of them would probably be under suspicion.
The kind of activities noted can include the following:

- No sale following a cash void
- Price overrides
- Under-ring of keyed items
- Returns without a receipt
- Employees ringing their own purchases
- Employees ringing their own returns
- Voids of own purchases
- Voids of other employees' purchases

- Voids before opening or after closing
- Multiple charge voids of the same account,
   or by the same employee, or on multiple dates
- Charge returns in excess of the charge purchases
   by account number over a period of time
- Multiple refunds for the same original transaction
- Refunds rung at registers other than the service desk
- Layaway cancellations other than at the service desk
- Excessive line item voids
- Manual entry of credit card numbers

This list is by no means complete. There are presently hundreds more defined queries available. Each successive release or software upgrade contains new queries and features, based on the experience of customers. In addition, many of these software developers offer customization services for companies to add extra capabilities unique to their environment. Recognizing and tracking these high-risk transactions over time and across the retail organization forms the foundation of the system.

After the software has detected a suspicious pattern, the analyst can zoom in on a particular area of interest.

For example, you can focus on:
- A particular store
- A group of stores
- A district
- A group of registers
- A particular time of day, such as lunch time, or end-of-shift
- A particular employee
- A group of employees
- An account number
- Transactions above a specified value

This information is displayed on the PC screen, output as printed reports or with the report control functions allow, designing reports that meet your needs to control the areas where you are most likely losing money.

Additional investigative tools include:
- Employee scoring
- Incident analysis
- Top ten store reporting
- Transaction analysis

An example of how such a system can work is to query the "Statistical Analysis of Voids" or similarly named report depending on the software company:

First you would produce a frequency distribution graph showing the normal frequency of voids within the organization within a sample time period. You need to manage to the norm. In a small number of abnormal cases, you may find that an employee has performed a considerably higher number of voids. Some of these can be quite innocent, in which the employee has performed a very small number of transactions, one of which may be a void, and some may be instances of fraud. Let's find out which is which.

The software system allows you to drill down, by clicking on a particular element of the graph, or perhaps using a pull-down menu to provide further details of the element.

As an example, say a particular employee has performed 44 sale transactions, 9 of which were voids, a suspiciously high number of voids. You or your analyst can drill down more to provide further details.

If we see that all of the voids took place on a single day, maybe you should investigate further. By clicking on the date in question, you can obtain details of any high risk transactions performed by the employee. If you see that a single high-value void occurred, it is not necessarily an indication of fraud, but certainly a cause for concern. You need to look at how the transaction fits in with all others performed by the employee by drilling down again.

If you query finds that the employee has rung up a sale of $318.26 at 10:47 am and approximately 2 hours later a 'void before total' transaction for the same amount was done at 12:43 PM, you now have enough information to decide whether to pursue a more in depth investigation, definitely monitoring future activities of the employee and calling the Store Manager for an explanation.

We think that such a revelation would prompt you to look further into the possibility of other historical potential fraud activity of the particular employee. You or your analyst may be well along the way toward fixing a big hole in your profit margin.

Another example of how the system works is to consider a simple case, based on pattern recognition rather than statistics. After selecting the Credit query category, you can select credit transactions which might be labeled "Credit Accounts: Manual and Swiped".

If you see a credit sale, where the card has been swiped, followed by one or more sales where the card number has been manually entered, it may well indicate credit card fraud.

A highly suspicious pattern may emerge if you see that the same employee has run up a number of credit card sales, all of which (except the first) were manually entered. Note also whether these were all on the same account number. Hint...they probably were!

No longer just suspicious, you have uncovered a case of fraud by the register operator that lets them exchange your cash for phony credit card sales slips. You now are in the position to take action on the employee, and also to make the appropriate adjustments to the customer's account, before you lose a customer who has to discover the multiple charges on their account.

Imagine how long it would have taken to go through individual register and store reports without the specialized software. The difference is that you would not have likely taken the time to do the research until the problem got so big that you immediately could spot the flow of profits out of your business on the P&L!

**Protect your cash
with accountable policies
and procedures!**

A well planned loss prevention program can help you recover lost profits due to theft, waste, high claims and bad planning.

Your Competitive Advantage is increased revenue to improve and expand your business!

It's Your Profit!

10%
5%

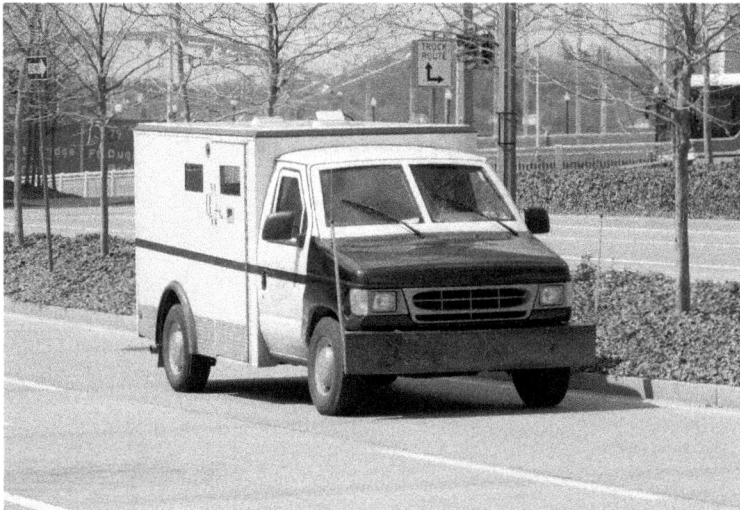

"Never Count your money
before you have it."

Thomas Jefferson
3rd President of the US
(1743-1826)

We have a lot to say about using armored car companies to transfer your deposits to the bank. For the most part, the reason for using this service is to transfer the risk of theft and robbery to a third party. Failure to pay attention to the contract details, however, can make recovery more difficult in the event that all of the money does not make it into your bank account for some reason.

Assume your risk analysis shows that it makes a lot of sense to use armored car service to do your banking runs instead of sending managers to the bank daily with way too much money. Also assume that your new safes have been ordered with a separate secured drop compartment inside to accommodate armored car.

The following information will apply to businesses that use the standard armored car service rather than the newer automated systems described in the cash controls chapter that utilize special safes with currency fed into safes with sealed cassettes.

You should establish a deposit drop log that provides two person controls over each deposit drop and a system is in place to have two employees witness the funds transfer to the armored car company courier.

Your research before establishing an armored car courier program should include discussions with a number of armored car (AC) service providers, recommendations from your CPP Loss Prevention professional and other merchants in your area.

You will find out that some armored car companies limit their liability to one container "said to contain" a specific amount of money not to exceed the agreed upon maximum amount. They take your deposit to your banks money-processing facility.

A substantial number of these companies will also provide "fine count" banking services whereby they transport your deposit to their own money processing facility, count the deposit, issue you deposit verification and transfer the funds to your bank electronically.

In fact, you may find out that your bank is already using the armored car company's facility to count their customer deposits. Your bank is marking up their processing charges from the armored car money room substantially in many cases. You should check your bank statement and see how much you are being charged for monthly processing fees.

Armored car companies with their own money rooms often have contracted with a number of banks legally naming them as a limited branch of the bank. Good news for you!

You may be able to negotiate a package deal with the armored car company to include more favorable costs and services:

•   AC Companies offer an "envelope account" allowing verification of contents for each of your deposit drops. This allows you to segregate drop responsibility to specific managers dropping their shift deposits. You can even have each register operator's sales proceeds be sealed in a plastic cash bag and dropped separately after the manager and operator verify

198457

INSTRUCTIONS:

1. USE A BALL POINT PEN TO FILL IN THE INFORMATION.
2. REMOVE THE RELEASE TAPE AND SEAL BAF FIRMLY.
3. ANY ATTEMPT TO OPEN WILL DAMAGE BAG.
4. TEAR OFF AND SAVE DUPLICATE SEAL NUMBER.

198457

DATE:_____ REGISTER #_____
STORE_____ DEPARTMENT:_____
CASHIER'S NAME_____ I.D. #_____
TOTAL AMOUNT DROPPED: $_____

CASH BREAKDOWN   TOTAL NUMBER

bills $100 x _____ = _____
50 x _____ = _____
20 x _____ = _____
10 x _____ = _____
5 x _____ = _____
1 x _____ = _____
2 x _____ = _____
COINS = _____

CASHIER'S SIGNATURE: _____
VERIFIED BY:_____ I.D. #_____

Signed and sealed is good!

the contents. (See cash control procedures)

- You can negotiate that the AC Company becomes your managers' witness at the time of transfer verifying multiple piece counts. You won't need a second employee to be able to verify what the safe contained when it was opened.

- You can receive daily reports regarding the deposit including amounts of each envelope drop and denominations count, total deposit count and over/short reports versus deposit ticket information.

In general, AC companies can do a lot for your loss prevention program to limit exposure of your people and money to theft and robbery. However, no program is perfect so you still have to pay attention to the fact that you can still experience theft in a number of ways while the money is transferred, en route to and at the money room. You need to protect yourself with clear contract language regarding dispute resolution.

First of all don't sign the AC Company contract without extensive modifications from your legal advisor. We are not lawyers and do not offer legal device, however we have experienced the ups and downs of dealing with armored car companies for many years.

Among the items your legal department may look at will avoid open ended or automatically renewing contracts. Contracts should have a beginning and an end. You can negotiate longer contracts as a bargaining chip to lock in a lower price for services - assuming that are receiving good service.

Contract addendum should specify the exact services to be performed, whether the AC courier is responsible for verifying the piece count as well as the amount "said to contain" in the couriers transit bag, cost of coin and change deliveries and specify that they must be paid "COD". They should provide you with a "Manifest" book to record their transfers

Pricing information should be specified and any holiday surcharge listed. The contract should very clearly state that you will not pay any non-contracted charges such as fuel surcharges, excess wait charges, return charges, etc. Armored car companies love to tack on extras without asking, the items just appears on your bill.

Most armored car companies vary their routes periodically even daily for security reasons. That means that you will probably not have the same pick up time or even the same AC courier every day. If you have specific times that you cannot accommodate the deposit transfer in a timely manner due to peak sales times requiring managers to completely focus on the business, list any "black out" times in the contract.

For instance, if your business is unable to accommodate deposit transfers from 11:30 AM until 1:00 PM, list the times. But, you must be flexible because on occasion, the truck routing will drop them on your doorstep at noon. Accommodate them if you can but don't let it become a habit because the secret is that very few of the AC companies clients want pick ups to occur at noon either. Your contract can also state procedures to follow that will result in the truck returning later in the day. You do not want to miss a pick up which will result in too much money left in the safe overnight until the next day.

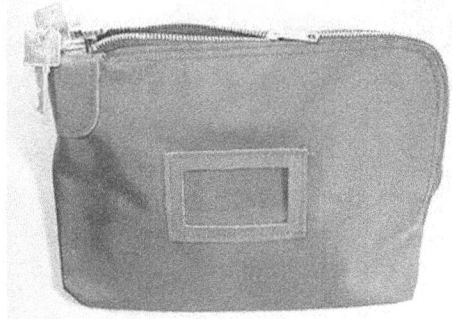

Take it to the bank yourself in one of these? Not so good!

Dispute resolution is a very important part of a contract. In our experience, we have encountered instances where theft occurred even with procedures in place. Money rooms all have extensive camera systems and counting procedures that are tied into processing computers that specify how each customer account must be processed by the teller. If a teller is unable to balance your deposit to the deposit ticket amount keyed into the system, a supervisor must be called for the recount.

It's all recorded on their video system. You must make sure that your contract allows you or your representative the right to view all security tapes; all drop and deposit bags and other documentation related to a disputed deposit shortage. This documentation should clearly identify security breaches whether yours or the armored car companies.

In one instance, a loss investigation found couriers had not paid attention to the piece count during deposit transfers allowing an employee to short the deposit by one-drop bag each day over a fairly extensive period of time.   The teller discovered the losses during the fine count but incredibly no one was notified so the first alert of trouble occurred in an over/short report sent to company headquarters accounting.

The contract allowed recovery of the losses but prosecution of the thief was not possible due to the signed paperwork that verified the piece count.

In other instances we encountered evidence that tellers at the money room opened all of the drop bags at once and ran the cash through the currency counting machine to save time. Shortages occurred and were identified using random bag numbers, not necessarily the bag that was short! A review of the money room security video revealed the contract violation allowing for recovery.

As you can see, half the battle is to be able to have policies and procedures in place that allow for resolution of the inevitable losses that occur. We are dealing with people and money and some will always yield to temptation.

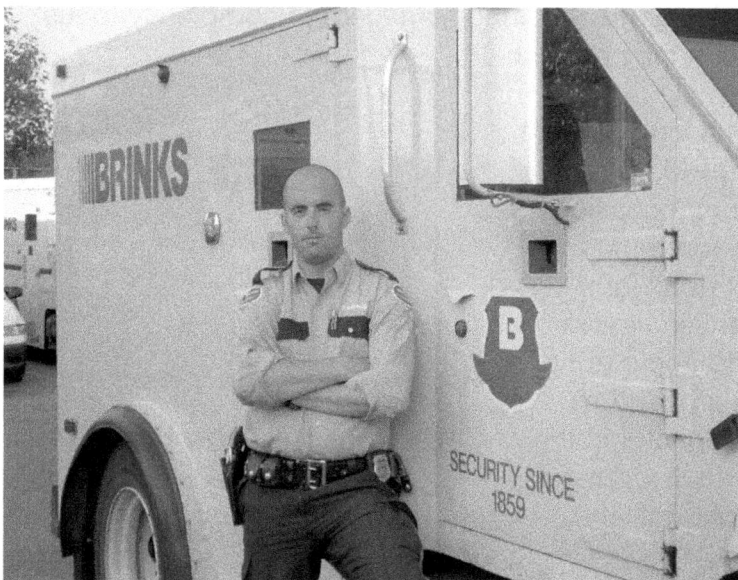

A proactive policy approach lets you be in the position of negotiating refunds instead of having to write off a loss.

Remember we told you that aren't lawyers. We are just very experienced in investigating and resolving losses that have occurred to our previous employers. So always get everything you can in writing and listen to your legal counsel.

Some other tools you will need include tamper evident sequentially numbered drop bags and large deposit transit bags. Don't buy them from the AC company. In fact, don't use them even if they are offered free; get your own logo printed on them from your own vendor. Once sealed, these bags show evidence if the sealed edge is pried apart. Using your own bags versus the generic AC Company imprinted ones removes a theft opportunity involving opening your deposit, pocketing a portion and replacing the bag with a new one.

The money room will always cut the bottom of the bag open leaving sealed edges intact. Bags are retained for an extended period of time and your contract should state that you are allowed to inspect the bags at any time. I have recovered money stolen en route to the bank by the AC courier when we could prove that bag had been tampered with. As you can see by examining our Armored Car Drop Log example on the next page of this book, the bag numbers play a major role in accountability.

Use of a deposit ticket is also recommended. The ticket should list each drop by bag number and amount. Have the manager putting the deposit together sign the ticket and arrange for a copy of the multipart form to sealed inside of the deposit bag in the money section for use by the money room.   One or two copies of the deposit ticket are usually placed in a pocket on the outside of the deposit bag and are removed when the bag is delivered to the money room by the truck. Of course, be sure and keep a copy for store records (this means use a 3 or 4 part form).   Your log may look something like the example that was created for a restaurant company. Note the directions are at the top of each form to reduce misunderstanding the correct procedures to use.

Armored Car Drop Log Manifest:

Use a new manifest for each business day. You *Must* place a cardboard between the form sets or the carbon copy will not be legible*. Each Pull / Drop must *be sealed* in a numbered tamper resistant envelope after the Cash Manager and the register operator have counted, verified the contents and signed the bag. Place your drop bag in a hard plastic [red/clear] sleeve. The Cash Manager and a witness must sign this log to verify the drop. **Look inside the drop slot and make absolutely sure that the drop has fallen into the inner compartment.** All armored car transfers must have a manager and a witness to verify the number of drops removed from the safe. Compare the drop bag number to the number listed on this log. The cash manager and witness will list the number of drops counted and sign the bottom line at the time the deposit is transferred to the armored car representative. All information must be completed on *Each* section of this form for your protection. **Do Not** include checks/credit slips in register operator cash bank down drops. **The Cash Manager and witness must return any drops from today to the armored car drop safe for tomorrow's pickup. List the number in the box and both manager and witness must sign.** The drop manifest cash total, deposit ticket total and the deposit amount keyed into the register *must* match. Checks/credit slips must be keyed into the register as separate deposits. They must be placed in their own drop bag at the end of the night along with a separate deposit ticket. Be sure and list the total of your check/credit slip drop in space # 43 below and include in the deposit Grand Total for the day.

Today's DCR Date: **Day of the Week:**

Drop #	Envelope Number	Amount	Time:	Cash Manager:	Witness:	Drop #	Envelope Number	Drop Amount	Time:	Cash Manager:	Witness:
1.						26.					
2.						27.					
3.						28.					
4.						29.					
5.						30.					
6.						31.					
7.						32.					
8.						33.					
9.						34.					
10.						35.					
11.						36.					
12.						37.					
13.						38.					
14.						39.					
15.						40.					
16.						41.					
17.						42.					
18.						**43:**					
19.						Check	Envelope Number	Checks Tot. #	Check Tot. $	Cash Manager	Witness
20.						Drop					
21.											
22.											
23.							Today's Cash Total:			$	
24.							Business Check Total: (+)			$	
25.							Travelers Check Total: (+)			$	

Total # of drops transferred to Armored Car today:	Cash Manager: Witness:	We are returning these drops for the next pick up:		Today's Deposits Grand Total: (=)	$
			Mgr.: Witness:	Armored Car Bag Number:	

* The white copy must be retained in the store. The completed store copies must be retained for one year.
The weeks* **Legible** yellow copies must be forwarded to Accounting .   ©2004 Security Wise Group

Cash Management Programs

Managing cash is a vital part of any retail business, especially stores handling high volumes of currency. To improve cash security and control, many retailers employ a cash-handling process built on a series of checks and balances. First, the cash is counted at the cashier level; it is then counted again by back office personnel, often twice and under dual custody; and possibly again by the manager as part of the deposit preparation process.

Some of the challenges inherent in this process are obvious; it is time consuming and the opportunities for mistakes are endless. Other challenges are less apparent, but equally detrimental to the retail environment. Cash not held in a safe is exposed, making it vulnerable to theft.

Moving your money needs a plan!

Poor cash controls, inattentiveness, apathy, and lack of proper cash-handling training can lead to counting errors, mathematical mistakes, transpositions, and reconciliation miscalculations. Employees are human, and humans make mistakes.

Counting, recounting, and reconciling cash can take hours a day. For retailers with multiple stores, cash handling can consume countless hours a month that otherwise could be contributing to sales, customer service and profitability. A study conducted several years ago at a previous employer of mine determined that the manual verification and counting of cash, along with written documentation of dual controls took approximately eight hours a day of employee and management time!

Manual cash handling translates to manual record keeping and limited access to information for cash forecasting and management. Manual systems are highly dependant on bank deposit slips stamped by bank tellers and do no reflect the actual cash fine count which may differ from the amount that you thought you deposited. The way it works from the bank standpoint is "you give us your money and we'll tell you how much it was". It can take several days to get fine count verifications depending on whether the branch fine counts your deposit or they send it off "said to contain" to a money room. Either way, they will seldom let you know about over/shorts until the bank statement is issued or they give you a settlement or variance report.

Manual cash handling is unpredictable. When a discrepancy or reconciliation error causes the team to miss the daily deposit cut-off, the retailer is denied use of those funds until they're collected and transferred to the bank. Furthermore many banks consider same day credit for your deposits to be a "loan" since they have not fine counted the money. They can actually add a banking fee for this!

The manual cash process offers numerous opportunities for robberies to occur and for thieves to strike due to exposure of too much tempting cash. While cashiers are closing out their tills, when employees and managers are counting the cash, and when the manager takes the bag of cash to the bank are all exposures and this threat can be frightening and can damage employee morale. Some companies have felt compelled to insist that managers take a witness/escort to the bank to make the deposit for the safety of the employees.

I have long considered manual transport of deposits to the bank by a manager to be risky behavior even when handled with appropriate caution. How have you handled the issue where the manager says that they put the deposit in the night depository and the bank says that they did not receive it? Lots of managers get fired over this issue whether they stole the money or not.

With manual cash handling, each store is responsible for its own deposits usually twice a day. Deposits taken manually should occur in the morning for the previous evenings deposit and before dark for the day deposit. Otherwise too much money can accumulate increasing the risk for armed robberies at the store. Each bank transaction generates a bank fee. These costs can add up quickly, especially for retailers with numerous stores.

We have found that in many cases, the consolidation of cash deposits and control of banking charges have often justified the use of armored car service due to the savings on bank charges and fees.

"Intelligent Safes", sometimes called "Smart Safes", can replace manual cash handling in retail stores usually installed at the point of sale (POS) or in the back office and automate the cash-handling process while providing secure storage out of criminal reach. In fact, these safes are so sophisticated, they virtually remove cash handling from a store's operations except for the few seconds between accepting it from customers and inserting it into the safe's bill acceptors. Once inserted into the safe, the cash is verified, authenticated, and passed into locked cassettes where it remains safe from theft and mismanagement.

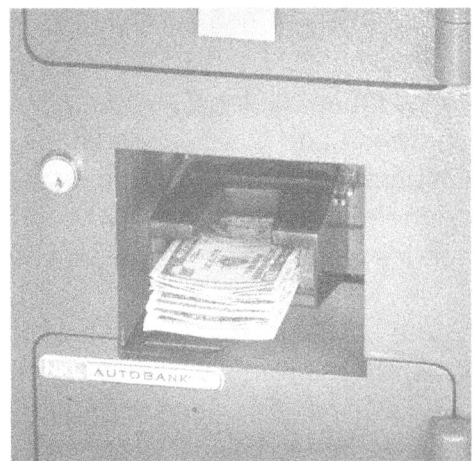

Intelligent safes do more than protect your cash. They also manage the cash process, counting and tracking cash activity at the cashier level for fast, accurate balancing—no counting, recounting, and verifying is necessary. The intelligent safes capture data electronically for aggregation across a single store or an entire network of locations.

The result is a complete cash management solution virtually eliminating on-site counting and verification. Remember our eight hours a day of management and employee time counting cash and verifying controls? How long does it take your manager to go to the bank every day? Do you have loss exposure not only of the cash in transit but who pays if someone runs into your manager's car on the way to the bank? For some stores, this can save countless hours a month, and multiplied over a number of locations, the increase in productivity can be staggering along with the reduction of risk exposure.

It works like this:

1.   Cash received at the POS is inserted into the intelligent safe where it is verified and authenticated, then passed into cassettes for safekeeping. It's the only time you handle the money.

2.   Armored transportation provider picks up cash and takes it to a cash vault for processing. Only the armored car people have access to the money and you have no need for transfer paperwork or written manifests since you are given a print-out of the transaction.

Only the armored car company has access to the money after it passes to the casette

3.   Network access connects locations enabling sharing of information and electronic transmission of deposit information. That means enhanced reporting is available to know where your money is at.

4.   Deposit information from multiple stores is aggregated and deposited to a single bank account usually electronically.

Many times the local armored car company also conducts the fine count money room operation and is actually a limited branch of a bank service company such as Chase or Citibank. In depth reporting is available and all of reports are available via a secure on-line connection for daily review by your accounting people. The amount and number of types of service available depends on who you use and the capability of the equipment that you use.

Some of the innovative technology available allows some service company's smart safes to interface via remote access to report cash totals for each cashier, each store and totals across all locations. The service provider, works with select financial institutions to facilitate credit based on these electronically reported totals, giving customers credit for their deposits faster than by manual cash-handling methods. In fact, most customers reportedly receive credit for their cash, hours, and in most cases, days before the cash actually reaches the bank. Meanwhile, the armored car service picks up the cash cassettes from the smart safe units according to the store's schedule, possibly on a daily basis depending on note storage capacity or longer.

The safes may hold several days worth of receipts allowing the store manager to reduce pickup frequency depending on your sales volume. Daily Credit totals can be transmitted upon day end, or at a predetermined time each day, giving retailers more flexibility and discretion in meeting bank deposit cut-off times.

Upon pick-up, the cash is verified and prepared for deposit. If discrepancies are noted at this time, the difference between the actual and reported amounts is debited or credited to the customer account as appropriate.

At this point, the cash system has accounted for every bill of the currency that you have fed into the cassette. That means it "is what it is" and your POS system balances with the cash amount that is going to the bank. No debit memos from the bank will be showing up at a later time and date like what happens now!

As your business grows and becomes more complex, you have fewer opportunities to directly supervise what is happening related to cash controls. The more locations that you have and the more managers that you employ increases the likelihood that controls will be violated and you may sustain a cash loss.

Furthermore the less you are able to supervise the cash function the more likely that bad manager habits can become a pattern that the dishonest will eventually take advantage of.

Counting out high volumes of cash in areas open to the public is very risky behavior!

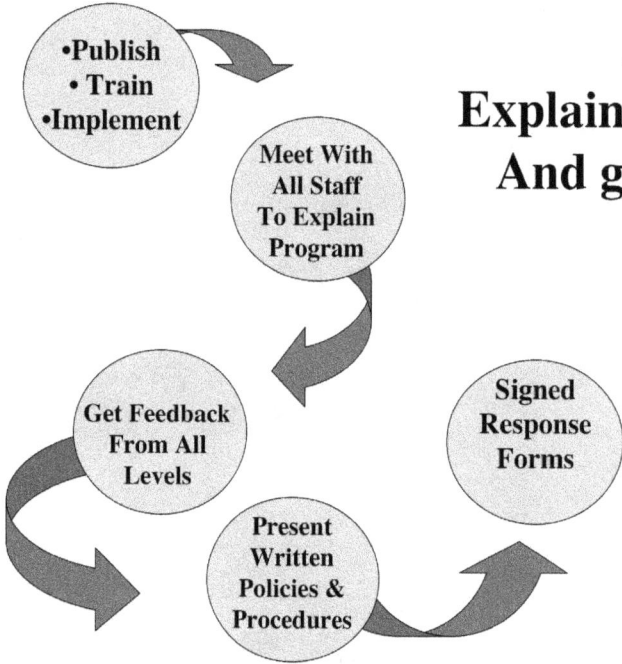

- •Publish
- • Train
- •Implement

Meet With All Staff To Explain Program

Explain The Purpose And get "Buy In"

Get Feedback From All Levels

Signed Response Forms

Present Written Policies & Procedures

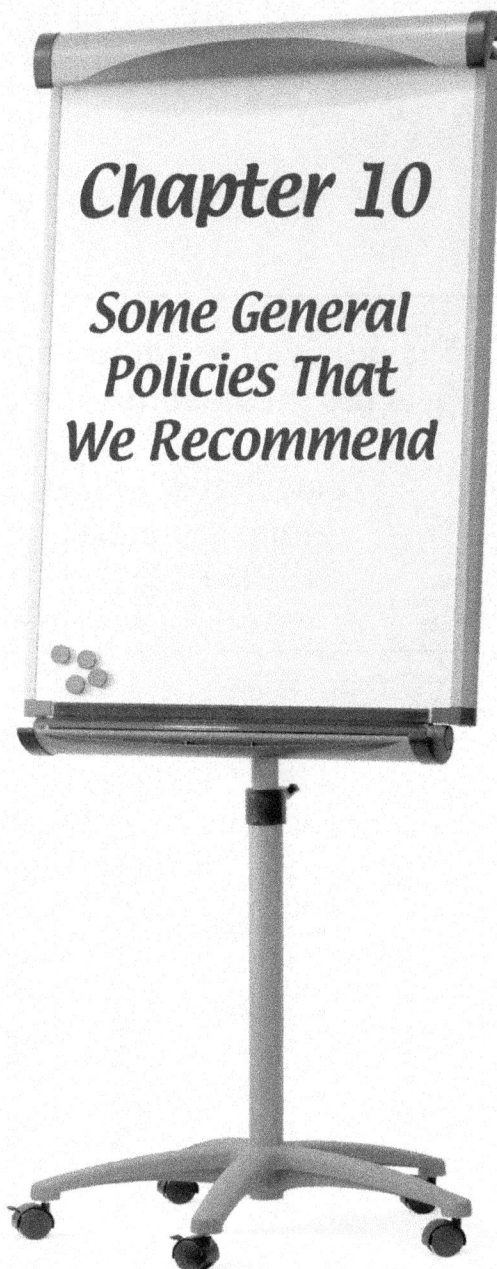

> "The policy of being too cautious
> is the greatest risk of all."
>
> Jawaharlal Nehru
> Indian Politician
> (1889-1964)

Loss prevention must be part of your "best practices" that you have identified as an important core competency to achieve in your written business plan. A number of companies who have failed to realize the importance of controls have declined or disappeared in recent years.

A 2006 story in the news related to the demise of the Radio Shack CEO, surfaces some thought provoking issues related to the loss prevention role in company operations.

The Chief Executive Officer was supposedly sacked for lying on his resume regarding some college degrees from institutions that were pretty academically anemic even if genuine. The schools involved are not important, other than to mention that they never heard of the guy. The Chief was a long-term employee, who apparently never had a background check as he navigated his way up the corporate ladder.

We think that the flap was more likely over performance and the fact that Radio Shack recently said that its fourth quarter 2005 earnings fell 62% and the company plans on closing 400 to 700 stores and two distribution centers as a plan to fix it's financial woes. Shares on the news tumbled 8% to a new three-year low.

Fast reverse back to the end of 2003. That year, Radio Shack announced that it was disbanding its entire loss prevention department comprised of 70 loss prevention professionals in favor of an outsourced solution. The reason given by the now departed CEO's administration was that "loss prevention was not a core competency" of Radio Shack and it would focus on its key strengths of merchandising and customer service.

An astounding statement on a number of fronts.

First of all, the outsourcing of corporate loss prevention, while not a new concept was certainly a major paradigm shift for the old brick and mortar business model. As a consultant company that welcomes business outsourcing sent in our direction, we were pleased at the precedent.

But wait, you have to ask yourself, how did a company the size of Radio Shack get to be where they are today with out developing a strong profit driven corporate culture including an evolving loss prevention program? The key word here is "evolving".

If loss prevention was not a core competency, what makes them sure that they will be able to select competent replacements for the disbanded security department? Isn't it just as likely that if loss numbers were unacceptable, the problem may well have been in selection, implementation and support of best practices policies and procedures?

Fast forward to 2006 and the news continues to be grim. Radio Shack has closed 40 stores as of the end of first quarter 2006 and is targeting a total store closure of 480 units. The consumer electronics retailer will suffer charges of $50 million to $90 million related to its store closings.

During the first quarter of 2006, profits plunged 85% due to weak wireless sales and inventory write-downs. Talk about a ship without a rudder! We wonder how much of the "slow moving" inventory is simply missing from the warehouse and is being written off to balance the books.

What of fiscal year 2007 and beyond? Time will tell. The need exists in all businesses, for a steady flow of executive education about security and risk, until it becomes unthinkable for a CEO to propose the neutering of a well-crafted security model. A strong program of internal influence and awareness is a best practice of untold value, whether the advice is coming from internal staff or the outsourced loss prevention consultant.

Taking short term and we think short sighted opportunity to cut costs, only puts a band-aid on the real problem that many companies experience if they have not created a corporate culture that includes loss prevention systems and controls. Your Competitive Advantage is to learn from the lessons of some large companies and identify and correct any similar hazards that may trip you up on your own path toward profitability.

SECURITY PROGRAM CONSIDERATIONS

We have identified a number of categories of loss risks to the average company. First on our list are those losses that occur due to the dishonesty, careless acts or risky behavior of your employees. We will discuss these loss exposures in Chapter Eleven. Next on the list are those policies and procedures put in place to defend against criminal acts or other harmful activities by outsiders which we cover in Chapter 12. Finally, we have a series of policies that are used to defend against the risks of both inside and outside threats.

This chapter will address these "general" threat events and those "general" policies that you need as barriers to loss.

LOSS REPORTING

We recommend that all companies should have a formal loss reporting system for your accounting system records and for required submission to your insurance company if a claim is appropriate.

Your policy should include the completion of an incident report form, by the manager in charge of the location, during the period of time that the loss or incident occurred. We think that it should be completed the day of occurrence and forwarded to the office where you have designated that the report be processed and stored.

An Incident Report form would be typically be completed for all crimes and cash losses over $100.00. The report form completion should be done by the manager conducting the initial investigation and should be time bound as to completion date. We recommend that the report occur at the completion of the initial investigation and be forwarded to the various levels of management where decision making can occur to insure that the exposure issues are addressed and follow up occurs.

INCIDENT REPORT

Date Prepared		Prepared by Name and Title		Store Name/#		

Kind of Loss:

		Date of Loss	Time of Loss	Day of Week	Amount of Loss $	
	Armed Robbery ☐	Senior Manager		Store Manager		
Burglary	Cash Over/Short ☐	Store Address		City	State	Zip
	Internal Theft ☐					
Incident	☐					

Police Information

Reported to Police Yes ☐ No ☐	Police Case #	Arrest? Yes ☐ No ☐	Money Recovered $
Police Department Name		Police Department Phone	Detective/Officer Assigned

Narrative
Outline the circumstances of the loss/incident.

Policy Violations

Policies Violated: Deposits not taken to the bank ... ☐ Unsecured cash ... ☐ Safe left unlocked ... ☐ Alarm not set ... ☐ Security procedures not followed ... ☐ Cash control procedures not followed ... ☐ None ... ☐ Other (explain) _____	What disciplinary action was taken? Name of employee:	Verbal	Written	Final		None

Robberies
This section should be completed in the event of a robbery

# of Robbers:	Type of weapon used:	Money taken from:	Injuries: (explain)
Male 0 ☐ 1 ☐ 2 ☐ 3 ☐ Female 0 ☐ 1 ☐ 2 ☐ 3 ☐	Pistol ☐ Shotgun ☐ Knife ☐ Assault Rifle ☐ Other _____	Registers ☐ Safe ☐ Drop Safe ☐ Other _____	

Action Plan
List actions to be taken by management to prevent future occurrences

A suggested procedure for reporting and processing crime events and losses for all crimes and cash losses over $100 can include the following:

• The Manager on duty calls the company office/senior manager for all crimes that occur on property or involve loss of a company asset off property, i.e. robbery at bank. You may want to include specific examples of when your company hierarchy needs to be notified of a crime loss.

• This call should be made before the Manager's end of shift.

PERSONAL PROPERTY

A few precautions can reduce your exposure to missing and stolen property claims in your business. People will commonly put down their packages, purses and other personal items in your business, become distracted and leave without them.

To save embarrassment and lawsuits related to mishandled customer personal property, a few rules will help.

**Always inventory
all found property!**

Do not accept responsibility for the protection, loss, or theft of customers' or employees' personal property. Encourage employees to come dressed for work and never bring valuables with them because you will not be responsible.

Employee personal property brought into the business should be kept in one approved location, but not in the manager's office. Many companies issue employee lockers and allow them to provide their own locks. If this is the case in your business, be sure to reserve the right to inspect the lockers for reasons of safety, health and security at any time.

Lost customer property found must be inventoried and placed in the safe for protection.

• **Attempt to contact owner if identification is available.**

• **Hold for one week maximum.**

• **Train employees to contact the manager immediately if they find customer property.**

• **Unclaimed property should be turned over to the local police in accordance with your state laws.**

- **Manager notifies the police and acquires a police case number for all crimes and for cash loses over $100.00.**

SECURITY SERVICES

Hiring security guards to work in a business presents issues that require analysis before a decision is made. Your companies' legal counsel must approve hiring and/or contracts for security guards. Because less obtrusive and potentially less volatile security solutions are available, security guards should be considered a last resort in most situations.

You should consult your CPP Loss Prevention expert regarding the need to implement security services in your business. You will receive help with the proper selection and deployment of the security personnel to your best advantage.

The decision making process must determine where and how the security guard is to be utilized for the most effective results. (I.e., If problems with loiterers and speeding in the parking lot, the manager should have the security guard patrolling outside, as opposed to sitting in the dining room.) This should be communicated to the security guard agency.

Managers should not be responsible for providing supervision to any guard. This is the responsibility of the guard agency. The issue here is the fact that the actions of your contract guards can increase your liability exposure significantly.

If you take over direct control of the guards, you effectively transfer the controls and liability of their employer, which is the guard service company, to you. There is a lot of case law regarding actions and omissions of guard services and you should get references from prospective companies along with copies of their liability insurance coverage.

All vendors working on your property must provide proof of adequate liability insurance. In the case of guard companies, since we are going to presume that you have the need for special levels of protection, the coverage should be related to what you could lose in a lawsuit that claims injury as a result of the actions of guards on your property. Ask your attorney.

Written agreements with security service vendors usually need to be carefully scrutinized and amended to remove some of the exclusionary clauses that the guard companies like to add. Our experience has been that getting acceptable performance from security guards can be a challenge to business owners.

Think about it. Let's say you want to hire a security guard company to deal with late night loiterers on your parking lot and stay overnight on the property to keep track of trucks coming and going at your warehouse. You contract with the vendor and they send a guard to your property the first night of service, he walks up to your night receiving supervisor and asks, "What do you want me to do?"

You may well have spent a lot of time with the guard company putting together post orders and a job description but don't be surprised if the guard wasn't trained in their duties. Also don't be surprised that you don't get the same guards every night because the service will often move people around a lot due to high turnover and poor training.

You may find that your receiving supervisor is spending a significant amount of time getting the guard into position each night and tracking them down when they are needed.

Many guard services provide poor training, poor selection and screening, have poor supervision, high turnover of low wage employees and high cost to you the business owner. You can do the math yourself. Most guard companies pay their people $8 to $10 an hour that they mark up to $18 -$20 an hour to you. Large security guard companies are very profitable.

Guards need very specific post orders and a lot of supervision.

Using the lower number, if you employee their guards for 40 hours a week, that comes to $720 a week. A years worth of service is $37,440. Considering the return on this investment, you could take the same money and invest in more exterior low light cameras and look into some remote controlled access control hardware.

Yes, there are many good security guard services. The problem is finding these services and maintaining the level of service that you require. Even up-scale security vendors with guarantees of higher paid and better quality people struggle to keep their people and maintain consistency. The reason the good security guard company employees leave is that many are recruited into proprietary company security departments that have good wages, benefits and promotion opportunities or join local public law enforcement.

Talk to your CPP Loss Prevention Professional about other approaches to dealing with problems using methods other than guard services. Compare the costs and look at the long-term cost of service versus equipment solutions.

In most cases, the use of off duty police is preferential versus hiring a guard agency if it is allowed in your community. Here is where your relationship with the local police precinct commander will come in handy again. Advise of your local legal counsel is urged when dealing with situations that you feel require you to hire guard agencies.

In any case, before any decision, contact your local police precinct and speak with the community services officer (COPE) or station commander regarding what your options are. In our experience, working with local law enforcement agencies has been very productive for a number of reasons.

First of all, it is true that police agencies are over worked and under funded and if you want to receive priority service you need to demonstrate to them that you will work with them to solve the problem.

This means that you may need to willingly file charges against individuals that have broken the law on your property but since they have not committed the crime or offense in the presence of the responding officer, you will may need to sign the complaint and appear in court.

If you take the technology versus the guard approach, you also have physical proof in hand in the case of video records that you can hand to the prosecutors. Nothing says it better than a thousand pictures!

What makes the most sense for your organization? People or equipment? Examine your plan, determine what you want to achieve and run the numbers!

We told you that you can protect your property in a number of ways beyond and better than using guards.

Interactive hosted guard service grew out of a need for affordable, live, 24/7/365 security coverage that integrated electronic systems with real people intervening when a security breach is detected.   It is basically live video monitoring. There are thousands of companies doing monitoring remotely from your business using digital cameras and internet protocols (IP), the problem is that those systems are basically proprietary with cameras being recorded but no one responding to crimes in progress.

Basically, when someone buys a CCTV system, they need one or two things. They need loss prevention for normal operating hours, and they also need after-hours security.

When someone enters your property at night the IP system is recording. The business owner comes in the next morning and finds the damage, and goes to his system to review the captured footage, but it's too late because the criminal is gone. With the new interactive systems, the manufacturer builds in artificial intelligence.

A perimeter is created electronically around your property and when that perimeter is broken, the system wakes up first one camera, and then more as the threat is assessed. In other words, what is occurring is a "motion interrupt". When the system video pixels are affected by the motion sensed from the arriving criminal it alerts the live operator that a security breach has been sensed that needs to be assessed and authenticated. Since everything is monitored live, the security breach is classed according to threat level and dealt with by the central station in real time. You have now essentially had an alarm occurring at the perimeter instead of the building interior after a break in and the alarm is being verified as it occurs.

The system can be used for video verification to cut down on false alarms, and it also gives its monitoring agents the ability to issue an audible warning to intruders once the perimeter is broken. The proactive approach, versus a typical reactive alarm system allows the on line system operator to verbally challenge the intruder before the break in, vandalism or other crime occurs.

These "smart" systems are different from the last generation of so called interactive systems which only came on "live" when a standard burglar alarm occurred, a manually operated "hot phone" call for assistance occurred or a scheduled video capture or live guard tour occurred. These new systems have a service cost advertised as low as $75 a month, based on the area of the perimeter and the amount of possible activity versus $200-$300 a month for the older systems.

In addition to the above, the next tier up the protection chain uses a system of providing each detection and communication device it's own IP address so that the integrated system knows what each device does. This next system assumes that you will have a physical response to the alarm using your proprietary monitoring station and guards to confront the intruder.

There are many high tech perimeter protection systems available to protect your business even up to the standards used by the military and you can have the best detection system available in the world, but if they can't communicate the information that your fence has been breached in a timely manner, the system is worthless.

All of the detection and delay technology must have the ability to "talk" to each other, or at least communicate via a software application package of some sort. In the past, every system had its own output that would be wired to a monitoring location. These monitoring locations rapidly became crowded with tens or even hundreds of devices that each had their own operating system and alarm mechanism. The poor security guard had to have an eye on 30 different systems at the same time, and worse yet, had to know how to operate each one using the correct proprietary communication codes.

Now, thanks to modern telecommunications, all the devices discussed can be combined into one system via the use of TCP/IP, Telecommunications Protocol/Internet Protocol. You can give each sensor in the intrusion detection system, such as the device that picks up vibration at the fence, its own IP address. This allows two-way communication to the sensor via our computer network, whether it is local (LAN) or remote via the Internet (WAN). This means that the operator can make adjustments to the sensor from the control location, or can be notified about something from the sensor. All this capability can be integrated into one operating system. That same system can perform all necessary security functions for the enterprise such as creating badges, keeping employee files, saving monitoring logs of employees coming and going, viewing closed circuit TV, and of course, running the intrusion detection system.

With this integrated capability, a fence breaching will instantly show up on a computer screen at the monitoring station, and a response can immediately take place. Since we are using IP addresses, the trespass action can even be sent to someone's PDA such as a Palm or Blackberry! The response can take the form of activating a camera and allowing the security guard to control it with a pan, tilt, and zoom control (PTZ), or turning on floodlights, sending out a vehicle with guards, activating a siren, or whatever is the appropriate response for a particular facility.

You could even take the non-aggressive approach and have a conversation with the intruder via a two way intercom!

Perimeter security measures are now so sophisticated, that you can set up an "intelligent" video system which will look for certain "situations" needing a response. You can program the intelligent video to alarm if someone is walking in the wrong direction, or if someone starts climbing the fence, or if someone drops a bag and it remains stationary for a certain period of time. Delaying an intruder easy access to the perimeter of your facility long enough to deny him access to our critical infrastructure is the key.

Finally, you ask, why is the perimeter so important, anyway? If you have good security at the door to the building, you can keep people out, right? All you need at the perimeter is a boundary line and a gate. The answer is that people with intention to harm only have to get next to the building to cause severe damage. Remember the Oklahoma City bombing. The perpetrators never even had to leave the curb.

Even if physical damage to a structure or facility is not an intruder's intent, vital data may also need to be protected and trespassers denied access to critical information. When you add a total system solution of perimeter security to any building or facility already secured by modern access controls, you create a modern "moat" that protects and secures your infrastructure, denying and controlling admittance to your grounds on your terms.

**You don't need to hire these guys unless
you have something serious to protect!**

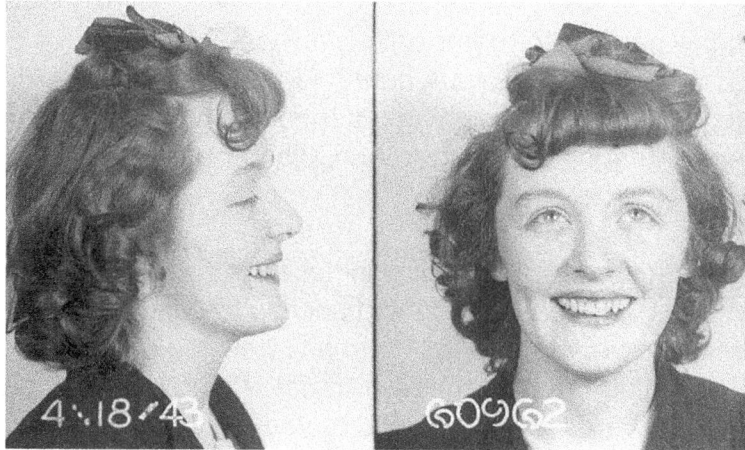

She had such an honest face!

DEPARTMENT OF POLICE

NEWARK, N. J.

ARREST FOR GRAND LARCENY

JOSEPH MANG

This fugitive is under indictment in this City for larceny of $3,300, funds of the Brewers Union Local, No. 2, of which at the time of his disappearance, December 1st, 1914, he was Business Agent.

DESCRIPTION

Age 46 years, 5-feet 11-inches in height, slender build, weight about 180 pounds, black hair, bald on top, black moustache (if wearing one), very large dark eyes, walks erect, decidedly soldierly bearing, native of Germany, speaks poor English.

Should any trace of this fugitive be discovered, kindly communicate; and if arrested wire and officer armed with necessary requisition papers will be sent immediately.

M. T. LONG,
Chief Police.

December 23, 1914

PLEASE POST CONSPICUOUSLY.

A fine old tradition of employee theft!

The topic of internal theft-that is those goods and services stolen by employees within a business organization must be separated from the loss exposure businesses experience from those losses perpetrated by those outside of the organization.

To begin with, it is a good idea to define what some of the crimes that you have experienced and read about every day are called and how they fit into the legal systems.

Embezzlement, is defined as wrongful use, for one's own selfish ends, of the property of another when that property has been legally entrusted to one. Such an act was not larceny at common law because larceny was committed only when property was acquired by a "felonious taking," i.e., when the act was committed with respect to property that was at the time in the legal possession of the owner.

Consequently, unfaithful servants, employees, agents, trustees, or guardians who misappropriated another's property could be sued only in the civil courts, on the grounds that although the defendant had legally come into possession of the property, he had breached his trust by wrongfully misappropriating it to his own use. To remedy this situation statutes were passed in England and the United States that either made embezzlement a distinct crime or enlarged the definition of larceny in such a way as to include all cases of misappropriation of property in the lawful possession of the wrongdoer. In most states of the United States embezzlement is a felony. Under acts of Congress, stealing of letters by postmasters, clerks, and letter carriers is considered embezzlement.

Larceny, defined in law, is the unlawful taking and carrying away of the property of another, with intent to deprive the owner of its use or to appropriate it to the use of the perpetrator or of someone else. It is usually distinguished from embezzlement and false pretenses in that the actual taking of the property is accomplished unlawfully and without the victim's consent along with the taking there must be a carrying-off.

It is also distinguished from burglary in that the theft does not necessarily involve unlawful breaking and entering. Statutes in some states of the United States enlarge the scope of larceny to include embezzlement and false pretenses. Grand larceny, usually a felony, is distinguished from petty larceny, usually a misdemeanor by the value of the property stolen.

An interesting trend we have been following involves the increase in the number of women who are being caught embezzling from their employers. Embezzlement by women skyrocketed 80 percent between 1993 and 2002, even slightly exceeding the number of those crimes committed by men in 2002, according to a New York Times analysis of federal data.

Experts say women are tapping the company till for several reasons. Some have a vice, such as a drug or gambling addiction or compulsive shopping. Others may have incurred large medical bills or made a bad investment and are desperate for cash.

The Association of Certified Fraud Examiners released a study recently of 1,134 occupational fraud cases investigated from January 2004 to January 2006. The median loss, regardless of gender, was $159,000.   Small business and non-profit organizations suffered the most.

Sadly, statistics and surveys conclude that as a business owner you are overwhelmingly experiencing more losses from inside versus outside. The National Retail Federation (NRF) that puts the problem of retail crime in perspective sponsors a major yearly statistical event.

Take it back..It's your profit!

The National Retail Federation is the world's largest retail trade association, with membership that comprises all retail formats and channels of distribution including department, specialty, discount, catalog, Internet, independent stores, chain restaurants, drug stores and grocery stores as well as the industry's key trading partners of retail goods and services.

NRF represents an industry with more than 1.6 million U.S. retail establishments, more than 24 million employees - about one in five American workers - and 2006 sales of $4.7 trillion. As the industry umbrella group, NRF also represents more than 100 state, national and international retail associations. (You can find them at www.nrf.com)

At a recent National Retail Federation's Loss Prevention Conference and EXPO, Dr. Richard Hollinger, a professor at the University of Florida, released the latest National Retail Security Survey.

The National Retail Security Survey is an annual survey of loss prevention executives that benchmarks retail shrinkage and operational information about how retailers are combating losses. The study, which surveyed 139 retailers in the first half of 2007 and uses data from 2006, is a partnership between the University of Florida and the National Retail Federation.

Note the fact that since only large companies generally employ "loss prevention executives" you can infer that these large cap heavy hitters are putting a lot of prevention dollars into the game to achieve the following numbers. It is generally understood based on many other surveys and sources that the average business shrinkage is really 3% to 5% of gross sales.

The NRF report is really a small numerical sampling of companies albeit using some very big sales numbers.

It is also noteworthy that the surveyed companies state that they spend on average .5% of their gross sales per year to pay for loss prevention systems and people that are responsible for the stated loss metrics. Are you spending anywhere near that for your security systems?

Consider for instance that the average unit volume for a Home Depot store is about 45M per year. A half of a percent of sales would be about $225,000. They are paying that cost to recover the one and a half percent difference between the average retail shrink loss of 3% and what they report as their actual shrink percentage of 1.6%. So the 225K investment returns 675K to their bottom line for each store in the chain. That's pure profit and they are also writing off their loss prevention program recovery costs!

If you're not spending some money to keep your profit margin, you are walking away from and accepting your loss as a cost of doing business. And generally, you can't write off a profit loss caused by bad management.

The NRF survey found that retail shrinkage* averaged 1.61 percent of retail sales last year, nearly unchanged from 1.60 percent in 2005. The survey, an annual event is now in its fifteenth year as a collaborative effort between NRF and the University of Florida. In past years the trend has generally been favorable.

Even though shrinkage as a percentage of sales stayed virtually the same, total retail losses increased last year to $41.6 billion due to higher retail sales in 2006 compared to 2005.

Hollinger, lead author of the report and a criminology professor at the University of Florida, acknowledged they have a lot of work left to do. According to the survey, the majority of retail shrinkage last year was due to employee theft, at $19.5 billion, which represented almost half of losses (47%). Shoplifting accounted for $13.3 billion, or about one-third (32%) of losses.

Noteworthy is the information that almost half of all losses were due to internal theft. It is a very good indicator of where you should be focusing your own efforts to control losses.

Other losses included administrative error ($5.8 billion and 14% of shrinkage) and vendor fraud ($1.7 billion and 4% of shrinkage).

The survey suggests that the phenomenon of organized retail crime is gaining more awareness within the industry. As retailers' understanding regarding the impact of these crimes continues to grow, roughly half of companies say they are now tracking organized retail crime activity. To combat criminals' brazen actions, retailers have been investing in new technologies to deter, detect and convict criminals.

According to the survey, most retailers' loss prevention systems include burglar alarms (95.7%), visible closed circuit televisions (87.1%) and digital video (84.9%). Retailers also conduct check screening (60.4%), use armored cars (69.8%), and operate point of sale data mining software (69.1%), and hidden closed circuit televisions (57.6%).

Retail theft not only affects the bottom line, when criminals steal from retailers, consumers pay higher prices, the safety of innocent employees can be compromised, and shoppers looking for popular merchandise often cannot find it. These trends suggest that retailers will continue to invest in new technologies to prevent and prosecute crimes.

Product categories identified in the survey that experienced the highest degrees of shrinkage include cards, gifts and novelties; specialty accessories; crafts and hobbies; and supermarket and grocery items.

Lessons From Losses – The Embezzlers

At the top of the criminal food chain resides the people who can potentially do you the most harm if you do not have systems in place to provide checks and balances. The typical embezzler is looking for you to provide them with opportunities like little supervision and minimal separation of duties within the business financial structure. This group of miscreants preys on the vulnerabilities of organizations big and small, charitable and commercial alike. It's about the money. It's about greed and it is a crime of the worst kind of abuse of trust.

As you will see, there are a number of conditions that must be present in the organization in order for their schemes to work. The first is the failure to separate the duties of accounts receivable and accounts payable. Another is to fail to conduct independent audits of the business records on a regular basis. Here are a few of my favorite examples.

In a rural, close-knit Oregon hamlet of 2,400, Pamela Kay was a familiar face to everyone in town.

She was known for her sharp financial sense on the city council, for her iron-fisted reign as bookkeeper at the Fire District, for showing off jewelry and for her grandiose displays of Christmas lights during the holidays at her home in one of the better parts of town.

But suspicions mounted down at the local bank when they saw her a bit too often. The tellers began asking themselves "How often is this lady paid anyway"?

Payday is in fact a twice-monthly occasion for salaried employees at the Rural Fire District but court documents released at the request of the media show Pamela Kay, who had been with the district for 24 years, ran on a different schedule, depositing eight paychecks to her Key Bank personal checking account in March alone.

As their suspicions grew, bank employees began keeping track of Pamela Kay's visits. According to records they submitted to investigators, Pamela Kay deposited 30 fire district paychecks into her personal account -- and cashed several more – over four and a half months, from December through May.

Pamela Kay deposited $52,892.68 in district payroll checks into her bank account, amassing nearly the entire amount of her $56,662 annual salary in less than half a year, court papers say. At the end of May, bank officials submitted their findings to the Oregon Government Waste Hotline, which forwarded the case to the County Sheriff's Office in June.

Pamela Kay not only cashed an undetermined number of payroll checks at her bank, but may have performed more transactions at a different bank, where she is believed to maintain other accounts, a County Sheriff's Office investigator wrote in his affidavit for a search warrant.

In July, County Sheriff's Office announced that Pamela Kay was the sole suspect in connection with several hundred thousand dollars that vanished over a period of several years. The Fire Chief estimated that $50,000 to $100,000 a year -- up to 4 percent of the district's budget -- went missing.

Court documents and interviews with the chief and others offer insight into how so much money could have disappeared without arousing suspicions of colleagues, the district board or even the district's accountants. The chief said Pamela Kay's books always appeared to be in perfect order, but he acknowledged that she had virtually exclusive and unsupervised access to district mail and finances and resisted even minimal oversight.

Payroll reports to the fire chief and district board always listed checks in numerical order, the chief said. "Every month was . . . just perfect," he said, but no one was watching to make sure the check numbers lined up from one report to the next. "The gap was between the months," The chief said.

Still perplexed, scratching his head and standing next to Pamela Kay's former desk, the chief pointed out a special machine the district uses to imprint dollar amounts and signatures on its checks. For security purposes, the machine requires two keys, and he said Pamela Kay kept them both. He said to investigators that once, when he suggested he should have the second one, Pamela Kay blew up and threatened to leave accusing him of not trusting her.

And with the benefit of 20-20 hindsight, everyone said there were many "Red Flags" that should have caused a quicker reaction.

When the district installed Quick Books accounting software earlier this year, she complained and refused to use it, the chief said. Also, Pamela Kay grew angry when the district employees asked her to supply line-item data from the budget.

She reportedly told him "We don't do that here, because if we did, you'd know how much money you had to spend, and you'd spend it all".

Pamela Kay often boasted to co-workers about an inheritance from a deceased relative; the chief said he heard it was a quarter-million dollars left behind by a rich uncle. They said that was how she explained some other conspicuous spending such as taking half a dozen coworkers out to lunch each week; offering financial support to family members, who sometimes visited her office asking for money; buying expensive jewelry; owning a vacation property, which she told The chief was north of Prineville in Crook County. Yes, there really is a Crook County in Oregon.

Did we mention the sheriff raided her home and found two stock certificates with 1,000 total shares of GE Corp. stock, a jeweler's receipt, more than $1,740 in cash from a black purse, and a small amount of marijuana with a pipe? Or that Pamela Kay also owned a motor home and a 19-foot ski boat?

As the investigation wound down and the amount of the loss began to sink in, her boss the fire chief, was heard to tell a local banker "Anything more from now on, don't cash."

As incredible as this lesson from losses may seem, it is anything but uncommon. Small government departments and especially non-profit organizations regularly report being victimized by employees generally due to the lack of decent accounting controls. The method of stealing this example highlights is very common because many organizations trust one individual to handle all of the financial affairs of the organization without any oversight what so ever.

Just think, all the chief had to do at a minimum, was to keep one of the check writer keys and follow the procedures in the simple Quick Books program.

As we told you, a number of organizational environmental factors are often blamed for the fact that so many non-profits, small governmental, religious and fraternal organizations also seem to be a favorite target of embezzlers. The cautionary tale that recently surfaced at a small Oregon school district highlights some typical issues. School districts as most of us know, are by nature locally controlled by a board that hires a superintendant to conduct the business administration of the district.

The superintendant is often free to hire employees with out a lot of input from anyone, which can invite cronyism and nepotism to influence placement of individuals who can then placed in a position of trust with little supervision.

When Connie Kennedy interviewed for the position of superintendent of the Nestucca Valley School District, board members assured her the district was in solid financial shape local press reports tell us. But less than two months later, as teachers and students were about to come back for another school year, Kennedy learned there was not enough money to make payroll.

The first hint of trouble came when the business manager informed Kennedy that they'd never completed the 2006-07 audit, which was due in December 2007. Then, she mentioned they were $400,000 short and would need to take out a loan to make payroll.

As it turns out, the school district wasn't so flush after all, but was in fact $1.47 **million** in the hole. The three-school district's budget was $7.5 million for 2008-09 and Kennedy was to determine that the books had not been balanced since a '05-06 audit so she didn't know how much money was in the bank.

Kennedy's new job was about to turn into a nightmare. She called the auditing firm and asked them where the past-due audit was. Kennedy was told that the auditors came out twice to do the '06-07 audit, and the books were in such disarray they were not able to complete it.   The audit firm had asked that the books be balanced before they were called again.

Kennedy had to hire a CPA to make sense of the records, costing another $10,000. She learned that auditors warned in the 2005-06 audit that there were problems with the bookkeeping, but a letter detailing the problems was missing. After obtaining a copy from the auditors, it was clear there were problems with not balancing the ledger and bank statement.

The overdue audit was finally presented to the school board which included in it 10 deficiencies, all categorized as "material weaknesses," considered the most serious.

One of those weaknesses noted the relationship between accounting employees. The business manager had apparently hired her daughter, who was in charge of accounts payables. Kennedy subsequently fired the two, along with the woman who managed accounts receivables.

Court records show all three have filed for bankruptcy in recent years and the Tillamook County Sheriff's Office has started an investigation to determine whether any crimes occurred.

It appears very likely that the trio saw opportunity when the old superintendant was replaced and no one noticed that there was a missing internal audit report – for a couple of years!

You would think that when people who are put in the position of trust in some organizations they would be smart enough to know instinctively that there are certain organizations that you probably should not steal from. Like a police organization? Right?

Well, meet Katherine Leese, the treasurer of FOP Lodge 53 and an officer with the Falls Township police, who allegedly stole more than $87,000, police said.

Leese told the judge, "It was a loan. I was paying it back."   As she exited a Bucks County court she tried to hide her face from the cameras.

Leese, 42, of Langhorne, PA was elected FOP treasurer in January 2006. According to the Bucks County District Attorney's Office, it was not long before she allegedly began dipping into the union funds. Her alleged thefts could be traced back 16 months; police said she transferred the money from the union account directly into her personal bank account. She had been an officer in Falls Township for nine years.

The County District Attorney said Leese allegedly has admitted to taking the money to make credit card and mortgage payments. Leese has been suspended from police duties pending the outcome of the trial needless to say.

But wait there's more, because hell hath no fury greater than a group of ripped off cops and the Bucks County Fraternal Order of Police has filed a civil suit against their former treasurer who embezzled the missing $87,000 from the fund set up to help families of injured and slain police offers. Yep, the Widows And Orphans Fund!

Court records indicate she repaid about $6,320.50 of the money before she was charged. The FOP lawsuit filed seeks the repayment of the remaining $81,212.50 Leese is charged with taking from the organization's Police and Fire Federal Credit Union account as well as costs, interest and attorneys fees. The suit requests a jury trial. The purpose is to identify and seize any assets that might be available to recover some of the loss and add civil repayment requirements to the potential criminal court order when Leese is sentenced. It's called hedging your bets!

I received the above information from the new FOP treasurer who immediately upon taking over, instituted a complete audit of all bank accounts and lodge assets so that moving forward, there would be no question about what was in the bank.

Small towns seem to attract these people like flies are attracted to honey. Consider the following example.

Deborah Perry loved to crochet, knit and cook, but those industrious fingers turned sticky according to the news reports alleging that she stole more than $270,000 from the Delaware County township where she worked. County detectives learned of her hobbies over the last eight months as they pored through years of purchases that Perry, the former treasurer for Thornbury Township, allegedly made with stolen municipal funds.

No, she wasn't spending the ill gotten gains on gambling or drugs, but rather on books about crafting, cooking and home décor- and what a collection it was! She filled her crafty library along with spending the money on purchases from gas stations, hardware stores and supermarkets, as investigators were to discover.

Perry, 51, had been dipping into the township cookie jar for several years and could have continued on for several more years except for one small thing. Her downfall started with some late-night calls to Township offices from her jilted boyfriend. At some time, he obviously became disenchanted with her and decided to drop a dime and get some revenge according to the Delaware County District Attorney.

The story was that after getting into an argument on the day after Christmas, Perry's ex-boyfriend, left messages at the township office saying that Perry had used township credit cards for personal items and that she'd given him two of those cards for his own use.

The ex-boyfriend according to court documents knowingly used around $40,000 of township funds and is not exempt from prosecution. The fact that he turned in Ms. Perry doesn't shift his own responsibility according to the D.A.

In fact the ex-boyfriend faces more than 70 charges, including theft, conspiracy and receiving stolen property. Investigators have not been able to locate him and a warrant has been issued for his arrest.

Perry, of course, faces similar charges – more than 350 of them. Her fraudulent activity from 2000 to 2007 totaled more than $232,000, in addition to the ex's $40,000, according to court documents.

After being arrested, Perry was remanded to the Delaware County prison, where she remains held on $250,000 bail, according to court officials.

Aside from fraudulent credit-card activity, forged checks and theft from petty cash, Perry, a 14-year township employee, allegedly created phony vendors to which she would write checks and then deposit the money in her own account.

According to township officials, township audits - which happen once a year - didn't catch the thefts because the auditors used a random sampling of transactions. The selected transactions most likely exceeded $500, and since Perry wrote checks and stole in smaller amounts, auditors never caught on, they said. I suspect that the statements from the officials were a little self-serving to cover their own lack of oversight of the city finances.

The theft should however prompt all organizations to re-examine their auditing practices to include smaller transaction amounts as well as verification of vendor information.

The township, which fired Perry, has since hired a certified public accountant from an independent firm to serve as treasurer. The outsourced CPA has instituted new procedures "which are probably advisable." Like we told you, separate receivables from payables.

According to the township officials, Perry always (get ready, here it comes) "appeared to be a trusted employee, and no one in the office had any idea what she was doing or why she did it." Although the township is bonded for up to a million dollars, officials plan to go after Perry for full restitution when the case goes to court.

She was eventually sentenced to 3 years in state prison and required to make restitution of $300,000.

I could go on and on telling you stories about embezzlers...

So let's re-address the key issue.

Why do employees steal? The experts agree that three factors must be present before an employee will steal from an employer:

- **Need or desire:**

A need to steal may be caused by such factors as medical expenses, divorce costs, gambling expenses, drugs, etc.

- **Rationalization:**

Most people need to rationalize or minimize dishonest acts. Rationalization is usually accompanied by such self-statements as, "I'm just borrowing." "Everyone else is doing it." "I deserve it because I work harder than..."

- **Opportunity:**

Opportunity means relatively uncontrolled access to an asset, such as the register operator has while the manager is in the office, merchandise has been left near the exit or in the case of an embezzler, and checks and balances do not exist.

Remove any of these three factors and an employee is less likely to steal. Can you affect your employees' needs to steal or their ability to rationalize? Probably not, but while you can't totally remove their opportunity to steal, you can control their opportunity to steal.

In almost all situations it simply makes more sense to control or deter employee theft than it is to investigate suspected theft. Most often you will have suspicions an employee may be stealing without having actually witnessed the act. Your suspicions may be founded, but suspicions are not proof.

You should never accuse an employee of theft unless you have actually witnessed the entire act. When you become suspicious of employee honesty because of red flags, comments from other employees or other reasons, but you have no proof, sometimes your best action is to bring the employees actions to the employee's attention, explain the problem, and state your expectations. Let them know, in essence that you know what they are doing and that you will be watching.

Some credible opinions and accepted theories regarding employee theft are:

- Opportunity, not the need, to steal is the primary cause of employee theft.

- A majority of employee theft goes undetected by management.

- Less than 10% of the employee population causes over 95% of the total losses from employee theft.

- Nearly every business experiences some degree of employee theft.

- Employee theft is often committed in reaction to favoritism, unreasonable discipline, inconsistency and other acts of poor or abusive supervision.

- A majority of honest employees look the other way regarding employee theft and fail to report it.

- Nearly 1/3 of all bankruptcies is caused by employee theft.

- Dishonest employees steal to the degree the system allows and don't stop until they are caught.

- A majority of the time, employees know or suspect employee theft is present, but will not report it because the "anti-snitch" attitude prevails over company loyalty.

- There is a direct correlation between drug abuse and employee theft.

- Based on a 5% net profit margin, it takes $20 in additional sales to offset every $1 lost to employee theft.

- The cost for a company to steal a trade secret from a competitor is a fraction of the cost to develop it in-house.

Let your employees know that you know how dishonest employees steal. This reduces employees' opportunity to be dishonest and increases their chances of getting caught if you are attentive to their actions. A very effective method is to conduct periodic surprise register bank downs to spot check cash accuracy versus sales data on the POS.

Employee theft is a serious infraction of policy and should be considered grounds for immediate termination. However, an employee should never be terminated immediately for theft unless the manager personally witnesses the employee steal, the employee admits to a theft or documented evidence is obtained proving the allegation.

Employee admissions should be obtained in writing, dated, and witnessed.

Employees who admit to theft should also be interviewed to determine the extent of their dishonesty or the involvement of other employees. Theft is also a violation of law in every state. Company general policy should be to criminally prosecute persons who commit crimes against the company. Prior to filing any criminal charge, you should consult with local legal counsel.

Lessons From Losses: Your Silent Partner!

Roy had a small problem. He liked to gamble. He liked it a lot. He especially loved to buy and scratch off those little lottery tickets from the neighborhood convenience store where you might win a million dollars or at least a $1,000 a week for life. Hey, it could happen!

Roy spent over $20,000 one summer on the tickets he told me and never won more than $500, which happened only once and $25 and $50 winning tickets a few times.

Yes, Roy had a real gambling problem. But the real problem was that Roy, who was a restaurant general manager, gambled with money he stole from his employer. Roy went through all of his own salary and to get more money that he needed, Roy made his store deposit a day late. The deposit, which was about $4,000, was used to buy more of those losing tickets.

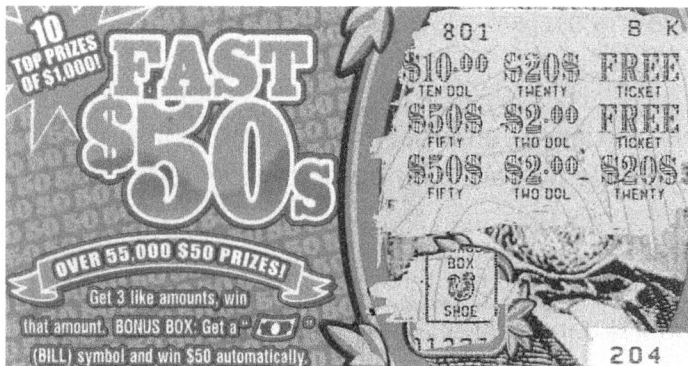

The way it works is that you give the guy at 7-11 a dollar, you scratch to reveal the numbers and... you lose a dollar!

Once he lost the $4,000 he knew that he needed to get the deposit money into the company bank account soon or he would be caught and fired. So, to buy time, Roy used the current days deposit funds to make up for yesterdays now stolen deposit. As long as his supervisor didn't check the deposit dates on the bank receipts against the records of the dates that the money was supposed to be at the bank, he had time to win back his losses. By buying more lottery tickets!

Needing another infusion of cash, Roy stole another deposit for a little over $5,000 this time using current funds to make up for the shortage. Now he needed to make up the loss of two deposits that were now showing up at the bank late. This process kept going until the company accountants finally noticed the pattern of late deposits and tossed down a red flag on the play.

Once the situation was investigated, it was determined that several stolen deposits, totaling over $20,000, were being juggled by Roy. When the scheme crashed, it was pretty obvious who was responsible and Roy shared the whole sad story with me.

The police took the confessed thief into custody and Roy had to do some jail time and later made some restitution when he got back on to his feet after getting a job elsewhere. Roy's boss was also fired for failing to monitor the store deposits thereby allowing the theft to go on for several months before discovery.

The real lesson from this loss is to "Trust but verify" as former President Ronald Reagan used to say. You must set up systems of checks and balances to insure that whoever is making your deposits is not the same person that verifies the bank records so that "late" deposits are addressed immediately. The problem of your company not receiving on time credit for deposit funds can, in fact, also be a problem at your bank, with an armored car company or with your managers.

Wikipedia articles on compulsive gamblers shares with us that there is an irrefutable correlation between pathological gambling and criminal behavior. A study by the U.S. Department of Justice demonstrated that 30% of pathological gamblers arrested in Las Vegas had committed a robbery within the past year; 13% had assaulted another individual.

The motive was simply to obtain money to pay for gambling, or gambling debts. Studies by Gamblers Anonymous members are even more troubling. 67% admitted to committing crimes or civil fraud to finance their gambling or to pay gambling-related debts. 47% admitted to having engaged in some form of insurance fraud, embezzlement or arson. Not surprisingly, pathological gamblers are much more likely to have sold drugs than other arrestees.

Compulsive gamblers fall in love with the excitement and action of gambling. Four phases of compulsive gambling have been identified; winning, losing, desperation, and hopelessness. At first, during the winning phase, the gambler is often successful. This success leads to fantasies of further successes; and resultant wealth, power, and prestige. They are certain they know how to beat the system. Their self-esteem becomes centered on being smarter or luckier than the average gambler.

Inevitably the compulsive gambler suffers financial losses which eventually lead to a damaged ego. In an effort to maintain their self-esteem they begin to rationalize losses and may blame others. During the losing phase the pathological gambler becomes more preoccupied with gambling. He begins to gamble alone, borrow money, skip work, lie to family and friends, and default on debts. This is the point in which pathological gamblers begin to "chase" their losses; gambling in order to win back money that was lost, "I'll get even tomorrow." This chasing behavior is a defining characteristic of the pathological gambler. Thus, a vicious cycle has begun; chasing leads to more gambling and additional financial losses. The gambler attempts to determine his handicapping abilities to assure that losses will be minimized. If the gambler has run out of money for "the chase", he now begins to tap into savings or to borrow money.

The more money that is spent or borrowed is again reflected in a belief that the only way to recoup or pay off debts is to gamble even more. Loans are due, bookies are seeking payment, and the entire situation begins spiraling out of control. Those who have jobs may embezzle from their employer. Others may make fraudulent loan applications or insurance claims. Many will resort to theft for the money. Initially, the pathological gambler rationalizes these crimes. He will repay it all... it is just a loan... he really isn't a criminal. A cycle of tapping all resources, pawning items, taking out loans, embezzlement, theft, lies, rinse, and repeat ensues.

During the desperation phase pathological gamblers lose all control over their gambling. Desperate gamblers see heightened gambling activity as the only chance for survival. Although desperate gamblers feel ashamed and guilty after gambling, fundamentally they cannot stop. They frequently resort to illegal activities to finance their addiction. At this point, the consequences of compulsive gambling invariably catch up with them; they get fired, divorced, forced into bankruptcy, or arrested.

INVESTIGATIVE GUIDELINES

Situations may develop in a company that require some investigative action. The situation may be specific in nature, such as a large cash shortage or it may be more general in nature such as a sudden increase in shrinkage or inventory variance. This section is not intended to teach managers how to become a professional investigator, but to provide general guidelines that can be used to help you solve problems.

The objectives of an investigation are to determine what happened, why it happened, when and where it happened, who did it, and to resolve the situation in a manner most advantageous to the company.

To learn from the incident and adopt measures to minimize recurrence of the situation. Report known losses or thefts to your senior manager, the police, and file a claim with your insurance carrier if appropriate.

Once a situation has been reported to the police, cooperate and provide assistance as requested. In most instances the police need your knowledge of facts and experience to successfully investigate and resolve the situation.

Many situations will require you to gather information, identify possible suspects, gather evidence, or interview employees. You can use the following steps as a guide to assist you in resolving investigative situations:

Note: This is not an interrogation! Interview your people to get the facts about what happened.

For example, a "missing deposit" should not be assumed to be stolen until you talk to the responsible manager and verify that the deposit is definitely not where it is supposed to be which is in the safe, in the managers possession, on the way to the bank or in the bank credited to your account.

• 	Identify the problem. A deposit is missing and there is not deposit ticket stamped by the bank.

• 	Identify who was supposed to take the money to the bank.

• 	Gather all relevant paperwork.

• 	Interview employees. You need to know what they know.

• 	Obtain written statements from all of the people that had access.

• 	When interviewing employees, start at the center and work your way out. That is with the responsible manager in this case and progress to others that may have observed what happened.

- Don't make promises that you can't keep. For instance if you promise an employee that their answers to your questions will be kept confidential you   need to tell them that the police may need to be informed of their information if it affects the police investigation.

- You may wish to let employees know that what they tell you will not be shared with other employees, then honor that promise. Employees will be reluctant to share information or suspicions if they don't believe you, or if you have violated the trust of others.

By the way, your policies should clearly state your expectation that all employees are required to assist with both your company internal as well as any police investigation as a condition of their continued employment. Refusal to cooperate with an investigation should not be an option.

When the police become involved, update them on the information you have learned. If the police are not involved, have you developed information enough to determine a crime was committed? If so, make a report to the police and request they investigate.

We have experienced many instances with our client companies where the police investigation was simply not going anywhere. Here is yet another example why the business owner needs to have a good rapport established with the local police precinct commander.

By offering to assist the police with the development of the case through the cooperation of your company and people, you are much more likely to move your case to the "front burner" and to a quicker conclusion.

Conclude The Investigation:

When you reach the point where no further information appears to be available you should the end the investigation. You may find that you have not learned enough to answer the old "who, what, when, where, why and how". You may be unable to prove any particular employees involvement. If this happens, do not overspend time trying to resolve a situation that is not provable. Recognize what caused the problem or situation and fix the problem using measures to deter the situation from happening again.

If you have lost a significant amount of money and you have adopted our recommended policies and procedures, you will at a minimum, be able to hold the appropriate people responsible for the loss occurring. The reason will be that some act of commission or omission occurred and a policy was violated that was the proximate cause of the loss. You can then take action based on your progressive disciplinary policy. Unfortunately, sometimes the real thief gets away, because they took advantage of the responsible persons pattern of policy violations. Yes, losses can occur with a one-time mistake, but we find that it is usually due to a pattern of violations of your cash procedures that gets noticed by a dishonest person and taken advantage of.

If your investigation leads to a confession or strong evidence against an employee for misconduct or procedure violations, bring your findings to your senior manager's attention so proper action can be planned and executed.

POLYGRAPH

The employee polygraph protection act of December 1988 severely restricted a private employers use of polygraph examinations.   Your company should not request or require an employee to take a polygraph examination. This law does not prohibit a law enforcement agency from requesting that one of your employees take a polygraph examination as part of a law enforcement investigation. Questions about polygraph should be directed to your local legal counsel.

In our experience, we have come to the conclusion that since they are not legally acceptable in court to prove or disprove guilt they are only useful to law enforcement as a tool to assist other criminal interrogation techniques. We recommend that you not mention polygraph to your employees as an option that might be used by your company to resolve an issue of who may or may not be responsible for missing funds.

Employee Search Guidelines

This topic is among the most sensitive issues you will encounter when dealing with employee dishonesty. You can get into a lot of trouble if your policy is not very specific about what your managers can and cannot do when investigating a loss.

There are occasions when managers may become aware of missing or stolen cash, property or other assets that belong to the company, its customers or its employees. Depending on the situation, it may be warranted to consider a search of the company and/or employees in an effort to locate, recover and protect the missing property or assets. The guidelines in this section are provided to assure that searches conducted by management employees are reasonable, lawful and nondiscriminatory.

Company Property:

Management has the right and authority to inspect, examine or search any and all property owned by the company. Search away and don't forget the dumpster!

Employees:

Management has the right and authority to request an employee's consent to a visual inspection of the employee's property whenever the manager has reasonable grounds to believe: - A theft has occurred. OR An employee may be in possession of contraband (drugs, weapons, etc.).

Searches of employees must be visual, not physical. Employees may be asked to open or empty pockets, knapsacks, etc., if a normal visual inspection is not adequate.

Don't even take a peek, unless you have another employee witness the search. Ideally, the witness should be the same gender as the employee being searched. Some employees may be embarrassed to have a person of the opposite sex see their personal possessions. The witness can help overcome this problem.

Employee searches should be limited to articles of possession that could reasonably conceal or contain the missing or stolen property. For example, if you were missing a case of beer from Pete's Food and Beer, it would be reasonable to request employee consent to a search of his/her car for the missing case. It would not be reasonable to search the car's glove compartment because it could not possibly contain a case of beer. It would be unreasonable to ask a female employee to open her purse for inspection if the purse was too small to contain the missing case.

IMPORTANT!

- ***Under no circumstances will an employee be asked to remove any article of clothing that covers their torso except an outer coat, shoes or hat.***

Let's be very specific and clear about this provision of your policy. If you think a physical search of an employee is necessary because you have good cause to believe that any employee is concealing missing or stolen property on their person, call the police immediately. It would NOT be reasonable or permissible to ask an employee to remove or open a shirt, blouse, slacks, etc. We have some real horror stories we could share with you about companies who did not heed this recommendation!

The vast majority of your employees are honest people and are not going to be involved in any misconduct. In fact, earlier in our book we have told you about the 80-10-10 Rule that relates to employee honesty. You now know that 10% will never steal, 80% are unlikely steal because of the systems policies and procedures you have put in place and the other 10% are fairly certain they will be caught and are therefore looking for work elsewhere if they are still employed by you for the moment.

It is very uncomfortable for most of us to have to conduct investigations related to employee honesty and we should be reminded to show our appreciation to them for their assistance in resolving the problem.

Should a search disclose the missing property or asset in the possession of an employee, managers should follow these steps:

- Confiscate the property if you are positive of its identity and ownership.

- Contact your Senior Manager.

- Call the police and report the crime.

Should one of your employees refuse to cooperate with a reasonable request to search, do not take any action without the approval of your senior manager. Your policy should not authorize that any of your managers may file charges against anyone on behalf of your company without the approval of senior management. The police have the right to file charges themselves based on the facts of the case. Employees caught stealing are subject to and must be terminated.

Since substance abuse is often the key motivator of employee dishonesty, we have added some comments and recommendations related to the topic in this chapter.

ALCOHOL & DRUG ABUSE

Your company should regard any misuse of alcohol or drugs by employees to be an undesirable practice, which results in poor health and unacceptable work performance. We have placed this subject in position in the book because substance abuse is a major motivation to steal from you.

Employees using any drug or alcohol in an improper manner creates an increased risk to the safety of themselves, their fellow employees and your customers. Managers should be aware that the use of drugs and alcohol in the work place is increasing, and such activity can lead to unacceptable performance, absences, accidents, injuries, reduced employee morale and drains on the profitability of the business.

RECOGNIZING THE SIGNS

Changes in attitude or attendance:

Change in normal capabilities: work habits, efficiencies, carelessness, etc. Poor physical appearance, including personal hygiene and inattention to dress. Change in work routine: frequent trips to the restroom, unexplained absence from work area, avoiding the manager, frequent non work-related visits by strangers or employees from another business. Association with known drug users.

Physical changes:

Blood-shot eyes, runny nose or irritation in eyes or nose, unsteady walk, trembling of hands or mouth, dilated pupils (enlarged dark center of eye), slurred speech, odor on or about their person.

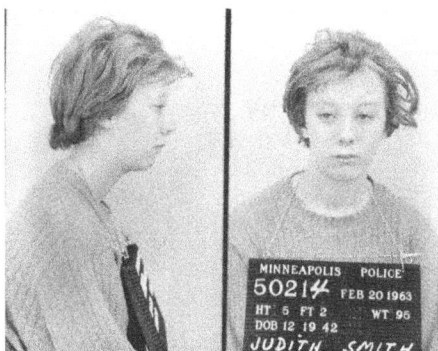

MINNEAPOLIS POLICE
50214 FEB 20 1963
HT 5 FT 2   WT 96
DOB 12 19 42
JUDITH SMITH

MANAGER'S ACTIONS

Should management suspect an employee of drug or alcohol abuse due to poor job performance, follow these action guidelines: Discuss the job performance or behavior problems with the employee to determine what the problem might be. Do not suggest suspicion of drug or alcohol abuse. There may be another reason for the employee's performance or behavior. If the employee's performance or behavior is obviously creating a safety risk, the employee should be sent home immediately.

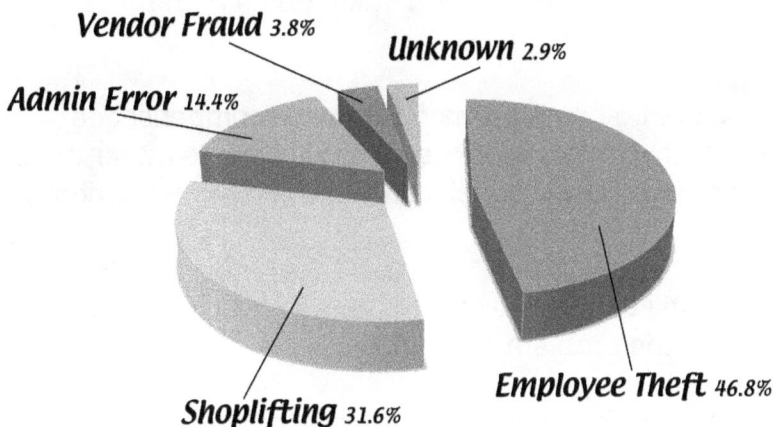

Vendor Fraud 3.8%

Unknown 2.9%

Admin Error 14.4%

Shoplifting 31.6%

Employee Theft 46.8%

This is where you are losing your profits!

IT IS BEST TO MANAGE THE BEHAVIOR.

Make notes on your observations and your conversation with the employee. Retain the notes in the employee's personnel file or other place of safekeeping and privacy. Contact the senior manager. If your company has instituted a drug-testing program, the employee should be referred to the designated program director for further action. If the situation requires follow-up, a suggestion to the employee to visit a physician may be warranted. Should an employee refuse to cooperate, the employee should be advised that his/her actions might be grounds for termination. Use common sense and discretion; these guidelines may not address all situations.

Workers Compensation Fraud Issues

Workers' compensation fraud costs Americans more than $5 billion annually, threatens the jobs of Americans, and hurts employers so much that in some cases, companies go out of business or are forced to move. It adds 10 cents to every dollar of your insurance premiums. It's pervasive, growing, and often very hard to detect.

The topic of Workers Compensation cost increases in the past several years hits an immediate hot button with most business owners and operators that we know. So if you are already hot about the topic of uncontrolled cost spirals of upwards of 20% a year, imagine how you are going to react to the effects of fraudulent claims on your bottom line!

The rising premium rates for workers' compensation insurance have increasingly pressured both insurers and employers. Despite workers' compensation reform legislation that has been enacted recently in states such as California, across the nation medical costs continue to grow significantly despite a decline in the number of claims filed. In a study by the National Council on Compensation Insurance (NCCI), "The medical share of total benefit costs in workers' compensation rose to approximately 55 percent on a countrywide basis, with some individual state shares approaching 70 percent".

There is a great deal of frustration voiced by business owners who are generally very action oriented individuals when it comes to controlling costs but because they lack a plan directing what steps can be taken to reign in the costs, just sit and steam as they write the WC insurance coverage check.

In Chapter Thirteen of this book, we go to great lengths to describe and recommend what prevention programs you need to have in place to reduce exposure to employee injuries. So there is plenty that can be done to reduce negative trends affecting injury claims costs and the price of your insurance coverage. He we need to take a look at the crime of fraud as it impacts your operation.

Because a significant percentage of claims start off as legitimate, workers' compensation fraud and abuse is hard to spot. Much of what you may be experiencing is abuse rather than fraud. An example of abuse would be such as a case in which an employee is malingering, delaying their return to work.

Our plan deals with abuse somewhat differently than it does for fraud, so we need to define our terms as we move into the realm of fixing the problem.

In criminal law, fraud is the crime or offense of deliberately deceiving another in order to damage them – usually, to obtain property or services unjustly. Fraud can be accomplished through the aid of forged objects. In the criminal law of common law jurisdictions it may be called "theft by deception," "larceny by trick," "larceny by fraud and deception" or something similar.

Fraud can be committed through many methods and is a threat to your business from both employees and outsiders, including mail, wire, phone and the internet which may constitute criminal fraud include:

- Bait and switch
- Confidence tricks
- False Advertising
- Identity theft
- False billing schemes
- Forgery of documents or signatures
- Taking money, which is under your control, but not yours embezzlement
- Health fraud, selling of products of spurious use, such as "quack" medicines
- Creation of false companies
- False Insurance claims
- Bankruptcy fraud is a US federal crime that can lead to criminal prosecution under the charge of theft of the goods or services.
- And many others

Outright fraud is less frequent and much harder to catch but often costs business owners dearly. The longer it takes to discover a fraudulent claim, the more money is paid out. That's why early detection of fraudulent and abusive claims is critical to containing the cost of Workers' Compensation. And the more insurers can decrease their losses, the more likely it is that their insurance rates will be lower as well.

Workers Compensation fraud comes in many guises. Some workers fake injuries at the workplace to get paid for staying home. In some cases that we were involved with, it was common to find an injury had been reported by an employee who was about to be terminated for poor performance issues. Other cases that were common involved a slip and fall reported by a female employee in the early weeks of pregnancy. Few doctors will send this person back to work anytime soon if the patient claims a history of difficult pregnancies and the danger of an early return risking the mothers or the baby's health.

Of course, few of these claimed events were ever witnessed by anyone.

Some exaggerate the extent of injury just to prolong time away from work, while others claim their injuries occurred at work, when, in fact, they happened off premises and are unrelated to work. In extreme cases, fraud is the result of organized crime, or collusion with unscrupulous doctors, therapists, and attorneys. There were reports of a ring of so called medical providers in California a few years ago that specialized in creating mental stress claims that were difficult to disprove given the medical diagnosis by apparently legitimate doctors who also blocked attempts to have the claimant submit to an Independent Medical Evaluation (IME).

How prepared are insurance payers to detect fraud and abuse? A surprising number of claim departments still rely on manual detection processes, which simply are not sophisticated enough to identify the many patterns and types of claimant fraud. Adding to that is the volume of cases on any adjuster's desk. With an industry average of 250 claims at any time, adjusters are often too overwhelmed to perform the detailed analysis needed to find complex patterns that indicate fraud on top of their growing caseload.

For many years, we periodically conducted file audits of our insurance carriers. The purpose of the audits was to verify that the claims were being handled according to the provisions of the service contract that our company negotiated. It was a very useful process that improved communications with the carrier and allowed us to see how diligently the claims adjusters were performing their jobs. The detection of fraud efforts was totally manual resulting in missed detection no doubt.

According to the Coalition Against Insurance Fraud, we have read that 20 percent of total fraud at most is detected, and much of this fraud is detected late in the life of the claim. This late discovery dramatically increases the total cost on payers. In addition, a high percentage of claims that are referred to Special Investigative Units (SIUs) often are not fraudulent leads. The time and cost to investigators to pursue suspicious claims that don't turn out to be fraudulent or abusive contribute to the high cost of workers' compensation.

In fact, many companies we found do not employ professional SIU personnel who generally have law enforcement investigation backgrounds. Instead, they rely on the services of contract private investigators to conduct activity surveillance. It was very common to find the work product of these guys in the form of a VCR tape stuffed into the file folder.

Another study noted that nationwide, fraud bureau budgets and head-counts have declined significantly in the past three years, while fraud referrals to SIUs are growing. With a growing volume of fraud referrals per investigator, properly identifying the patterns typical of truly fraudulent or abusive cases has become a huge challenge. So your insurance company agrees that the need is clearly identified but not surprisingly doesn't want to pay for the service. That means in the long run you pay more for undetected fraud.

That's why some insurance companies have adopted sophisticated analytic software called predictive models. Adjusters can spend significantly less time reviewing and processing claims, while spotting truly suspicious claims faster with greater accuracy. The advanced software technology known as neural networks predictive models can enable carriers to identify fraudulent, abusive and high-risk claims much earlier and with a higher degree of accuracy than any other known method. It can do this while swiftly and accurately processing the majority of claims without adjuster intervention. We think that this innovative wave of the future approach is something you need to check on to see if your carrier is doing it on your behalf.

The same predictive models are largely responsible for the dramatic turnabout in fraud detection in the credit card industry. Today, predictive models are used to screen 85 percent of U.S. credit card transactions for fraud, resulting in a 50 percent reduction in industry losses. This same technology, used so successfully by 65 percent of the world's credit card issuers, is now increasingly being deployed to contain the spiraling costs of Workers' Compensation.

In a few seconds, predictive models can scan thousands of data elements simultaneously to find subtle, complex, and hidden patterns of suspicious behavior. While human experts are capable of identifying some red flags and simple fraud patterns, these sophisticated modeling techniques are required to find more complex patterns of fraud. The computer model was developed based on historical examples already determined to be fraud and abuse claims, neural network predictive models can learn which subtle patterns are associated with a high likelihood of fraud and which are not.

As claims mature they leave a trail of data. During our file audits, all of the files contained activity data such as the first report of injury form, payment transactions that indicate workers' compensation payments, medical services bills and diagnostic reports, vocational rehabilitation, and other important claim events such as return to work and closure evaluations.

These patterns of activity provide the raw material that is used by the predictive model to score each claim from 1-1,000. Normal claims will typically have scores of 300 or less. But a high score is a signal that the claim is out of profile when compared to its peers. Each time the predictive model scores a claim, reasons are produced to explain the model score. This can provide useful information to assist in the analysis of a claim being suspected of being fraudulent, abusive, or exceptional by looking at the reason codes returned with the score.

We found that the typical Workers Compensation file was a pretty sparse document with the basic facts covered. Even if the injury was lost time compensable, it told a pretty clear story like "injury occurred, treatment was rendered, maximum medical benefit was achieved and the person went back to work".

The questionable claims we found were inches thick often with multiple lengthy diagnostic information sections and miles of claims notes by the adjuster attesting to and memorializing the numerous phone calls and follow up with claimant and various providers.

Many of these fraudulent or abusive claims don't look all that remarkable at first, even to the eye of a well-trained adjuster. Clues may be subtle and submerged in an ocean of data. In the case of fraud, opportunists who initially file legitimate claims may eventually fall prey to the temptation to exaggerate or misrepresent their cases. In fact, the majority of insurance fraud starts out this way.

Predictive models are accurate because the technology recognizes patterns from the data itself, not from preexisting assumptions on what the data means. As a result, the system provides high-quality referrals to investigative units, further reducing losses. In addition, neural networks also are the only systems investigative units take on referral, further reducing losses. In addition, neural networks also are the only systems sophisticated enough to detect fraud types that have not been seen before. Claims are scored frequently to detect any change in the status of the claimant.

Not surprisingly, only a small percentage of claims account for the majority of claims costs. These more costly cases include fraudulent, abusive, as well as legitimate claims that for various reasons require special handling. These exceptional situations could include a claimant who is not acting fraudulently or showing abusive behavior, but instead is someone in need of aggressive case management. It was not uncommon in our claim file audits to find cases of injured employees who had simple fallen through the cracks. They were getting checks, but they were not getting better because of the need to get more aggressive injury management.

Predictive models don't replace the skills and experience of an adjuster. Instead, the power of predictive analytics augments the work of adjusters to work more efficiently and effectively. In a fraction of a second, predictive models can consider thousands of variables simultaneously, looking at complex relationships between data and deciphering subtle clues that might be missed by even the most seasoned adjuster.

The process of predictive analytics, we are told is used continuously and automatically throughout the life of the claim. Predictive models can recognize patterns from the data itself, not assumptions about it, so when the data indicates something new, the software updates its detection criteria.

Early detection is just one of the total benefits. Armed with evidence of fraudulent or abusive activity, claim adjusters can be proactive in managing claims more effectively. Often, fraud or abuse can be stopped quickly by a call or letter to the claimant, helping them understand that their activity is being monitored. Once contacted politely, malingering injured workers often stage miraculous recoveries from their injuries. This preemptive effect also prevents claim costs from growing.

We have read that insurers using predictive analytics software technology to detect fraudulent and abusive claims have experienced a return on investment of 20-to-1, or up to $300 per claim in savings. In comparison tests, 55 percent of claims were identified by models weeks or months before they were discovered manually, and the software often discovered suspicious claims or claims needing case management that would have been missed by insurance claims analysts.

All companies frustrated with how their Workers Compensation claims are being managed should take an active partnership role with their carriers. Just having the ability to effectively communicate with the insurance adjusters about what you know about a claim that you think might be fraud or abuse will help the process.

As we discussed, many insurance carriers in our experience are simply not all that sophisticated in identification of fraud. As a business owner, you have a vested interest in not becoming a crime victim of any type, be it fraud, theft or embezzlement. It really does pay to get to know these people!

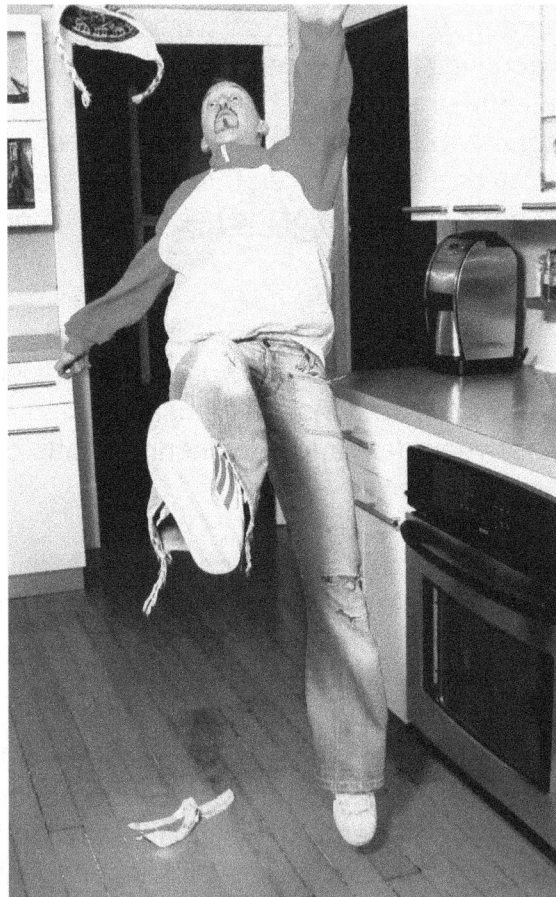

Unusual claims are not necessarily fraud but you have to investigate!

"The louder he talked of his honor, the faster we counted the spoons."

Ralph Waldo Emerson

DATE OF ARREST   3-5-54
CRIME   Burglary 3rd & 1 PC
DISP. MSP Indet. 0-10 Prob 5 yrs.
JUDGE Carroll   DATE 4/15/54.
AGE 35(4-27-18   HT6-1 5/8WT.148
HAIR   ch
EYES   blue   COMP. med
BUILD   sldr   M. OR S. M
TEETH Upr plate;lwr 1&r 2 bic,mos ou
OCCUP.   moulder
MARKS—SCARS
III. Nose tilt to left; sm pig mv
      abv lt gl mouth.

CASE HISTORY By Ball- with Wm Clerk burglarized gas station at 48th & Lyndale N.

NATIVITY:Milwaukee,Wis   F. P. CLASS   5 0 29 W MII 19
RESIDENCE   615 E. 16 St.   I 18 T   OI 19
NAME   NO.
NAUS, RICHARD   CC#50-B   4/27/18   43413

**The good news is that most
of these guys are not too bright!**

Anyone can be a victim of crime!

External threats to your business can take a variety of forms that include direct and violent attack against your people, business assets and your reputation. Failing to take reasonable action to deter criminal activity on your business property can result in all kinds of ugly consequences including death, injury and expensive litigation that are often accompanied by extensive negative media coverage. The basis of much of this litigation revolves around not what you did but rather what you did not do

The failure to provide reasonable care as a basis for negligence litigation or as it is often called premises liability, can depend largely on how a jury perceives what the level of care should be based on expert witness testimony and what other similar business enterprises like your commonly do to prevent such criminal acts from occurring on their premises.

Your company policies should address your plan to use barriers and policies and procedures designed to reduce your exposure to criminal activity.

ROBBERY PREVENTION

Robbery Defined:

The taking or attempting to take anything of value from the care, custody, or control of a person by force or threat of force or violence and / or putting the victim in fear.

Who Are These People?

There are many things, which can be done to deter armed robbery. Having established routines, which show a potential robber that you and your employees are alert, is the best prevention available. There are some robbers who will rob you regardless of your routines. If your losses are small, robbers will be encouraged to go somewhere else. Conversely, if your losses are large, robbers may be encouraged to return to your business. A number of studies have been conducted by researchers who have interviewed convicted armed robbers in order to formulate defensive tactics to reduce or prevent the crime.

The results of the surveys are startling in many ways.

There is very strong statistical evidence that the majority of robberies are committed by criminals with inside information about your business.

Believe the fact that the person who robs your business is very likely a current or ex-employee or has been given information about your operations by one.

- *83% did not think that they would be caught*
- *80% did not know what their sentence would be*
- *55% said it was longer than expected!*

This means that your best practice cash control procedures will be known to the criminals who desire to know such things and you have the opportunity of deflecting the crime to some other companies more vulnerable business. Good procedures harden your business against crime losses.

Education
- **Elementary only**   9%
- **Some High School** 39
- **High school grad**   31
- **College and above** 21

and individuals on the street.

The studies reveal that robbers are not necessarily uneducated. Over half of the surveyed robbers had at least a high school education but declared ignorance about being caught and how long they would be incarcerated.

Note as well, that the robbers generally hit businesses that were less than 2 miles from home almost 60% of the time. And they got caught when they robbed convenience stores

We recommend that you take a look at how you operate your business in terms of good loss prevention habits and what may be a risky behavior pattern.

Like all of your other activities, robbery prevention can be broken down according to day parts. These routines include the use of good judgment and can be made a part of your daily activities.

Before You Enter

The first person to unlock and enter the business in the morning must be a Manager or Shift Supervisor. Hourly employees must not be permitted to unlock the store and enter before a Manager or Shift Supervisor arrives. There are pre-opening robbery prevention routines, which need to be followed: Schedule at least one person to open and enter the business with the manager. Look for suspicious persons or cars. Before leaving your car, circle the building and look for signs of tampering at doors or windows and for other signs of forced entry. If you see any of the above, do not leave your car or enter the building. Immediately go to the nearest off-premise telephone and call the police.

Once you have determined it is safe and you have entered, keep all doors and windows locked. Doors can be unlocked for employees as they arrive. If you see signs of forced entry, leave at once, call the police and your Manager.

Before You Open For Business

Current Conviction for Robbing This Location:

	Location	%
1.	Convenience Store	24
2.	Street Robbery	22
3.	Home	7
4.	Car Jacking	6
5.	Gas Station	6
6.	Fast Food	6
7.	Donut Shop	5
8.	Bank Teller	3
9.	Liquor Store	2
10.	Bar	2

If it is necessary to open the rear door, you, as a manager should do it. You can then be assured it is necessary, and that it is being done as safely as possible. Management must not allow any exterior door to be opened while cash is being counted and verified in the morning.

Do not permit anyone other than on-duty personnel in the business. Minimize outside activity. Do no allow employees to enter/exit through the back door.

While You Are Open

Once the business is open there are numerous good habits that deter robberies: Place cash pulls in to the time lock compartment of your electronic lock safe after your last trip to the bank to minimize cash available. All $20 bills should be placed in the drop box located at each register immediately after accepting them.

There should be no more than four $10 bills in the cash register at any given time. Drop excess $5's and $1's in the drop box as they accumulate. Cash pulls are made from the drop boxes hourly and placed immediately into the safe. The idea is to maintain the original amount of currency in the drawer at all times if possible

55% said that they were high on drugs at the time of the robbery for which they were serving time.

19% lived less than a mile away From where the robbery occurred

40% lived less than 2 miles away

71% considered themselves amateurs.

Make bank deposits as required. We recommend tamper-evident plastic deposit bag in a briefcase, a paper bag, or disguise it in some other way. These bags should be purchased pre-numbered so that the deposit bag number can be written on the deposit ticket.

Stagger the times you make bank runs. Vary the route you take to the bank. You and your employees should stay on the alert for people loitering in the business, on the lot, and at the bank. Yes at the bank! Just because your business is in a safe neighborhood with no history of robberies, don't be surprised if you find out that the bank is located in a not-so-safe neighborhood with a serious history of robberies. Bank parking lots can be a favorite hangout for crooks that are looking for a quick score by robbing an unsuspecting manager going to the bank.

Among The Top 10 favorite places to rob according to the inmates:

		%
1.	Street Robbery	46
2.	Convenience Store	41
3.	Gas Station	27
4.	Fast Food	22
5.	Home	21

We recommend that if you are sending managers to the bank with deposits, they use the night depository exclusively. The bank will not likely be giving you credit for the deposits that you make the same day that you make them.

The reason is that they don't have to and will give you credit when the "fine count" is completed. Any checks you have deposited will be subject to clearing before you receive credit.

Lessons From Losses – Robbed On The Way To The Bank

This lesson tells a story that is just plain wrong on several levels.

The story begins with Blake age 18 and Bethany age 17 who worked at a Georgia pizza restaurant. The employees told police they were robbed of two night bank deposits at knife point by two men on the way to the bank after the restaurant closed about 2:00 AM early one Thursday morning. It was the practice of the restaurant to take the closing cash and checks to the night depository every night and on this occasion the deposit contained about $350 in cash and $900 in checks.

By 4:30 AM, police figured out the story was false and had obtained confessions from the pair that they had lied.   According to a sworn police statement, Blake told police he set up the "robbery" after receiving a call from a friend suggesting the idea.

Blake said he arranged to meet his friend the morning of April 26 and that the friend and another man took the employees' night deposit bags as well as two speakers from Blake's trunk. The money was to be divided later among the group. A few minutes after the men left on foot, Blake called the police, who became suspicious when Blake and Bethany's accounts of the robbery differed.

Blake later confessed but told police that while Bethany was aware of the robbery plan she did not want to be involved. Bethany told police she lied because she didn't want Blake to get in trouble and she was afraid of losing her job.

On Tuesday, police arrested the good friends Terryance and DeMario, who were charged as the two other people involved in the theft. Terryance is also alleged to have threatened one of the pizza restaurant employees with physical harm if he was connected to the theft. He is in custody at the Macon County Jail under $50,000 bond. DeMario, who is on parole for previous theft and burglary convictions, was remanded to the Macon County Jail under $20,000 bond.

Blake and Bethany were deemed eligible for pretrial release and face an additional disorderly conduct charge for filing the false police report. They were scheduled to be arraigned in county court a few days later.

Let's begin by making a few comments about directing hourly employees to go to the bank at 2:00 AM. There simply is no justification for send employees to the bank at close as it is just too dangerous. In this case, the lack of judgment on the owners part created an opportunity for all kinds of bad things to happen.

These two young employees could have been, in the event of a real robbery, the victims of a violent crime that could have resulted in their injury or death. At a minimum, some mental trauma is bound to result.

Instead, because of bad banking procedures, they were presented with what they believed was an outstanding opportunity to steal the owners money. As is true about the adage that too many cooks in the kitchen spoil the stew, it is doubly true when too many crooks steal the cash and in this case the actual amount was embarrassingly small.

Cash in a commercial venture such as a restaurant, should be kept overnight in a safe adequately rated to protect the contents. Deposits should be prepared by management and transported to the bank at least daily for low volume establishments and twice for higher volumes during daylight hours or once daily if armored car transport is used.

We should also mention that in the case of the 17 year old participant, labor laws in many states prohibit minors from working past midnight on school nights. Just what you need, another labor law violation fine!

Be aware that we have experienced many false robbery claims by employees who claim to have been robbed to cover up an actual theft.

Back to prevention:

During slow periods, keep your employees busy and spread out performing cleanup and other tasks. Potential robbers may become discouraged and leave because they don't feel they can get control of everyone. It is for that same reason that busy stores are not a good target for lone robbers. Surprise and control are needed for a successful robbery and if one of your employees is able to get out and call the police, it can ruin his whole day!

Pay attention to your customers. Good customer eye contact and rapport is very discouraging to a potential robber. By directing your attention on the customer, you will not only provide customer satisfaction, you will also discourage robbers by giving them the attention they do not want.

Obstructing the view inside is not good!

Unless deliveries are scheduled, never open the back door after dark. Unnecessary outside activity such as parking lot clean up or trash runs should be discouraged after dark. After dark trash runs should not be made using the back door.

Prior to dark, you and your employees should move your cars to a well-lit area near the door you use to exit. Immediately before locking all doors check to assure no one is hiding inside the business.

Keep all doors and windows locked. Do not let unauthorized persons or off duty employees in. If someone is asking for help, tell him or her you will call the police. Do not open the door to talk to them. After close, the manager and employees should leave together for security reasons. It's all about staying alert to possible criminal behavior.

A manager should not work alone in the business. A minimum of two people should be in the business at all times. Working alone is an invitation to be robbed. Please, for the sake of your employees, insist on this rule being followed. We have personally been required to handle the aftermath of a number of armed robberies involving the manager staying alone after close. Two instances resulted in the death of the manager.

Let's face it, if you work alone, you become a target because you provide the criminal with all of the elements that are in their favor.

- **You can be easily surprised. If the business is closed, all it really takes to get in is a brick through the window.**

- **You are alone so can easily be controlled.**

- **You have money.**

Additional security precautions can be considered for your business that can enhance your safety at night. When you leave at night, you have a special exposure to robbery and good common sense dictates that you exercise caution.

- **Lot lights should be on - use a timer device to delay lighting shutdown.**

- **All closing employees and the manager should leave together.**

- **Depart the parking area without delay.**

DURING A ROBBERY

This is one of those worst-case situations that you need to address in your policies. Your policy should be written to focus on the safety of your employees, not on protecting the money. Train your employees to cooperate fully with the robber. Do not resist in any way. Remain calm. Do exactly as you are told.

Do not lie to the robber. Never let the robber be surprised. He or she may be as nervous as you are and a surprise could be dangerous. If you have to reach for something where your hand will be out of sight, tell the robber why. If an employee member is out of sight, perhaps in the restroom, tell the robber. If you have a time lock safe, point out signs to the robber. This will help to establish credibility for you when you tell him how long it takes to open the safe.

AFTER A ROBBERY

Immediately call the police and give them as much information as they request. Stay on the line until the emergency operator tells you that you can hang up.

Next, go take care of your employees!

Request that any customer witnesses remain; however, remember you cannot require them to stay. Keep all employees in the business. Do what you can to preserve the crime scene. Place newspaper or a bag over any objects the robbers) touched. This will identify evidence areas and help protect any fingerprints.

Have employees write down a description of the robbery and try to not let them compare notes or descriptions. When the police arrive, make sure that they are given all copies of any written description of the crime and the criminals.

You will no doubt be the focus of some media attention. We recommend that your policy address who is authorized to talk to the press and what presence on your property you will allow the media. The trucks from the local news teams will quickly make your parking lot look like a three ring circus if you let it happen.

In our experience, crime such as robbery, even when no physical forced is used and no one gets hurt, creates some level of psychological trauma in many of us. Some managers and employees will quit due to the experience, others may take time off and some others will seem not to be affected negatively. We think that it is important to be as supportive as possible, offer encouragement and even consider the use of psychological counseling if necessary. In the event that the robbery is violent and injuries or death occurs, counseling availability is a must in order to get peoples lives back on track.

Your CPP Loss Prevention professional can help you in a number of ways. The first is to help you to establish a disaster plan that addresses violent crimes such as robberies and evaluation of your physical security and equipment. After a violent crime occurs, they can help you to do the right things when dealing with the crime loss and consult with police investigators to expedite solving the crime.

Lessons From Losses - Robbery

After the dining room of the fast food restaurant closed one night at 10:00 PM with the drive through window open until 1 AM a robber pulled up to the window, ordered food and when the window opened to take the payment, the suspect vaulted through the open window with gun in hand demanding money.

The suspect forced the manager to open the safe and also took her around to the various cash registers and under counter drop safes which unfortunately had not been banked down allowing the robber to flee with a large cash haul that should not have been available since the office was equipped with an electronic armored car safe which is where all of the drawer and deposit cash was supposed to be.

Not surprisingly, after the success at one restaurant, the robber hit another store in the same chain a few miles away but only got available currency from one drawer amounting to a few hundred dollars since drops had regularly occurred.

Devices like automatic window openers are convenient but can leave you exposed to skinny athletic robbers if the opening is too wide. This is a very common type of entry used in fast food robberies. Windows can be adjusted to open only wide enough to receive payments and hand out food bags. Windows are also available that require cash to be placed in a revolving opening portion of the window that keeps bullet resistant glass between the people on the outside and the employees on the inside.

Most important, robberies are very often committed by people with knowledge of the business you're in. It has been estimated that 80% of fast food robberies are committed by their employees, ex-employees, assisted by your employees or have worked in your industry and know it well.

With that in mind, if you practice "loose" cash controls and procedures you increase your risk exposure to robbery, as your employees, of course, know about these sloppy practices. For example in this illustration, the registers were not banked down when the operations in the dining room were closed for the night. This was determined to be a regular practice and a lot money was regularly left exposed that should have been in the deposit section of the armored car safe.   Late night operations are inherently risky and made more so if it is known that you have extra cash available.

BURGLARY

Commercial burglaries are a common and frequently devastating crime that we used in our first loss example in Chapter One. As you noted, the loss that we described, spurred the business owner into a complete re-evaluation of their loss prevention programs.

Burglary is the entering of a building with the intent to commit a crime. Among the items that we have recommended that can be done to discourage a potential burglar included:

The Problem

Arrest reports reveal that the average burglar is male and ranges in age from 18 to 40 years old. Many of them started doing residential burglaries when they were young and some progressed to commercial crimes. The most popular items to steal are computers, electronics, wallets, purses, jewelry and petty cash boxes.

Most burglaries do not require forced entry. Most of the time the burglar enters through an open door or window, a skylight or roof vent. Many burglaries take place during business hours.

Are You Exposed To Burglary?

Burglary is typically defined as the unlawful entry into almost any structure (not just a home or business) with the intent to commit any crime inside (not just theft/larceny). No physical breaking and entering is required; the offender may simply trespass through an open door. Unlike robbery, which involves use of force or fear to obtain another person's property, there is usually no victim present during a burglary.

Turning for information to the Department Of Justice Uniform Crime Reporting (UCR) Program they list three sub classifications for burglary: forcible entry, unlawful entry where no force is used, and attempted forcible entry.

*   **In 2005, law enforcement agencies reported an estimated 2,154,126 burglary offenses in the U.S.-a ½ percent increase compared with 2004 data.**

*   **An examination of 5- and 10-year trends revealed a 1.8-percent increase in the number of burglaries compared with the 2001 estimate.**

*   **Burglary accounted for 21.2 percent of the estimated number of all property crimes committed in 2005.**

Anyone Can Be A Target!

*   **The average dollar loss per burglary offense in 2005 was $1,725.**

*   **Of all burglary offenses in 2005, 65.8 percent were of residential structures.**

*   **Most (62.4 percent) of residential burglaries in 2005 for which time of occurrence was known took plce during the day, between 6 a.m. and 6 p.m.**

Night burglaries are almost always commercial locations

* Among burglaries of nonresidential structures when time of occurrence was known, 58.0 percent occurred at night.

So what the statistics tell us is that you are most likely to be burgled at home while you are at work and your business is most likely a target at night when your at home!

Whether you're designing a protection strategy for your business or your home, the key strategies apply: Check Locks, Windows, And Doors.

There is not such thing as a completely foolproof lock, but a modern double cylinder type dead bolt will deter most burglars. Follow our lock recommendation chapter for more information.

Follow key control policies and procedures that we have recommended. Devise a security system for all keys. Keep a record of who has keys. Engrave all keys "Do not duplicate" even if you have a patented keyway. Changing locks annually or after an employee has been terminated is a good best practice.

Make sure window locks are designed and located so they cannot be reached and opened if the glass is broken.   To deter a "smash and grab", move merchandise away from the windows after closing.   Protect door panels and glass from being kicked or knocked out.

Install metal lining on exterior wooden doors to resist drilling or sawing. Add, "shim plates" over door edges to protect exposed lock bolts.

Check Outside

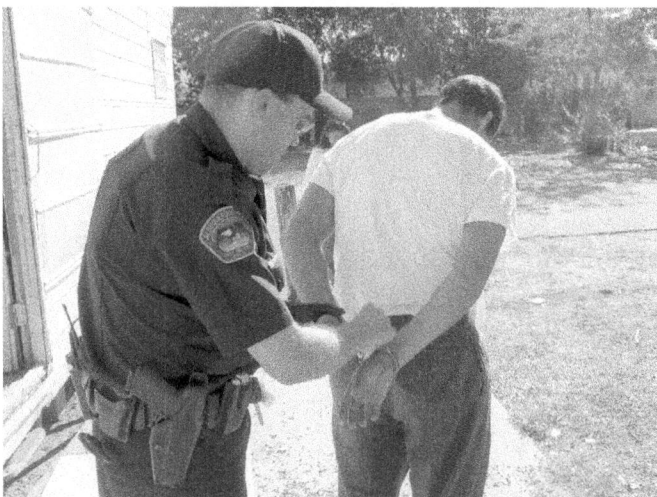

Daylight burglaries are usually residential targets

• A clean well-lighted secure building is seldom a target for break-ins. Keep weeds, shrubs, flowers and trees under control to eliminate hiding places for the burglar.

• Do not store lumber, pallets, or crates near building. They offer easy access to upper windows or the roof.

• Keep ladders locked up. Why supply crooks a way to get on to your roof?

• Keep all alleys clean and well lighted and make sure fire escapes and exits are designed for difficult entry as well as quick exits.

Lighting Makes A Difference!

Statistics show that three out of four commercial burglaries are committed against buildings with inadequate lighting. Follow these tips for top security:

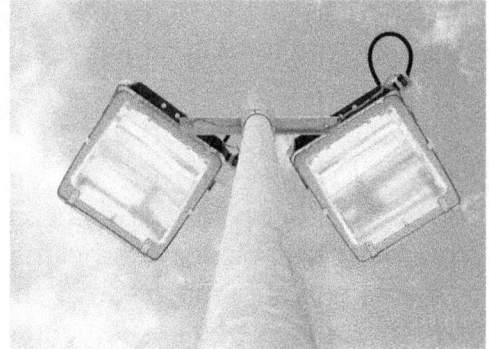

- **Install outside lights at all entry points, behind the building and in alleys.**

- **Install passive infrared-switched floodlights outside to illuminate intruders.**

- **Play it Safe and anchor the safe so it cannot be carried away.**

- **Never leave combinations where they can be found.**

- **Change the combination when you change employees.**

- **Bank frequently to keep cash at a minimum.**

- **Have enough security lighting to insure that your business is never dark.**

- **Leave some lighting on inside to allow police and passerby to look in and see suspicious activity.**

With the right barriers and good surveillance, your business can almost be burglar proof!

SHOPLIFTING

We advocate "deterrence marketing" as a combination of measures that makes it apparent even to people who have never shopped a store that it is the wrong place to attempt to shoplift. Use Cameras, Electronic Article Surveillance systems, signs and good common sense training for your employees.

First some common sense regarding shoplifting losses.

The average shoplifting apprehension recovery at large retail establishments is around $114. The average employee internal theft case recovery is $1,400. Apprehension of shoplifting suspects by your employees exposes your business to significant financial risks and the very real physical risk of injury to your employees. If, on the other hand, you injure the suspect during apprehension, you may be subject to a personal injury Lawsuit.

The old approach of "Hook 'Em and Book 'Em" as your only response to a shoplifting problem is high risk and low return.

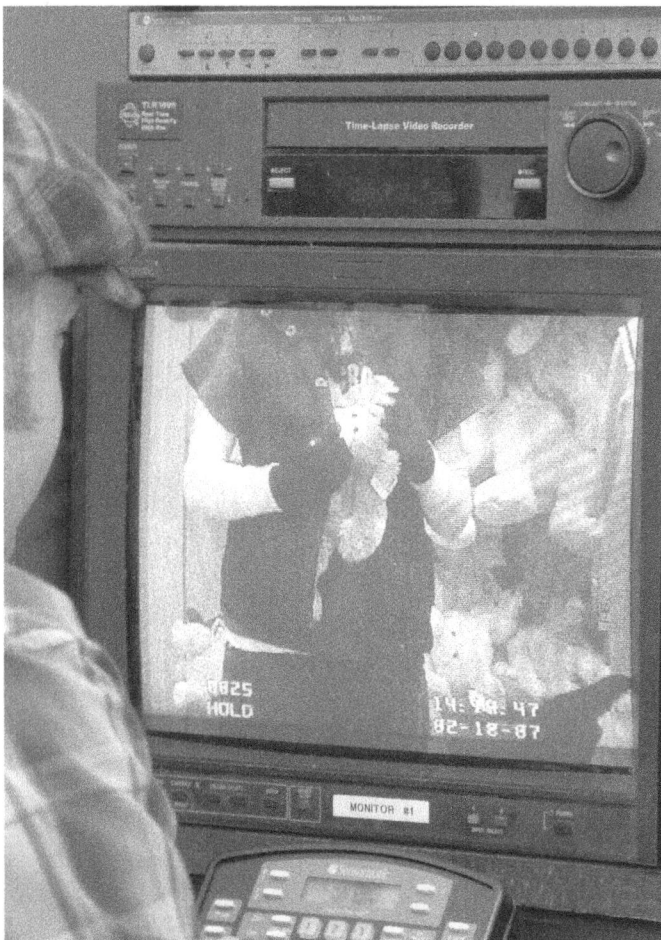

If you focus on apprehension.

• If a store has a policy of not detaining a shoplifter, it becomes known and the store can becomes a target.

• If a store detains but doesn't prosecute, that becomes known and the store becomes a target.

• If the store detains but don't prosecute up to a minimum amount, it becomes known you can steal with immunity up to that set dollar amount.

• If the store has a policy of arrest and prosecution, irrespective of the amount stolen, the police, prosecutor and courts will object and you will lose the case (see "Lawsuit").

What shoplifters use.

Shoplifters use the following to conceal items:

• 	Bulky clothing: coats, pants and maternity outfits.

- Packages, bags, backpacks and purses are hiding places, and sometimes they may have false bottoms.

- Special props include hollowed-out books, fake casts, umbrellas, secret pockets, belts or hooks under coats.

Foil lined booster bag used to conceal and defeat electronic tags

- Folded newspapers or magazines are used to hide small or flat items.

What to look for

- Be aware of customers' hands — and their pockets, purses, handkerchiefs.

- Notice open packages, purses, shopping bags, backpacks.

- Watch for customers who are nervous, have wandering eyes, are loitering or lingering in hidden areas.

- Watch groups of people, especially if a person tries to distract you.

Most shoplifters cannot succeed unless they get some privacy. This is why one of the best ways to stop shoplifting is to greet customers as soon as they walk in, and then be attentive to them the rest of the time.

1.   **You must see the shoplifter approach the merchandise**

2.   **You must see the shoplifter select the merchandise**

3.   **You must see the shoplifter conceal, convert or carry away the merchandise**

4.   **You must maintain continuous observation of the shoplifter**

5.   **You must observe the shoplifter fail to pay for the merchandise**

6.   **You must apprehend the shoplifter outside the store**

Reasons to focus on prevention rather than prosecution.

• If the store arrests and prosecutes and the offender is found not guilty in trial, the store can be subject to a Lawsuit (false arrest/malicious prosecution).

• If the store arrests and prosecutes and for a wide variety of reasons (e.g. the manager/ employee wasn't subpoenaed or is no longer employed and can't be located) and the court or prosecutor dismisses the case, the store can be subject to a Lawsuit.

• If the store detains and subsequently releases without a signed "admission", the store can be subject to a false arrest Lawsuit.

• If the store detains and releases with a signed "admission", the store may be subject to a Lawsuit claiming the agent extorted the signature, i.e. made promises or threats to obtain the confession.

• If the store detains and calls for the police and they arrive after a long delay (because transporting or citing a shoplifter has a low priority) the store can be subject to a false imprisonment Lawsuit for holding a person for an excessive amount of time.

• If the store detains, arrests and prosecutes because they have a "perfect case" in every way, including the written admission of the person arrested, the case can still be lost in trial for any number of reasons, and the store may be subjected to a Lawsuit.

Shoplifters assume they won't get caught. Your strategy is to make theft from your store look very difficult and risky. The following tips require thought and ingenuity, but cost very little.

• Alert employees are your best defense. Establish written procedures for them to follow if they suspect shoplifting, and make sure they are familiar with shoplifting laws.

• Make sure you can see everything that goes on in your store. Keep counters low, no more than waist-high. Mount mirrors in corners so there are no blind spots. Cameras should be placed with an unobstructed view and be focused to record facial features of a suspect for identification purposes.

• Arrange counters and display tables so there's no direct route to the exit. Some stores put turnstiles at entrances so the only way out is to pass the checkout counter. Place expensive items in the center of the store away from exits.

• Arrange displays so that missing items are easily noticed. Place small items in neat rows or clearly defined patterns. Attach inventory alarm tags to expensive merchandise. Reverse alternate hangers of hanging garments to prevent "grab and runs."

• Announce and observe a policy to prosecute shoplifters considering all of the above listed points. The threat of being caught, questioned by police, put on trial and maybe even put in jail will help to discourage shoplifters. Do not get into physical confrontations with shoplifters if you can avoid them. Your Policy should advocate few arrests, made when deemed necessary, such as a known shoplifter, and/or when the crime can't be prevented.

Many department stores and specialty stores not only try to deter theft attempts, through the use of cameras and item surveillance, but they also employ store detectives or specific security personnel, who thieves know will apprehend them if they are caught trying to steal. However, small to midsize retailers without a loss prevention professional on staff should use store detectives only after a consultation with a professional who can point out the risks, training requirements, personnel selection and proper procedures to use.

Lessons From Losses – Shoplifting

Stacy was having a bad day by all of the witness accounts. Several store employees told investigators that Stacy entered the store with an item marked with a sticker indicating it had been paid for, then switched the sticker to a more expensive item and tried to leave with it.

Employees told investigators Stacy had walked out the store with a package of diapers, a pair of sunglasses, a BB gun and a package of BB's. A number of employees chased Stacy out of the store to the parking lot on the hot Sunday afternoon.

Three employees caught Stacy, who twisted and turned until his shirt came off and he broke free and then ran again. A number of witnesses to the event, who followed the chase, then saw four or five employees hold Stacy on the ground. Stacy was pleading with them to let him up.   A witness said one of the store employees had Stacy in a choke hold as other employees pinned his body to the ground. Employees struggled with Stacy before he was handcuffed.

Caught in the act!

There was a struggle, and when they finally succeeded after getting him detained in handcuffs, he continued to struggle investigating officers were reported to have said.

About 30 people were reported witnessing the struggle with many telling the store employees to let him up that it was too hot.   Another employee brought a rug for Stacy to lie on, but one of those holding Stacy said he was fine where he was.

About five minutes of being held down, Stacy told his captors that he could not breathe and to call an ambulance. Witnesses told police that one employee had his knee on the man's neck and others were putting pressure on his back. Finally Stacy stopped moving and the employees got off him one witness told investigators; "They wouldn't call an ambulance."

Witnesses reported that Stacy had stopped breathing but were told that he (Stacy) was just on drugs. When told that his fingernails had turned gray, they finally called an ambulance.

Investigators have no indication that Stacy was intoxicated. They also said a review of surveillance tape showed that nine minutes had elapsed between the time employees got Stacy under control and the time EMS showed up. According to 9-1-1 records paramedics arrived two minutes, 19 seconds after they received the call. Paramedics performed CPR on Stacy en route to the Medical Center Hospital, where he was pronounced dead.

Stacy was found to have had a previous shoplifting incident with the same retailer. Stacy was on probation and had been banned from returning.

His death was ruled a homicide caused by asphyxia from neck and chest compression. The autopsy report listed a contributing factor as overheating with methamphetamine toxicity. The methamphetamine may have contributed to Driver's death, but didn't cause it. A grand jury in July 2006 declined to indict anyone in the case.

A civil jury none-the-less awarded the family $750,000.

Need we say more about taking a serious look at your policies and actions related to retail crime prevention? Be consistent and train your people well.

RESTITUTION GUIDELINE

Your written policy should include the provision that your managers are not authorized to promise suspected criminal offenders that restitution will be accepted in lieu of prosecution. If, in your best business judgment, you believe accepting restitution in lieu of prosecution may be the best course of action, the company senior manager must approve before any promise or commitment is made. Do not accept any form of restitution (unless restitution is court ordered) once a crime has been reported to the police without the direct and specific approval of company senior management. We think it is also a good idea to discuss the restitution option with the investigating police detective before making the decision. Some departments welcome closing the case with a civil compromise and some may discourage the practice.

VISITOR ACCESS CONTROL

Some considerations are required regarding whom you allow into your business after hours and where visitors may have access. You need to sensitize your employees to understand that for reasons of safety and security, your company does not allow unauthorized persons to wander around the business without a designated company employee as an escort.

There is the consideration that a criminal likes to see an environment where they can enter supposedly private areas of a business without being challenged.   You also have to be aware that persons that are not your employees are unaware of hazards and are prone to being injured. That means that you have liability exposure and can be sued!

You should admit only authorized persons into the business before open and after close. Do not let off duty employees, loitering before or after shifts, friends, relatives, job applicants, etc. into the business.

Stress to all employees that you do not admit unauthorized persons into the back areas. They should challenge persons not known to them with a cheerful "May I help you?" And be escorted to a manager.

Request identification from persons you do not know that want access to the work areas, or into the business during closed hours. If you do not know the person or you were not aware of the visit, check with your Manager before allowing access.

SHORT CHANGE ARTISTS

A few simple guidelines will prevent a short change from occurring: Always get the customer's money first. Be certain that each transaction is completed before handling another change transaction. Short change scams involve getting the register operator to perform change making functions in the middle of a sales transaction.

We recommend that your cashier training include the injunction to conduct one transaction at a time. Each sale should be completed and the register drawer closed and requests for different change denominations should be politely be deferred until after the current transaction.

The manager must handle any discrepancy between customers and register operator. If you have been practicing good cash control procedures such as those that we recommend including conducting frequent draw pulls, a quick count of the drawer contents will determine if the drawer is in balance.

Return Fraud

Just so you know, according to a National Retail Federation survey return fraud amounts to 3.7 billion dollars during the holiday season alone. Nearly 8.93 percent of holiday returns this year will be fraudulent.

The NRF's second annual Return Fraud Survey found that executives anticipate the loss, which is up slightly from 8.67 percent in 2006. Retailers will lose $10.8 billion overall in return fraud this year, NRF found. Since many retailers offer more lenient return policies during the holiday season to accommodate their customers, unfortunately, retailers must constantly balance the desire to take care of their customers with the undisputed fact that criminals are constantly looking to take advantage of return policies.

According to the survey completed by 60 large company retail loss prevention executives in October 2008, nine of out 10 retailers have had stolen merchandise returned to stores within the past year. Retailers also report being victimized by returns of merchandise originally purchased with fraudulent or stolen tender and returns 83.1 percent of the time. Returns using counterfeit receipts occurred 51 percent of the time, the survey found.

The report also found that the return of non-defective used merchandise is also climbing and affected nearly 66.1 percent of retailers. That is up from 56 percent from last year. According to the survey, 81 percent of retailers will be implementing the same return policy as last year, while 15 percent will tighten their policies. Remember that many of these Large Cap companies who have "loss prevention executives" are spending on average .6% of their sales on security systems and personnel. Are you investing in programs to prevent losses to your business?

COUNTERFEIT AND ALTERED CURRENCY

This issue should be addressed in any company environment where cash is handled simply because of how prevalent and common it is to find counterfeit currency. We recommend that along with the general statements found in your policy manual and employee handbooks, you provide each person who handles your money with training designed to allow them to quickly verify the authenticity of the money that they question.

We recommend that when receiving large bills such as the most popularly counterfeited bill, the $100, that a manager checks the bill for authenticity. Counterfeit rings will often test a business to see if the currency is checked and if not they will flood the business in a short period of time with bogus bills. For this reason, all cash handlers should know how to quickly check every bill $10 and over. Everybody needs to recognize the absence of color shifting ink, security strips and watermarks.

Oops! Accepted by a quick serve restaurant

A counterfeit bill is an imitation or copy of a country's currency. A counterfeit bill may be very difficult to distinguish to an untrained eye. Your local law enforcement office can give you assistance if you believe you have received a counterfeit bill. "Raised" or "altered bills" are created when corners of a higher denomination bill are pasted over the corners of a lower denomination bill, usually on the face. This is why register operators should place bills face down on the register. If you suspect you have received a counterfeit bill, try to politely return it for another. If they have left, write down their description and contact the police.

VANDALISM

Vandalism during open hours can be minimized. Assure that employees are attentive to guests. Those who may vandalize will note the increased chance of being caught. Pay attention to restrooms, as this is the most frequently vandalized area of the business during open hours. Have any and all graffiti removed immediately.

VAGRANTS & LOITERERS

A business with loitering problems should consider posting signs that state that loitering is prohibited. This kind of policy needs to be enforced in a polite and firm manner. If a loiterer refuses to leave, call the police.

If the police ask you to file a complaint against the loiterer, refer to your "Disorderly Activity" section for help. Loiterers on the parking lot need to be addressed. Contact your local police department. They can tell you about what options you may have to solve the problem.

Many departments have a community-policing unit (COPE) that specializes in dealing with the sorts of problems that business owners have to deal with. Your local precinct commander is someone that you, the business owner should get to know. Mutual cooperation and understanding goes a long way toward getting maximum help when you need it.

DISORDERLY ACTIVITY/ VIOLENT PERSONS

If a person is being unruly or offensive to other customers or employees, your manager on duty must be trained to take immediate action. An employee should be alerted to call the police in the event the situation gets out of control. Use care in your approach to the disorderly person. Request the person(s) causing the disturbance to stop their disorderly conduct.

If the disorderly person does not stop, or begins again, ask the person to leave the property. If the person refuses to leave, or the person's words or actions suggest possible violence, or the person becomes violent, your manager should back off and CALL THE POLICE. Ask customers to leave if the potential for harm exists.

Your manager and/or your employees should not attempt to physically control or restrain the disorderly or violent person. When the police arrive: Explain the situation. Ask the police to have the person leave. If the police have not witnessed a violation of law, they may not be willing to tell the person to leave without hearing you ask them to leave. The police may not be willing to take the person out unless you file charges as a representative of the company.

**Activity not so good
for your business!**

Your policy should make it clear under what circumstances your managers are authorized to file charges against a person. You may wish to consult with your attorney regarding your policy so that you can include as many of the potential reasons to file charges as possible. A list comes to mind besides the disorderly person that might include: shoplifters, intoxicated persons, employee's accused of theft, etc.

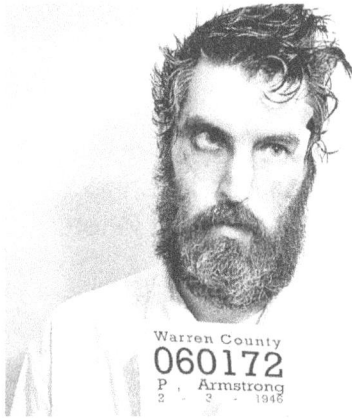

It is preferable to obtain advice from counsel prior to filing charges, but this may not be practical due to circumstances. If it is not practical, or you cannot reach someone for approval, you should allow your manager to file the appropriate charge recommended by the police if you believe it is necessary to return the business to an orderly condition.

Call the police to deal with scary people!

Filing criminal charges against an individual is best handled by the police following their investigation. However, some jurisdictions simply will not assist you with the filing of misdemeanors and you will have to visit the prosecutor's office and file the charges yourself. Again, seek the advise of your attorney because failure to follow through with your complaint can result in a lawsuit against you.

CRIMES AGAINST YOUR CUSTOMERS

Your company policy needs to address what to do in the event that a crime against a customer is witnessed or reported to one of your employees. Train your employees if they become aware of any situation or condition, which could affect the safety of a customer, they should take immediate action to prevent a problem from happening.

Examples of these conditions may include suspicious persons on the lot or inside the building, disorderly persons, etc. The appropriate action could range from asking suspicious persons to leave, to calling the police. If one of your customers becomes the victim of a crime, you should act in a responsible and concerned way.

Crimes you may see include; assault, robbery, intentional property damage, fights, purse snatching or any other situation that would cause a reasonable person to call the police for help. Upon learning a crime may happen, is happening, or has happened, the manager on duty must call the police immediately. If it can be done without agitating the victim, get the following information: Name. Address. Telephone Number. Description and value of property stolen. Description of injuries, if any.

Do not discuss liability. If you are unable to get information from the victim, you can get a copy of the police report later. Have all employee witnesses write a description of the incident as they remember seeing it. It is best if they don't talk to each other about their statements.

All written statements should be retained by your company unless requested by police. Always keep a copy of everything for your records.

Supply chain and your inventory losses.

As we told you earlier, the National Retail Security Survey conducted each year for the last several years attempts to quantify how much retail merchants are losing to theft and other losses that affect the bottom line. The loss was stated as $41.6 billion the most recent number available at the time of this books publication, due to higher retail sales in 2006 compared to 2005 and the study expresses loss as a percentage of sales.

According to the survey, the majority of retail shrinkage last year was due to employee theft, at $19.5 billion, which represented almost half of losses (47%). Shoplifting accounted for $13.3 billion, or about one-third (32%) of losses.

Almost as an after thought the study states "other losses" included administrative error pegged at $5.8 billion and 14% of shrinkage and vendor fraud of $1.7 billion and 4% of shrinkage. What? Eighteen percent of sales and 7.5 billion dollars is an after thought?

Having worked for many years for large corporate enterprises, I was always astonished at the size of the numbers that were attributed to the "miscellaneous" and "other "categories of accounting losses.

When you have that large of a number that does not fit any major category isn't it time to take a look at the circumstances creating these losses and come up with a new category? Once the problem has a description and a name, your CPP loss prevention expert and the creative business owner can come up with a number of defensive strategies to attack the problem.

For many years working for those large international companies, I watched many instances where managers were terminated for misstating inventory balances to hide a shortage. These guys would often have a boss who would not tolerate the bad news of an expanding food cost variance. That's what restaurant companies call raw product inventory shortages. So rather than surface the problem with the boss and work on solutions, the loss was carried as in stock inventory.

**Your Profits start here...
Control your receiving area!**

Few things will get you fired faster in most companies than cooking the books to cover theft, waste or mismanagement.

So the manager, not necessarily responsible or profiting from the theft, covers it up until on hand inventory numbers builds to a noticeable and unacceptably high level or a surprise inventory audit by the boss discovers the loss. We have seen instances where the loss discovery necessitated write off of over 5% of sales.

Often when unexplained inventory loss occurs, initial inquiries include going to the invoices and comparing the charges to the bills of lading copies received at the time of deliver. Discrepancies may be discovered that the store did not receive credit for returns or piece counts received do not match the invoice numbers.

Lessons From Losses – Where's my stuff!

Sally worked as a department manager for a subsidiary group of grocery stores that were owned by a large national chain. She was a 20+-year veteran of the organization group of stores, which was acquired by the national chain about 5 years ago.

Following the acquisition, the parent company brought to the group a number of computerized accounting systems previously unknown to the formerly family owned markets. The monthly inventory continued to be a pretty straightforward affair with items to be inventoried listed on a worksheet in the appropriate designation of pieces or pounds depending on the item.

Before long problems began to appear through out the system of stores related to deliveries and failure of the warehouse to credit the operating departments for returned or "miss picked" (wrong) items. As the number grew without credits being received, records did continue to show the discrepancies at the stores but not at the district office.

Part of the problem in this large organization involved the fact that the warehouse management was responsible for their own profitability results and were reluctant to show the now accumulated returns, which would skew their own profit margin as the return items were added to what was becoming a problem of their own. The warehouse operation was actually a separate outsourced company contracted to procure and deliver products to the subsidiary markets.

Compounding the problem was that all store deliveries occurred at night and were palletized and shrink-wrapped to facilitate quick on and off loading using forklifts and pallet jacks. The store stock "receivers" signed for the pallets of products and broke the orders down at a later time.

The result was, of course, that no delivery piece count verification occurred even though that was clearly the policy. It probably didn't take the warehouse long to discover that the store's receiving system was a very loose program and they were able to take advantage of the situation by purposely shorting deliveries if they wanted to in order to redirect the stock to a "cash customer" either at the warehouse door or at the end of the route.

The reaction of the company was interesting. A number of memos from the district manager began to arrive telling the store managers that they were short "thousands of dollars" worth of inventory and an explanation was required immediately. Each store was given a break out by department how much each department was short in dollars and to respond with the reason and what has been done to fix the problem.

Sally received her allocation of the loss and was told to supply the answer. Sally was told her shortage was over $3,000 for her department alone! Sally said "can't they tell me at least which stock items are at variance? I have hundreds of items that will need to be researched!".

But, no they couldn't, they were only interested in the big picture dollar amount.

Your inventory controls have to start at the lowest common denominator. The number of items on the shelf and proceed backward from there to the stock room, the warehouse and upstream to the rest of the supply chain. Losses can occur at any link of the chain where controls either are ignored or do not exist.

In this Lesson From Losses, the system was huge and computerized but fell apart very quickly due to accounting issues with issuing credits on returns and the failure of the receiver system to properly check in the broken down stock deliveries to determine if the bill of lading matched the physical case count.

In this case, hopefully the company will recognize the fact that the problem cannot be addressed due to several missing pieces of information and the need to revisit policies and procedures.

Could this "Management Theory" happen at your company?

A company had a vast scrap yard in the middle of a desert. Management said, "Someone might steal from it at night." So they created a night watchman position and hired a person for the job.

Then management said, "How does the watchman do his job without instruction?" So they created a planning department and hired two people: one person to write the instructions and one person to do time studies.

Then management said, "How will we know the night watchman is doing his tasks correctly?" So they created a Quality Control department and hired two people: one to do the studies and one to write the reports.

Then management said, "How are all these people going to get paid?" So they created positions for a timekeeper and a payroll officer, and hired two more people to fill them.

Then management said, "Who will be accountable for all of these people?" So they created an administrative section and hired three people: an Administrative Officer, Assistant Administrative Officer, and a Legal Secretary.

Then management said, "We've had this command in operation for one year now and we're $18,000 over budget. We have to cut back on overall costs."

So they laid off the night watchman!

Creating and maintaining a
safe work place is a core
management competency

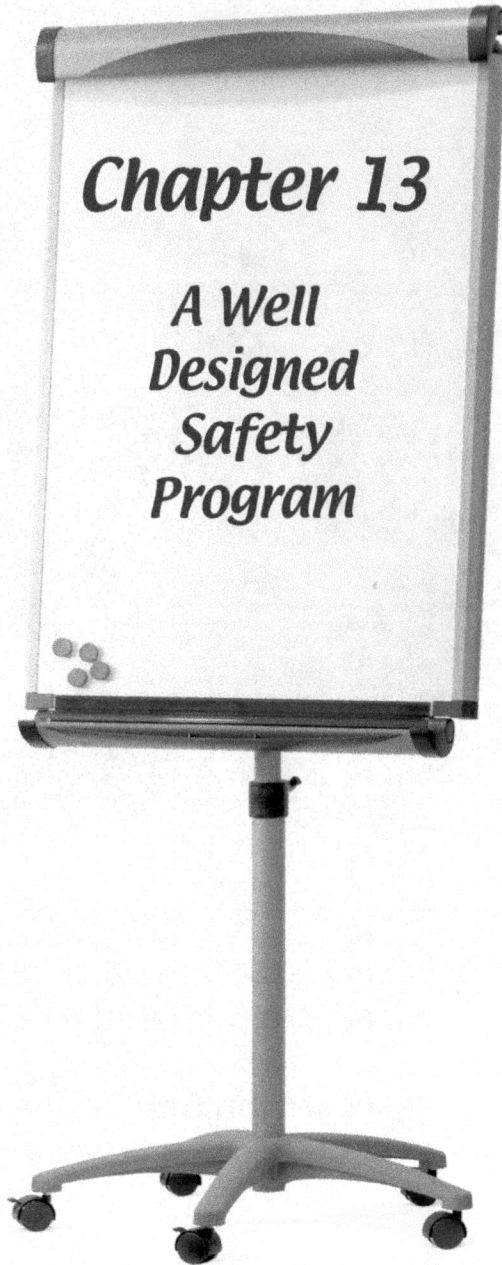

Chapter 13

A Well Designed Safety Program

"A discovery is said to be an accident
meeting a prepared mind".

Albert von Szent-Gyorgyi
US biochemist (1893 - 1986)

The purpose of this chapter is to provide the small to mid-sized business owner with some of the procedures and practices used by large companies who spend a lot of money on loss prevention managers, safety awareness programs and employee training programs in order to try and control losses due to Workers Compensation and Customer Liability Claims.

All of the preceding chapters of this book have related to security topics so why are we throwing in a chapter about "safety"? The answer is that fixing safety loss exposure is just another best practice that your business should incorporate to improve your profit margin. Why leave even more profit on the table and walk away, when there is something you can do to recover it?

Customer claims and Workers Compensation injuries are "bolt out of the blue" expenses. Since you don't know when accidents will happen or even if they will happen, it is tough to budget for these potential losses. We have experienced claims where a little old lady slips and falls down in a restaurant dining room, breaks her hip and cost the business owner $80,000.00 to settle the lawsuit.   These are not isolated incidents, they happen every day in all kinds of business environments.

But wait, if you budget for good hazard identification and safety awareness and you reduce your exposure to claims doesn't that make more sense than not planning and hoping for the best? It does make sense and in the long run will also save you money on Workers Compensation and liability coverage insurance.

The fact is that you pay Workers Compensation and liability insurance based on your loss experience. So do the big companies. The really big companies are often self-insured.

If you are experiencing Workers Compensation accident and claims frequency higher than the industry average, your insurance carrier will assign you with a "modifier" number that multiplies your premium. The higher your modifier number, the more you pay and some insurance companies will cancel your coverage if they think you are too high a risk and force you to pay for "pool" coverage that states set up.

The only way to get your premium costs down is to have over 3 years of better than average frequency. So if you have good rates now, the way to help keep them that way is to get started on a company safety program now.

By establishing a safety program we mean that you will want to promote a company culture that encourages safe work practices. Your new program will need a few items to get started.

- **A safety policy that sets the expectation of a safe work environment.**

- **Rules and procedures to reinforce good behaviors and to hold people accountable.**

- **Training tools.**

- **Awareness programs.**

- **A way to measure and reward success.**

- **A loss analysis of your claims history.**

- **A plan to reverse negative trends**

There are many specific safety requirements depending on the type of business you operate. Federal and State OSHA regulations require specific safety procedures for many industries. You need only contact your local office to obtain more information.   Or on the web it is "http://www.osha.gov".

A few words about OSHA have been added to the Third Edition of this book. We have found that many small to midsize companies have never had a contact with anybody from OSHA and have not really looked into the published safety rule requirements that OSHA has written that impacts their industry segment.

You will possibly move along in blissful ignorance just as you may have been doing unless one of the following occurs:

Do you have back door hazards at your business?

1.   An accident occurs at your business and an employee dies on the job.

2.   An accident occurs at your business involving multiple victims and injuries.

3.   OSHA receives a credible complaint of on-site dangerous working conditions.

4.   Your industry has a high frequency of industrial injuries such as construction or manufacturing and you may be targeted for a routine inspection.

All things being equal, it makes a lot of sense to know what all the rules are so you can make a good faith effort to follow them. Oh yeah, by the way, besides federal OSHA rules, many states have their own state occupational safety and health department and some may have rules that exceed the federal standards that have to be followed. For example, Rhode Island requires that hazard communication training be conducted and documented for all employees every year.

You may have tasks requiring special protective equipment for hazardous tasks such as welding or machinery operation. Each business must supply and maintain personal protective equipment appropriate for each type of employee task. An example would be that in food production environments, tasks requiring usage of knives, requires that the user be equipped with a suitable cut resistant glove.

The information in this book is of necessity directed to general safety issues common to most retail establishments. <u>You</u> need to contact OSHA for the requirements that impact your business.

Two key areas of concern to you are the top issues that many businesses fail to follow that result in the most frequent citations being issued by OSHA.

1.   **Failure to train and communicate a Chemical Hazard Awareness Program in compliance with the Right To Know Act.**

2.   **Failure to post Material Safety Data Sheets (MSDS) for all chemicals found in your place of business.**

These are requirements in all business environments even though the only chemicals in your business are cleaning materials such as floor cleaner like Mr. Clean and glass cleaner like Windex. All manufacturers under this act are required to supply you with MSDS upon request.

The best place for the training documentation is in the policy and procedure sign-off sections of your employee handbook that you retain in every employees personnel file.

The training documentations should include but may not be limited to:

1.   **A general description of the Right To Know Act.**

2.   **The Purpose of Material Safety Data Sheets (MSDS) and what information is on the sheet.**

3.   **Where the MSDS book containing the sheets is located.**

4.   **A complete description of all chemicals in use at the business, explanation of the use label, safe use rules of the product and what personal protective equipment, if any, is required while using or working with the chemical.**

5.   **An explanation of how chemicals must be stored at your business and safe storage rules to prevent contamination of other products or merchandise.**

6.   **Other hazardous materials such as combustible gases and fire extinguisher chemicals.**

Moving forward, it is important to know what your company loss experience is. You will need to obtain a **"Loss Run"** from you insurance provider detailing your last 3 years of claims.

Separate Workers Compensation claims and other customer liability claims that you have experienced.

An accident is any unforeseen or unexpected event that may or may not result in injury or damage to property or equipment. A reportable accident according to OSHA rules generally will include employee injuries that require treatment beyond on-property first aid. If they go to the doctor, it's "an accident".

You need this information to identify trends that you can reverse using procedures and policies directed at changing unsafe behaviors and hazardous conditions. To jump-start your program, you need to attack the problem starting with the three most important issues.

1.   **Workers Compensation and customer claims that happen frequently in your business.**

2.   **Claims with high potential costs that happen infrequently in your business.**

3.   **Claims by type that are common in your industry whether you have experienced them or not. You need to determine your level of risk.**

Businesses with multiple locations will want to sort the claims by location, date, claim type i.e. "Customer" or "Workers Compensation" a brief description of what happened, estimated claim cost, actual claim cost to date and whether the claim is open or closed. Setting up a simple spreadsheet in Excel will allow you to produce regular reports for distribution to your managers.

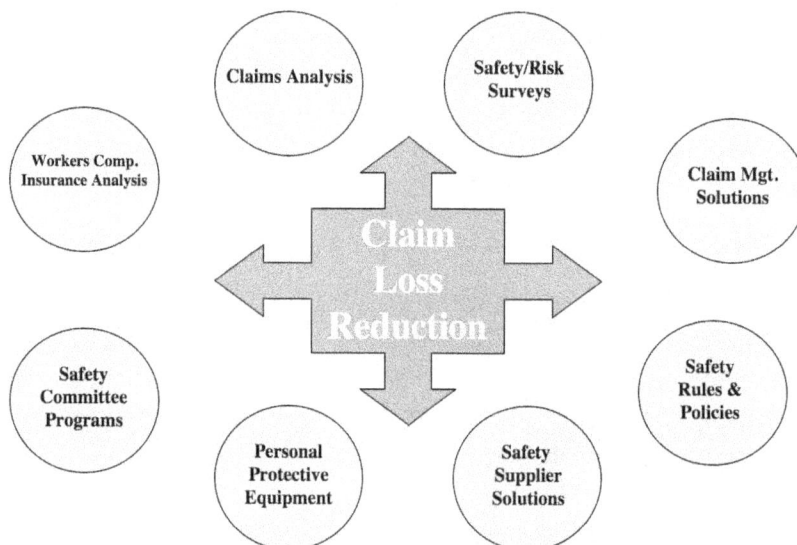

After you have had a chance to see your loss run history, you should be able to identify not only what claims have occurred but also what they cost to close and whether any trends are apparent such as a higher frequency at a particular company location.

If you have multiple locations, let's say you are a 12-store fast food restaurant franchise; don't be surprised if you find out that 80% of your claims for Workers Compensation are occurring in 20% of your stores.

We recommend that the business owner assign the record keeping task and program management to some one in your organization who can take on the added responsibility for a year. It has been our experience that the company Safety Coordinator role is a great manager development tool you can use to improve the selected manager's knowledge and productivity.

You need one person that you can hold accountable for results that you can measure your program with.

A great starting point to your safety program rollout is a statement of your company safety goal. Sort of like "See the end before you begin". A Mission Statement will provide your employees with a clear statement that safety procedures and policies are now part of your company culture and from the top of the organization down, the rules will be enforced.

The ultimate goal in accident prevention is "zero" disabling injuries and no lost work-time. However, there are many barriers to achieving this goal, the most important of which is the human attitude. Most people feel that "it won't happen to me" or "it couldn't happen here." You can do more to protect yourself and your employees by constantly thinking and practicing accident prevention than you can by memorizing all of the rules, regulations, and safeguards ever written or invented.

That is another way of saying that these best practices need to become part of your corporate culture and not just another program or goal to be focused on for a while then you can move on to the next priority.

The initial focus of your accident prevention efforts should be directed toward dealing with your loss experience. These are all of the injuries and claims that have been affecting your profits and insurance costs but most importantly have been affecting your people!

Management Commitment and Employee Involvement

As the owner or manager of a small business, your own attitude towards job safety and health will be reflected by your employees. If you are not interested in preventing employee injury and illness, nobody else is likely to be.

At all times, demonstrate your personal concern for employee safety and health and the priority you place on them in your workplace. Your policy must be clearly set. Only you can show its importance through your own actions.

Demonstrate to your employees the depth of your commitment by involving them in planning and carrying out your efforts. If you seriously involve your employees in identifying and resolving safety and health problems, they will commit their unique insights and energy to helping achieve the goal and objectives of your program.

Consider forming a joint employee-management safety committee. This can assist you in starting a program and will help maintain interest in the program once it is operating. Committees can be an excellent way of communicating safety and health information. If you have few employees, consider rotating them so that all can have an active part in the safety and health program.

The men and women who work for you are among the most valuable assets you have. Their safety, health, and goodwill are essential to the success of your business. Having them cooperate with you in protecting their safety and health not only helps to keep them healthy— it makes your job easier.

A policy statement might look something like the following:

OUR COMPANY COMMITMENT TO SAFETY

We are committed to the safety and health of our employees and customers. It is our intention to follow and comply with all safety laws and ordinances and our policies and procedures.

No job is so important that we cannot take the time to perform it safely and maintaining a safe work environment is our primary concern.

We owe each other a duty of care to follow safe work practices everyday and we are all expected to take our role seriously:

- **Wear personal protective equipment as instructed.**
- **Promptly report accidents.**
- **Work to correct safety hazards.**
- **Make safety an important part of our job every day.**

As a small business employer, you have inherent advantages, such as close contact with your employees, a specific acquaintance with the problems of the whole business, and usually a low worker turnover. Probably you have already developed a personal relationship of loyalty and cooperation that can be built upon very easily. These advantages may not only increase your concern for your employees but also may make it easier to get their help.

Some practical and useful safety guidelines to serve as habits and rules that will help you to achieve a safer attitude and a safer work environment are described on the following pages. We think that adding a structured safety program can add to your Competitive Advantage.

Here are some actions you can take:

• Post your own policy on the importance of worker safety and health next to the OSHA work place poster where all employees can see it.

• Hold a meeting with all your employees to communicate that policy to them and to discuss your objectives for safety and health for the rest of the year.

• Make sure that support from the top is visible by taking an active part, personally, in the activities that are part of your safety and health program. For example, personally review all inspection and accident reports to ensure follow-up when needed.

• Ensure that you, your managers, and supervisors follow all safety requirements that employees must follow, even if you are only in their area briefly. If, for instance, you require a hard hat, safety glasses and/or safety shoes in an area, wear them yourself when you are in that area.

• Use your employees' special knowledge and help them buy into the program by having them make inspections, put on safety training, or help investigate accidents.

• Make clear assignments of responsibility for every part of the program that you develop. Make certain everyone understands them. The more people involved the better. A good rule of thumb is to assign safety and health responsibilities in the same way you assign production responsibilities. Make it a special part of everyone's job to operate safely. That way, as you grow and delegate production responsibilities more widely, you will commit safety and health responsibilities with them.

• Give those with responsibility enough people, on the- clock time, training, money and authority to get the job done.

• Don't forget about it after you make assignments; make sure personally that they get the job done. Recognize and reward those who do well, and correct those who don't.

• Take time, at least annually, to review what you have accomplished against what you set as your objectives and decide if you need new objectives or program revisions to get where you want to be.

The following bullet points are topics for your safety rules manual that you can use to explain the importance of safety to your employees and how they fit into the equation.

The items that we have listed may not pertain to your business in particular but are generally found to cover many businesses. You may need more or less. Keep it simple and make sure that it relates to the hazards and requirements of your type of business.

Messy and disorganized invites accidents!

• **Reducing accidents means reporting to work physically and mentally rested, prepared to perform your job safely and properly.**

• **Always report any unsafe condition or unsafe act to your supervisor as soon as possible.**

• **Whenever you're performing your job, keep your mind on your work.**

- **Report any injury to your supervisor as soon as possible.**
- **If you are taking a prescribed drug, which may have a side effect, inform your supervisor before beginning the day's work.**

- **Use of illegal drugs or intoxicating beverages while at work (or reporting to work under the influence of these substances) may be cause for your dismissal.**

- **Shoes**
  It is recommended that approved safety shoes be worn to protect your feet.

- **Eye Protection**
  Proper eye protection must be worn when the nature of the operation presents a potential eye or face injury.

  Examples of these hazards include:
  Flying objects, dust, hot or splashing liquids, harmful rays, caustics or acids.

- **Gloves**
  Appropriate gloves, mitts and aprons shall be worn when handling hazardous chemicals, hot items and abrasive materials. Gloves should be replaced when the signs of wear are apparent.

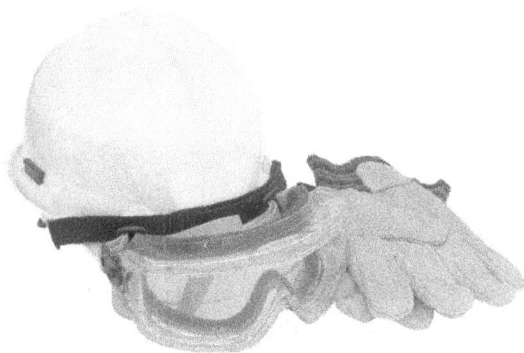

  - **Respiratory Equipment**
    Approved respiratory equipment shall be worn when the worker is exposed to toxic chemicals or dusts, spray-painting, or other inhalation hazards.

  - **Jewelry**
    The wearing of rings or other jewelry is not recommended on the job, particularly if working around moving or rotating parts or anywhere food is being prepared.

Keep required safety equipment available at the designated "Safety Station".

Work Area Housekeeping

- Good Housekeeping is an essential part of every job. Work areas, aisles, walkways, and equipment shall be kept clear of loose materials, tools, and scraps.

- Materials, supplies and merchandise shall be stored in an orderly and secure manner.

- Spills such as grease, water, or oil shall be cleaned up as soon as possible; a delay could result in an accident to you or a fellow worker.

- A safe access shall be maintained to work areas. Short cuts should be avoided. Never block aisles, traffic lanes, or fire exits with equipment or materials.

Hand Tools.

- Always know how to properly use hand and power tools before starting the job by following operating instructions and using the proper accessories. If you are unfamiliar with how a tool operates or is to be used, get the advice and instruction of your supervisor.

- Tools should not be used for other than their intended use.

- Keep all cutting tools sharp.

- Tools shall be kept in a safe condition without broken or damaged parts.

- Never use tools, which have burred or mushroomed heads and never carry loose tools in your pockets.

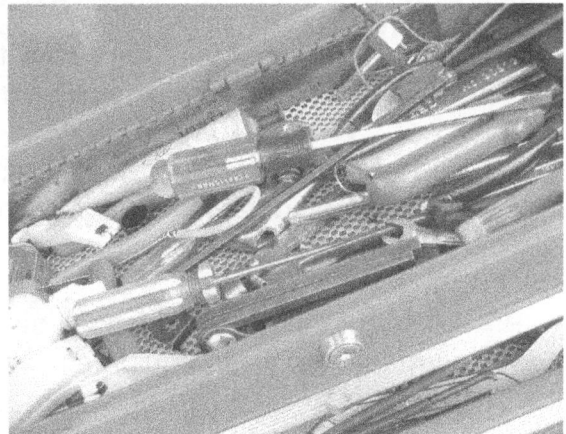

- If tools or equipment are found to be faulty, report them to your supervisor and return the equipment to the proper place where you found it.

- Never leave hand tools lying around loose where they may fall on someone below.

- Remember, use the right tool for the job.

Equipment & Machinery

- Supervisors shall allow only properly trained employees to operate power equipment or machinery and shall give proper instructions in their safe operation.

- All electrical equipment and machinery shall be properly grounded. Control switches shall be properly located at the point of operations best suited to control the equipment.

- You should never adjust, repair, clean, or oil machinery or equipment while any of its parts are in motion. Use lock out switches to prevent accidental start-ups. Be sure all of the components have stopped.

- Always replace guards after repairs have been made.

- Always perform proper maintenance on all machinery and equipment to prevent premature failure or possible accident. Have all safety guards in place while testing repaired equipment.

- You should regularly inspect for cracks, stretching, etc. on cables, chains, clamps, hooks, and other equipment that are frequently placed under stress. Spreading, crimps, or cracks are warning signs of danger. If you feel the equipment is damaged or creating a possible hazard, report this to your supervisor immediately.

Tag-Out Procedure

- A lockout device and universal "Danger" tag shall be placed on all energy-activating devices of machines or tools needing repair, or receiving routine maintenance.

  - The responsible trade should write the reason(s) the machine is not operable on the tag and sign it before placing the tag on the equipment.

  - Before starting maintenance or repair, the equipment should be checked to make sure all energy has been released or disconnected.

- Each trade should remove its tag after the equipment is repaired and notify affected personnel. When more than one trade is involved in repair or maintenance of such equipment, a compound-locking device shall be used.

- A lockout device and tag shall be placed on the junction box of stationary permanently- wired equipment with the energy activating device placed in the "off" position. This lockout/tagout procedure should reduce accidents caused by the unexpected start-up or release of energy.

- The equipment shall not be put back in service until after the last trade removes its lock and tag.

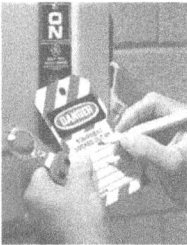

Fire Protection

Learning the location of fire extinguishing equipment and fire alarms in your work areas is important. Do not cover or hide fire protection equipment and fire alarms from view.

Sources of ignition, such as cigarettes, matches, portable heating equipment, unguarded light bulbs, etc., are prohibited in areas where explosives, flammable liquids or gases, or other combustibles exist. (I.e., near chemical exhaust outlets, flammable liquid storage areas, sump pump areas, and refueling areas)

- Always obey "No Smoking" signs.

- Never check for possible natural gas leaks with an open flame.

- Flammable liquids shall be kept in approved safety cans for use in small amounts and for transportation. These containers shall be clearly labeled and stored in a separate, protected area.

- Refueling a small engine that is running or is hot can be dangerous and should be avoided.   Always clean up spills that occur during refueling before re-starting engines.

- Rags that contain oils or solvents shall be kept in covered metal containers until they can be safety disposed of.

Electrical Safety

It takes very little electric current to kill ; less than one-tenth of an ampere. With good contact, 115 volts is sufficient voltage to cause death. There have been fatal electric shocks where voltage as low as 60 to 70 volts was involved.

- No electrical work should be performed "hot" when it can be done "cold."

- Switches, fuses, circuit breakers, and other control devices in areas where explosives or other flammable liquids or gasses exist shall be the type designed for use in these areas.

- All electrical equipment should be periodically inspected.

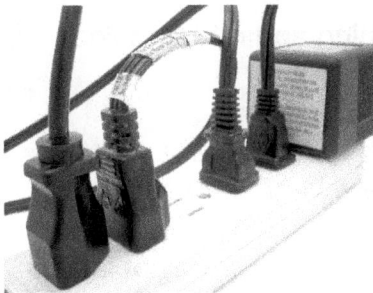

Avoid using extension cords!

- Suitable means should be provided for identifying all electrical equipment and circuits, especially if two or more voltages are used on the same job.

- All electrical tools and equipment should be properly grounded or be of the double insulated type. Spliced or damaged electrical cords shall not be used until properly repaired.

- Electrical cords on power tools and extension cords shall have heavy-duty rubber insulation.

You should never use electrical equipment when standing in or near water. In places such as bathrooms, kitchens, laundries, and out-of-doors, where a person having wet hands or standing on a wet surface is likely to touch objects that may be energized, a ground-fault circuit interrupter (GFI) shall be installed in the circuit to prevent electrical shock.

- All exposed electrical wires should be considered "hot" or "live" until checked by a qualified electrician.

- Electrical repairs shall be made only by qualified and trained personnel.

- Standing on metal ladders or wearing metal hard hats near high voltage electrical power can result in death or serious injury.

Ladder Safety

Although there is always a risk in working on elevated areas, it is a fact that the vast majority of accidents involving ladders result from the failure to exercise care. Proper training, as well as routine inspections and maintenance, can substantially reduce the number of ladder-related injuries.

- On any job requiring a ladder, use only approved sturdy ladders that you can place on a firm base.

**Bad ladders injure
a lot of people!**

- Inspect the ladder prior to EVERY use. Do not use ladders with structural defects; properly tag with "Do Not Use" and withdraw from service.

- Use a ladder only for the purpose for which it was designed (refer to manufacturer's labeling and recommendations).

- Use only non-conductive side rails around live electrical equipment.

- Wear protective clothing and rubber-soled shoes.

- Carry ladders parallel to the ground. Tie ladders down securely when transporting.

- Barricade traffic areas in the vicinity of ladder use, and lock, barricade or guard doorways in which a ladder is placed.

Keep the area around the top and bottom of the ladder clear. When ever possible, angle out the base one-fourth of the ladder's working length. The ladder should reach at least three feet above the landing.

Extension ladders shall be kept from slipping or tipping by tying off the ladder at the top and securing the ladder at the bottom. Portable ladders in use shall be tied, blocked or otherwise secured to prevent their being displaced.

Face the ladder while climbing and use both hands. You should lift equipment and materials with a rope specifically for that purpose and you should not carry the equipment up a ladder with one hand. Carry smaller tools in pouches around the waist.

Do not load the ladder beyond its maximum intended load and never allow more than one worker on the ladder at a time.

Back Safety

According to the Bureau of Labor Statistics, more than one million workers suffer back injuries each year, and back injuries account for one of every five-workplace injuries.

The amount of force placed on your back under certain conditions can be surprising. Anytime you bend or lean over to pick something up without bending your knees, you put tremendous pressure on your lower back.

Think of your back as a lever. With the fulcrum in the center of the lever, it only takes ten pounds of pressure to lift a ten-pound object. However, if you shift the fulcrum to one side, it takes much more force to lift the same object. Your waist actually acts like the fulcrum in a lever system, and it is not centered. In fact, it operates on a 10:1 ratio. Lifting a ten-pound object actually puts 100 pounds of pressure on your lower back.

When you add in the 105 pounds of the average human upper torso, you see that lifting a ten-pound object actually puts 1,150 pounds of pressure on the lower back.

Given these figures, it is easy to see how repetitive lifting and bending can quickly cause back problems. Even leaning forward while sitting at a desk or table can eventually lead to back-related problems.

- **Avoid Lifting and Bending Whenever You Can.**

- **Place objects up off the floor. If you can set something down on a table or other elevated surface instead of on the floor, you won't have to reach down to pick it up again.**

- **Raise/lower shelves. The best zone for lifting is between your shoulders and your waist. Put heavier objects on shelves at waist level and lighter objects on lower or higher shelves.**

- **Use carts and dollies to move objects instead of carrying them yourself. (It is better on your back to push carts than it is to pull them.)**

- **Avoid lifting over your head, and avoid reaching across a table or out the back of a truck.**

- **Avoid working in awkward, uncomfortable positions on tasks that require you to bend over for long periods of time.**

Proper Lifting

Over 250,000 industrial workers and office workers injure themselves each year through poor lifting techniques. The practice of stooping over from the waist to lift, accompanied with the added factors of uneven footing, poor balance, or awkward positioning is a direct invitation to eventual injury, because undue strain is thrown on the back and abdominal muscles.

The following rules should be observed for safe lifting:

1.   Determine if you need help. Consider the distance and the objects weight.

2.   Look over the pick-up and delivery area for (1) tripping hazards, (2) slippery spots, (3) small doors, (4) sharp corners, (5) blind spots, etc.

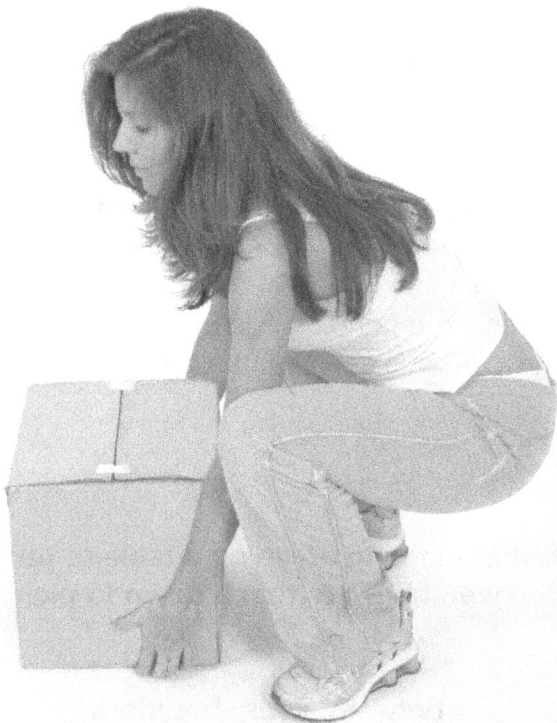

3.   Inspect the object for sharp corners, wet surfaces, slivers, etc.

4.   Place feet correctly with one foot close to the side of the object to provide stability and one directly behind the object to provide lift or thrust.

5.   Keep the object close to your body.

6.   Get a correct grip or hold on the object by using a full grip not just your fingers.

7.   Keep your back straight, this does not mean vertical, just aligned head to pelvis.

8.   You should tuck in your chin when lifting to insure alignment from head to pelvis.

9.   Do the actual lifting with your legs only.

10.   Just as important as lifting correctly is the ACT OF LOWERING CORRECTLY.

You should lower objects in the same manner as you lifted them. This is essential!

The body should never be turned or twisted while under the stress of heavy

weight.   Instead, you should turn your whole body if you desire to change your position after you have made the lift.

Slip and Fall Injury Prevention

In many retail and restaurant environments, the most expensive injuries are the result of slip and fall accidents. We will start our discussion by noting that all businesses have a very large liability exposure if steps are not taken to reduce the number and likelihood of slip and fall injuries that occur due to unsafe conditions.

According to some legal opinions, from a customer claim standpoint, the following warning seems to apply.

A "slip and fall" injury is a personal injury that occurs when a person slips or trips, usually on an area that is unexpectedly slippery, wet, or uneven. If a person slips and falls on the property of another due to preventable, unsafe conditions, the property owner may bear legal liability for the person's injury."

Property owners are not always legally liable for accidents that occur on their premises. In general, property owners have certain responsibilities that are owed to their guests, employees, or customers. When a personal injury occurs due to an unsafe condition on the property, the owner may be liable if:

- He or she caused the unsafe condition (by spilling liquid and not cleaning it up, digging a hole that is difficult to see, etc.).

- He or she knew about the condition, but did not take steps to correct it or to prevent harm to others (by failing to clean up a spill, not posting a sign near uneven ground, etc.).

- He or she should have known about the danger, because a "reasonable" property owner would have found the problem and taken steps to prevent injuries (by neglecting to properly maintain the premises, not inspecting a facility regularly, etc.).

In determining whether a property owner's actions or inactions were reasonable, the court must consider how long the unsafe condition existed and whether the owner had time to discover and remedy the problem. The jury may also consider whether the steps taken were appropriate or reasonable and whether the carelessness of the victim played a role."

And this about Workers Compensation claims:

Both federal and state laws impose certain safety standards on employers, and some of these are meant to guard against slip and fall injuries. Workers' compensation laws hold employers strictly liable for job injuries. In exchange, the law limits the amount of damages that can be collected.

Slip and fall accidents can occur when the walking surface "coefficient of friction" changes abruptly. This means that a person walking steps from a relatively good walking surface to a relatively bad one.

In other words a slippery condition such as water, grease or other spilled material is encountered on the floor and as we step forward, we lose traction and as weight is transferred to the forward foot the person flies into the air and lands awkwardly potentially causing an injury.

There are some very specific things that you can do to reduce occurrences of slip and fall injuries.

1. **Insure that all walking surfaces are clean and dry.**

2. **Use mats at all entrances and in areas where spills are common.**

3. **Clean as you go. Make sure that all spills are promptly cleaned up and notify every one of the wet condition using wet floor cones or signs.**

4. **Insure that your employees wear slip resistant shoes.**

5. **If you have tile floors that have become slippery over time due to wear or contamination from grease or other reasons, inexpensive treatments are available to renew and protect the surface from re-contamination.**

Additional sections that you may wish to add to your program are procedures related to:

*   Fire prevention and response to fires.

*   Fire extinguisher types use

*   Severe weather response.

*   Disaster plans and response

*   Specific operations procedures for the specialized equipment and machinery that you use in your business.

*   Emergency medical procedures and response.

*   Driver education

- Forklift operation and safety

Accident Prevention and Planning

There are a number of other strategies that you can implement to prevent accidents and claims. A key strategy, that we recommend, is to mobilize your employees and form an accident prevention committee. At the start of the chapter, we told you about the value of appointing a Safety Coordinator for your company who can organize and manage your program. Here is where you can start getting your employees involved by using awareness programs to address the accident history of your operating units.

This activity has the built in effect of creating awareness and when you structure it properly and give it the top down support of all levels of management, you will see a reduction in your claims.

A basic activity of your accident committee members is to perform a monthly safety inspection and meet regularly to discuss claims and what has been done to prevent future occurrences. The following pages describe creation of an action plan. It is designed to be a management plan that identifies problems and assigns tasks that are designed to increase awareness, change unsafe behaviors and reduce your claims experience.

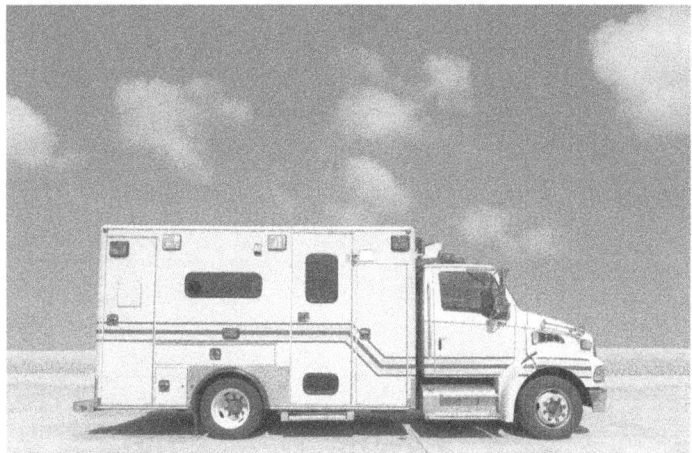

You know it's going to be a bad day when EMS takes an employee away!

The purpose of creating an action plan is to identify a problem, set measurable goals designed to reverse the negative trend and identify who will be responsible to complete action steps. The plan should be posted for all to see and progress reported regularly.

You can identify the stores that have been selected to participate in the creation of an action plan to reverse a negative loss trend. Base selection on the number of reportable Workers Compensation and/or General Liability customer accidents occurring the last calendar year and identify the store as a "Target Store". The following activities can help you identify any hazards and create safe behaviors.

Manager Meeting

- The store General Manager (person in charge) will call a meeting of all store managers. Bring to the meeting this guide and a blank "Safety Audit" form. You will also need a copy of your store Claim Detail for last year. Stores usually get this information from the insurance carrier/broker. The purpose of the meeting is to discuss the restaurant accident history, determine what types of accidents have been occurring and write an action plan to prevent future accidents.

- After the GM discusses the purpose of the meeting, all of the previous years reported claims will be discussed using the claims listing or Claim Detail Report.

- Talk about what happened and whether there were any injuries serious, what did they cost, and what sales are needed to replace the cost of these accidents.

- Discuss any hazardous conditions that contributed to the accident.

- Using the Safety Survey tour the store with your managers and conduct a safety inspection.

Get the whole team involved in the hazard survey process!

Store Safety Survey

Store Number_____ Completed By: _____ Date: _____

		Points		Points		Comments
	LOT & GROUNDS - 10 pts. SCORE					
A.	All uneven walking surfaces/curbs highlighted or highly visible	0	N	2	Y	
B.	Parking lot entrance, dumpster pad and parking area free of surface defects	0	N	4	Y	
C.	Parking lot area clean and free of slip/trip hazards	0	N	2	Y	
D.	Handicapped ramp and parking provided per local code	0	N	1	Y	
E.	Electrical boxes, landscaping lighting and signage free of exposed wires	0	N	1	Y	
	II. SALES FLOOR -28 pts. SCORE					
A.	Floor mats used at customer entrances from street or lot	0	N	2	Y	
B.	Company approved floor cleaning procedures followed	0	N	4	Y	
C.	Carpet free of rips and trip hazards .	0	N	4	Y	
D.	Tile floor (including restrooms free of slip/trip hazards)	0	N	8	Y	
E.	Handrails and Watch Your Step" signs at all steps .	0	N	2	Y	
F.	Customer exits marked and equipped with panic hardware per state fire code.	0	N	2	Y	
G.	Hanging plants, lights and ceiling tiles secured	0	N	2	Y	
H.	Displays and furniture free of defects and hazards	0	N	2	Y	
I.	Wet floor cones available for tile or hard surface floors.	0	N	2	Y	
	Ill. BACK ROOM - 50 pts. SCORE					
A.	Floor is clean	0	N	5	Y	
B.	Only approved cleaning chemicals used/stored properly	0	N	2	Y	
C.	Floor cleaning equipment available and in good condition	0	N	4	Y	
D.	Floor surfaces free of slip/trip hazards	0	N	4	Y	
E.	Hot water heater area free of clutter or combustibles	0	N	2	Y	
F.	Area free of electrical hazards (exposed wires, broken plugs, etc.)	0	N	2	Y	
G.	Compressed gas cylinders secured by a heavy strap or chain	0	N	2	Y	
H.	At least two fire extinguishers present, accessible & inspected within last 12 mo.	0	N	3	Y	
I.	Warning signs on all machinery	0	N	2	Y	
J.	Heavy duty flashlight/emergency lighting present	0	N	2	Y	
K.	Heavy inventory items stored on middle storage shelves	0	N	4	Y	
L.	Fire extinguishing pull boxes inspected/identified/accessible	0	N	2	Y	
M.	Back door area meets company standard - panic hardware, etc	0	N	2	Y	
N.	Stepstool or stepladder provided in storage area	0	N	3	Y	
0.	All electric panels/breakers boxes meet company requirements	0	N	2	Y	
P.	Non-skid surface or floor mats on all potentially wet floor areas	0	N	2	Y	
Q.	All required state and federal posters posted and visible	0	N	2	Y	
R.	First aid kit fully stocked and accessible	0	N	2	Y	

S.	Crew trained (with documentation) on all company safety policies & practices	0	N	3	Y	
IV. SAFETY EQUIPMENT -12 pts. SCORE -' ****SPECIAL ATTENTION****						
A.	Respiratory equipment	0	N	2 OK		
B.	Rubber gloves (18" or longer)	0	N	2 OK		
C.	Safety glasses/goggles/shield	0	N	2 OK		
D.	Required hardhat	0	N	2 OK		
E.	Required safety equipment – Other [state type]	0	N	2 OK		
F.	Leather gloves/ cut resistant gloves	0	N	2 OK		
	If any piece of safety equipment is missing, or in poor condition, it is an automatic "0" pts					

Items Needing Correction:	Scoring:	Your Score
	90 – 100 = A	
	80 – 89 = B	
	70 – 79 = C	
	Below 70 = F	

Plan Development is next.

The work sheet on the next page will work you through the meeting agenda of developing a written plan. Sections #1 & 2 will have you list all of your reported accidents and what was the nature of the injury.

Section #3 is where you will list your plan activities and who will be responsible.

Actions must be measurable and based on fixing a hazardous condition or educating employees and be "Time Bound" This means that you have to state when it's going to be done by.

Writing plans, setting goals and identifying accountabilities will give your company a set of measurable tasks that can be completed and serves the purpose of addressing the loss issue and gives the managers direction and expectations.

Post your plan where everyone can see your intentions and post the results so that everyone can see the value of their efforts.

By involving your people in the process, clearly stating the benefits and rewards to all of your employees, you are more likely to change attitudes and behaviors that will make your safety program a success. And you get to keep the profits!

The following sample plan is so that you get the idea of what type of items should be on your survey form. We recommend that you make your custom form up yourself following the meeting process so you are sure to include all of the hazards that exist in your company environment.

Business Accident Prevention Action Plan...

Unit Name:_____#_____Date:_____

This unit had _____reported Workers Compensation, _____General Liability [Customer] claims last year. The management of this unit is pledged to making this a safe place to work and have written the following *Action Plan....*

1.   **List all of Last Years Accidents.**   2. **List the Injury [i.e. cut, bruise]**

_____   _____
_____   _____
_____   _____
_____   _____
_____   _____
_____   _____
_____   _____
_____   _____
_____   _____
_____   _____

3.   **List Activities /Actions to Prevent Similar Accidents in the Future...**

When?_____**Who?**_____**What?**_____

_____
_____
_____
_____
_____
_____
_____
_____
_____
_____
_____

Signatures:

GM_____Manager_____Assistant__
_____

Hazard Communication Program

What is a hazard communication program?

The law, sometimes referred to as "The Employee's Right To Know Act", requires all employers to identify potentially hazardous chemicals in the workplace and using a written program, communicate any potential risks of the chemical to its' employees. **Failure to comply is the #1 OSHA citation issued to businesses.**

All businesses appear to be included, not just companies that use chemical processes in product manufacturing or construction. The best approach is to inspect your business and identify all types of chemicals you use or keep on hand. This might include any cleaning supplies, insect control, any compressed gas [i.e. helium for the balloons for the kiddies & CO_2 for the soda system] contents of your fire extinguishers, paint, varnish, glue and in some states even cooking oil [it burns].

Your supplier is required by law to provide you with a Material Safety Data Sheet for each commercially packaged chemical. They need to be accumulated in a binder or folder and posted for all of your employees to access in each of your locations.

Basically, the federal hazard communication standard is different from other OSHA health rules because it covers all hazardous chemicals. The rule also incorporates a "downstream flow of information," which means that producers of chemicals have the primary responsibility for generating and disseminating information, whereas users of chemicals must obtain the information and transmit it to their own employees. In general, it works like this:

Chemical Manufacturers/ Importers

• **Determine the hazards of each product.**

Chemical Manufacturers/ Importers

• **Communicate the hazard information and associated protective measures downstream to customers through labels and MSDS.**

Employers

• **Identify and list hazardous chemicals in their workplace**

• **Obtain MSDS [Material Safety Data Sheet] and labels for each hazardous chemical, if not provided by the manufacturer, importer, or distributor**

• **Develop and implement a written hazard communication program including** labels, MSDS, and employee training, on the list of chemicals, MSDS and label information.

- **Communicate hazard information to their employee through labels, MSDS, and formal training programs.**

Employers must establish a training and information program for employees who are exposed to hazardous chemicals in their work area at the time of initial assignment and whenever a new hazard is introduced into their work area. At a minimum, the discussion topics must include the following:

- The hazard communication standard and its requirements.

- The components of the hazard communication program in the employees' workplaces.

- Operations in work areas where hazardous chemicals are present.

- Where the employer will keep the written hazard evaluation procedures, communications program, lists of hazardous chemicals, and the required MSDS forms.

The employee training plan must consist of the following elements:

- How the hazard communication program is implemented in that workplace, how to read and interpret information on labels and the MSDS, and how employees can obtain and use the available hazard information.

- The hazards of the chemicals in the work area. (The hazards may be discussed by individual chemical or by hazard categories such as flammability.)

- Measures employees can take to protect themselves from the hazards.

- Specific procedures put into effect by the employer to provide protection such as engineering controls, work practices, and the use of personal protective equipment (PPE).
- Methods and observations—such as visual appearance or smell—workers can use to detect the presence of a hazardous chemical to which they may be exposed.

Keep It Simple

As noted above, the information about chemical hazards must be shared before an employee has a chance to be exposed. This means during new employee orientation you can discuss the contents of your program with your employee and obtain a sign-off that training has occurred. If chemicals are used in your business to process or manufacture you will need to be very specific and use the MSDS sections to conduct training for each chemical.

The following 2 pages illustrates a Hazard Communication Training Guide.

HAZARD COMMUNICATION TRAINING PROGRAM

Instructions:

1. Read and understand the information in this guide.

2. Your instructor will show you the Material safety Data sheets (MSDS) located in the employee area and explain the information on the sheet.

3. Your instructor will show you all of the chemical products in the store, what protective equipment that should be used and safe handling procedures.

4. Your instructor will conduct a quiz showing that you understand and will comply with the company safe handling of chemicals rules.

DEFINITIONS:

Hazardous Chemical: Any substance or mixture that can cause negative effects on the health or safety of a person. The two negative effects are: Physical and Health.

Physical Hazard: A chemical reaction is possible. An example is a flammable liquid can ignite if exposed to heat.

Health Hazard: The potential to directly affect a person through contact. Contact can be instantaneous (acute) or over time (chronic).

Irritant: Having the potential to cause irritation, especially physical. An example is that smoke is a common eye irritant.

Corrosive: Having the capability to cause corrosian. Many acids are corrosive.

Toxic: Capable of causing injury or death. Many chemicals can be toxic if injested.

Exposure Limits: Permissible Exposure Limit (PEL) which is calculated on an eight hour exposure without effect.

Allergic: A reaction of the body to a chemical resulting in physical symptoms such as a rash or breathing difficulty.

DISCUSSION QUESTIONS

What is the "Employees' Right to Know" act?

What is the purpose of a MSDS?

Why should you never mix different cleaning products?

Where should cleaning products be stored in our location?

If storing cleaning solutions in a spray bottle, what should be on th bottle?

What are the hazards of compressed gas?

How should compressed gas cylinders be store?

Who should you contact if you have any questions or concerns?

To our employees:

It is important to remember that some of the chemicals used in our business must be treated with care. If used properly, following the manufacturers instructions, these products pose no danger to employees.

This training program was designed to comply with the "employees' Right to Know Act". The act requires all employers to create a written program which lists the identification, use, storage and handling of potentially hazardous chemicals.

When employees are required to perform a potentially hazardous task such as special cleaning of equipment, a training session must be conducted by the manager to inform you about the cleaning chemicals use and the precautions to take. Precautions may include the use of gloves and eye protection. whenever a new chemical is introduced additional training must be provided.

Any questions or concerns should be brought to the attention of your manager.

Material Safety Data Sheets (MSDS)

Provide information on chemicals including:
- Manufacturers name, address and emergency phone number.
- Hazards identification.
- First aid measures.
- Health hazard data.
- Employee protective safety equipment

Storage of Chemicals

- never store chemicals within three feet of an open flame or other source of ignition such as a water heater.
- Never transfer chemicals to an unmarked container for storage.
- Store all chemicals in a separate area so they cannot contaminate merchandise or stock.
- All chemicals must be properly sealed after each use.

Compressed Gases

Compressed Gases in the form of carbon dioxide, welding gases, helium and fire extinguisher propellant, must be handled with caution.

All compressed gas containers should be firmly secured in an upright position using a chain, strap or mounting hardware.

Chemical Labeling

Chemical manufacturers are required to provide permanent labels on storage containers. The labels must explain how to correctly use or mix the product, if there are any hazards associated with the product and first aid procedures to use.

All secondary chemical dispensers such as spray bottles, must be labeled for content unless they are emptied and cleaned after each use.

Hazard Communication Training Check List.

- Employee has been shown and knows the location of Material Safety Data Sheets and understands information concerning potential hazards associated with each chemical.
- Never use unmarked spray bottles/tanks.
- Use proper chemicals for each job.
- Use proper dilution ratios.
- Never mix different chemicals together.
- Wear proper employee protective equipment.
- Knows proper storage of chemicals.
- Proper use and storage of compressed gas containers.

Training Date: _____

Trainer: _____

Employee: _____

Completed forms shall be filed in the employee personnel file.

For most small companies conducting retail activities, the sample training guide may help you comply with the law. The sample guide we included on the previous two pages of content can be copied using 2 sided printing, folded, used during training and finally filed in the employees file. To get a PDF copy contact us using the E-mail provided in Chapter 16.

Please note that each industry will have different requirements and you must consult with OSHA to obtain your own requirements.

Incident Investigations

There are few, if any, successful loss control programs, which do not have a procedure for investigating incidents. Regardless of the company, the product involved, or the service rendered, there will always be incidents and near misses. Through the conscientious investigation of all incidents, with appropriate corrective action taken, both the frequency and severity of these incidents can be reduced.

Incident investigations are usually best handled by the immediate supervisor involved. We recommend that all incidents be investigated, including "near misses". Near misses actually forecast serious injuries. Employees should be taught to report all unsafe acts or conditions to their supervisors, even if no incident occurs. Employees should also be encouraged to provide solutions to these problem situations.

As a first order of business, investigations should be made as soon as possible after the incident, and it should be made clear that investigations are "fact finding", not "fault finding". This approach is essential to an open and cooperative response.

Secondly, if the investigation is to be a meaningful part of your total loss analysis, it must distinguish between symptoms and causes. This can best be demonstrated by example:

Description of Incident:	Employee fell
Unsafe condition(s):	Water spill on floor
Unsafe Act(s):	Employee failed to clean up spill, or was inattentive
Correction:	Cleaned up spill and instructed employee to be more attentive.

The limitations of these types of conclusions are serious. It completely overlooks root causes, such as: How long was the spill overlooked? Why wasn't the supervisor alerted? Was the source of the spill corrected? Are spills a chronic problem? Personnel responsible for your incident investigation should be trained to avoid these limitations.

All investigations should be summarized in a written report. Here is what you need on the report form:

1.   Name of injured employee, date, and time of incident or near miss.
2.   Worker's occupation, department/job name, and other personal data (or description of equipment, material, etc., in the case of property damage).

Incident Investigation Report

Name of Injured Employee	Date of Incident/Near Miss	Time of Incident

Workers occupation, department, job title (or equipment description in the case of property damage)

Nature of injury, damage or near miss:

Medical treatment received:

Is this a lost time injury?   Yes ___   No ___

Location of Incident (be specific)

Safety policy violation?   Yes ___   No ___   If yes, describe the violation:

Description of what happened:

Analysis of why it happened, including contributory or indirect causes:

What should be done to prevent future occurrences?

Corrective action taken to date and action planned for the future.

3.   Nature of injury, damage, or near miss.
4.   Location of incident.
5.   Description of what happened.
6.   Analysis of why it happened, including contributory or indirect causes.
7.   Recommendations on what should be done to prevent reoccurrences.
8.   Action taken to date and action planned for the future.
9.   Follow-up notes.

NOTE: A written incident investigation procedure should be included as part of your loss control program. This procedure should supply the information necessary for the proper documentation and follow-up of internal incident investigations. The purpose of a written operating procedure is to ensure that every incident which has the potential or has actually produced a loss (either human and/or material) is investigated so that preventative action can be taken.

General Liability Claims

Good lighting is good for business and reduces claim frequency

All small and mid sized companies have the potential to find themselves on the receiving end of a lawsuit for something they either are alleged to have done or for failing to do something that the plaintiff said that they should have done. The results of the defendants actions, of course, was the proximate cause of an injury either physical or financial in nature and the plaintiff seeks a remedy – read money!

The vast majority of these claims are in the category of premises liability issues. Many of these legal actions started out as general liability (GL) claims for relatively minor problems that could have been fixed easily and early on if they had been dealt with properly in the first place.

Typical of these are instances where customers claim to have suffered a slip and fall or other injury on your business property. Others relate to auto or other property damage that occurred while they were a customer.

Many of these claims are frivolous and some can be outright fraud looking for a payoff to make it go away. All customer claims, however must be taken seriously at the time they are received and you need a system in place to record everything important and to insure that the reported information is forwarded to your insurance carrier in a timely fashion.

All of your managers and supervisors must be trained to handle these accident and claims incidents in an appropriate and professional manner. It's a very good idea to have a written system for all to follow in the event of a customer accident or reported claim.

Your customer claims procedure should always start with the obvious. Is any one hurt? Is there need to call for medical aid? Them follow through by making the calls that summon assistance. We recommend that even if the customer refuses help and in the judgment of your manager on the scene that medical help is appropriate, call 9-1-1 anyway. It is much better for the apparently injured person to refuse help from the arriving EMT's if they insist that their injury is minor.

The idea is to provide reasonable care. Few things are less defendable than to have one of your managers refuse to summon help when it should have appeared to the average reasonable person that help was needed. A delay in assistance can often exacerbate an injury that could have been stabilized earlier.

We also have to share with you, that at least in our experience with large companies, the first notification that an injury has occurred often arrives in the form of a letter from an attorney stating that they represent an injured party and to forward the information to your insurance carrier. If this occurs, simply make a copy for your files and forward it.

On the previous page we have provided an example of an incident report form. Follow the instructions, copy it for your files and forward all information to your insurance provider.

As a general rule it is best to view all claims and litigation threats from the standpoint of the big picture for claim defense. In isolation, settling individual claims might make sense. From a precedent or business standpoint, however, settlement might be questionable, especially if paying nuisance-value cases could spur additional non-meritorious claims. Settling dubious claims can brand an organization as an easy mark in the litigation arena, giving incentive to other attorneys and plaintiffs to feed from the proverbial trough. Nothing makes the sharks start circling like the smell of blood!

In many situations, your attorney will tell you, defending every case like you are going to trial makes sense. In an amazing amount of the time, plaintiffs' attorneys don't want to go to court and throw the dice in front of a jury either.

In other settings, such a policy invites disaster. If you lose a trial, your ability to keep an outcome confidential disappears. If you take every case to trial and lack a strong defense, you commit the litigation equivalent of Russian roulette.

Insurance companies and their claims personnel often can make fragmented decisions that are tactically sound but strategically unwise. This is common because rarely are all of a policyholder's claims handled by the same adjuster. Often, office management farms out claim assignments on an individual account amongst many different adjusters, depending upon staff schedules, availability, workload, and experience.

It is a very good idea to get to know the manager and adjusters in the local claims office if you have a significant number of claims that need to be tracked. You can meet with these people and gain an overall understanding about how they will handle your claims, whether they will "index" the claimants for other prior claims and under what circumstances they will get their special investigations unit people involved.

Due to the claims handling discrepancies out there among carriers, somebody must think strategically about claim defense and make specific decisions based on that foundation. If you do not have your own risk manager, we recommend that you look at outsourcing this function. Your risk manager can enforce that big picture and, in addition, fashion account guidelines requiring a more cohesive approach to claim assignments by an insurance company or TPA (third party administrator).

Slips, trips and falls are potentially your most expensive customer claims!

Sometimes it can be a far simpler process if you have the organizational resources to handle all claims like one company we know. The company, a large food service organization has a system in place that clearly reduces claims costs dramatically.

The process involves requiring all of the operating units to call in all claim information on the day it is received to a hotline number. The internal policy is to call all claimants within 72 hours of the receipt of the information to express concern and to get complete information about what happened with out admitting liability. Preferably before an attorney gets involved.

Store free product coupons and a sympathy letter are automatically sent and an amazing number of these claims go away without further payment. Even if the event is found to be serious, it hurts nothing to express sympathy toward the customer's problem and to gather as many facts as possible which are then forwarded to the insurance carrier or the TPA for resolution.

The key here has been the reduction of attorney involvement with genuine claims being handled expeditiously.

**Your safe work habits also
applies to projects at home!**

You have to plan *BEFORE* the disaster strikes!

Chapter 14

Crisis Management

"We live in the midst of alarms, anxiety beclouds the future; we expect some new disaster with each newspaper we read."

President Abraham Lincoln

The previous chapters in this book and the many activities of risk assessment and systems surveys have led us to the place where we can again return to square one and take a serious look at what to do if one of the worst case scenarios that we discussed in Chapter 1 happens.

Why should you go through the process of creating a disaster plan? We discussed some of the things that all businesses can be exposed to directly such as weather disasters and we have had a lot to say about what you need to do to defend against criminal attacks. Other concerns that must be addressed include determining how you need to respond to cases of product tampering or potential highly publicized such as strikes, product recalls and even events such accidents with multiple victims or crimes such as armed robberies that result in the serious injury or death of an employee. It can happen to you!

Protests and demonstrations on or near your property disrupt business and can result in physical damage and bad press. You have a plan...right?

Even though you may not see yourself as being the direct target of a criminal attack, you my be located next to another company enterprise that is. You could end up being shut down as the collateral damage of an attack on your neighbor.

Sound far-fetched? Think about whether you have neighboring companies in close proximity to your business that have international exposure to all sorts of anti establishment protesters such as anti-abortion, anti-globalization or groups such as the Animal Liberation Front, who like to stage attacks on medical labs and drug manufacturing facilities or the Environmental Liberation Front, who like to burn down new houses under construction and torch car lots with high SUV sales.

Criminal attacks aside, what's your plan if you are a small grocery chain that just found out that your fresh meat supplier has been identified as the purveyor of E.-coli contaminated products and the health department visits you because a number of customers have gotten sick? Any number of supply chain crashes can occur and you can be left holding the bag because you are the last stop in the chain and very visible to the media and the public. You are the collateral damage due to the actions or inactions of others not under your control and that's why you need a plan! It may never happen but if you have a plan on the shelf that you can quickly pull down and implement, you have just reduced your exposure to further loss, decreased the time it will take you to recover, reduced negative publicity and a whole lot of stress to you and your employees.

It Happened To Me

For me, the most difficult event in my loss prevention career occurred a few minutes prior to 11:00 PM on 5/24/2000. John Taylor and Craig Godineaux walked into the Wendy's restaurant on Main Street in Flushing NY. Taylor, an ex-employee recognized the assistant manager Jean August and engaged him in conversation while ordering food. As August completed closing out the register and walked downstairs to the manager's office, Taylor followed him a few moments later. All of this was recorded on the CCTV system, as was the scene of the employees all walking downstairs followed by Godineaux. The videotape stopped at 11:05.

The manager gave the safe contents consisting of the store change funds, which was mostly a lot of coin rolls and small bills to Taylor. Store bank deposit cash had been dropped by the managers hourly throughout the day, store records proved, into a time locked portion of the safe only accessible by the armored car company.

They had all of the money available, but the pair wanted no witnesses. In all, 7 employees had plastic bags put over their heads, were pushed into the walk-in refrigerator and were shot execution style.

After the crime, Taylor and Godineaux left the restaurant and caught a bus home. They believed that they left no witnesses behind, but miraculously two employees were alive. One was eventually able to drag his wounded friend upstairs and caught the attention of passersby who summoned police.

Along with the two witnesses, they also left behind a mountain of latent prints and other forensic evidence that allowed for NYPD and Suffolk County Police to have the pair in custody less than 36 hours after the crime. When Taylor was arrested, he still possessed the store videotape, the murder weapon and most of the proceeds of the robbery, which was mostly in coin.

I was notified about 5:30 AM on the 25th of May, and drove from Long Island to Flushing where I encountered the most horrific scene that I have ever seen in my life. I stayed at the crime scene assisting NYPD detectives for the next two days. That role was part of my written disaster plan checklist.

During my years in law enforcement I saw a lot of terrible events but nothing like this. Five dead and two alive, one of which was not expected to live at that point but later we learned that he would survive. We had to deal with the families, the employee survivors and a lot of blowback issues that would keep us occupied for months.

We provided counselors for everyone who needed it, paid for all of the funeral expenses and initiated a company wide appeal for funds to support the victim's families. We took over the 6th floor of a nearby Sheraton Hotel and were able to keep the press away from our people while we tried to adjust to the events of the day. Cameras and reporters were everywhere. On the street in front of the restaurant, people had started coming almost immediately to leave flowers and candles at the front of the store. The looks on their faces and the comments of dismay and horror were unforgettable.

NYPD detectives were superb in their support and empathy. They provided us with the information that we needed and we did the same for them.

After the Crime Scene people were done, I went into the scene with the investigating detectives and was able to provide additional evidence that helped to identify the two animals that did the crime. As noted above, one was an ex-employee, which is what we expected given the nature of the crime. I made many other trips into the crime scene to assist with other information requests.

In jail, Taylor and Godineaux couldn't wait to implicate each other. They were described as without remorse for their crime. Today, Godineaux is doing life without parole and Taylor resides on death row working through the mandatory appeals process.

The crisis that I experienced had many of the elements that any business can face no matter how well you plan your loss prevention program. We faced the gut wrenching reality that 5 of our co-workers had been murdered and two others would

Taylor doing the perp walk

need long term medical and psychological care. We had, for two days, unknown criminals who were on loose and could potentially attack our other business locations in the area that continued in operation and a lot of really scared employees. The other employees who were not on shift the night of the robbery were all totally traumatized.

Our Crisis Plan called for previously arranged relationships with professional psychological counselors, extra security personnel, corporate and outside public relations experts, human resource specialists and facilities staff to secure the now closed building. Many of these people were company employees but the same level of support can be put together using outsourced expertise in many communities with help and planning.

I'm telling you that your worst case scenario *can* happen!

The next few pages will help you to get started by giving you some directions to kick off the planning process.

One starting point is to consider what defines the word "Crisis" for my company? The answer will depend on the category of enterprise be it retail, services, supply chain or what ever. Any number unplanned events or a sequence of events can have a negative impact on your ability to continue business operations. Your plan, in the same way, needs to be able to address any number of types of catastrophes that can strike your company be it a natural disaster, crime, social unrest such as riots or mass public demonstrations, financial crashes, regulatory actions by government agencies such as health departments or OSHA.

ICM (Institute For Crisis Management) defines a crisis as: "A significant business disruption that stimulates extensive news media coverage. The resulting public scrutiny will affect the organization's normal operations and also could have a political, legal, financial and governmental impact on its business." The following shares a number of the agencies views of Crisis Management.

The basic causes of a business crisis can include:

1.   Natural disasters such as weather storms, earthquakes or volcanoes
2.   Criminal acts resulting in death or serious multiple injuries.
3.   Mechanical failure such as ruptured pipes, metal fatigue or a major crash in the manufacturing process.
4.   Human errors, accidents or poor judgment. Such as the wrong valve was opened, miscommunication about what to do, etc.
5.   Management decisions/indecision such as a controllable problem escalates due to lack of planning, procedures and processes.

Many times the crises falls in the last category and are the result of management not taking action when they were informed about a problem that eventually would grow into a crisis. Crisis events generally fall into two basic types based on the amount of warning time.
Sudden Crisis

A sudden crisis is defined as a disruption in the company's business which occurs without warning and is likely to generate negative publicity and may adversely impact:

1.   Employees, stakeholders, customers, suppliers or members of the public.
2.   Company facilities, franchise operations or other business assets.
3.   Sales, net income, stock price, etc.
4.   Our reputation and good will.

A sudden crisis may be:

- A business-related accident resulting in significant property damage that will disrupt normal business operations
- The death or serious illness or injury of management, employees, contractors, customers, visitors, etc. as the result of a business-related accident
- The sudden death or incapacitation of a key executive
- Discharge of hazardous chemicals or other materials into the environment
- Accidents that cause the disruption of telephone or utility service

- Significant reduction in utilities or vital services needed to conduct business
- Any natural disaster that disrupts operations, endangers employees
- Unexpected job action or labor disruption
- Workplace violence involving employees/family members or customers

Assessing the Severity of a Sudden Crisis

The following crisis classifications have been established to ensure consistency in assessment of any sudden crisis situation so that the proper level of communications response can be provided.

Sudden Level 1

Can be handled by on-duty personnel responsible for responding to and managing this kind of situation. Actions taken by employees or first responders should be listed in your action plan related to the type of emergency.
Example:
A careless employee leaves oily rags in the storeroom of an office building. Spontaneous combustion occurs. Luckily the fire is discovered and extinguished quickly by one of the building maintenance men or other on-site personnel.

Sudden Level 2

Can be handled by the personnel who respond, with support from other employees on duty or who may have to be called in from their homes.
The fire is out but heat and smoke damaged office furniture in the storeroom.

Sudden Level 3

Requires additional resources and people beyond the regular personnel. These managers and employees may be from other facilities or the corporate office, and may be supplemented by outside vendors or consultants. Clean up of the damages will need additional support personnel or outside fire damage remediation experts.

The fire was not discovered in time and spreads outside the storeroom. The fire department is called and puts out the blaze but it has severely damaged three offices. Two TV news stations cover the story and report that the fire was thought to have been caused by a careless employee.

Sudden Level 4

The situation is out of control and will impact an extended area and numerous people indefinitely. Business will have to be curtailed or discontinued and employees diverted from their normal duties until it is resolved. Other employees may have to be furloughed, vendors ordered not to make deliveries, etc.

Local emergency response agencies will be actively involved. State and federal agencies also may be called in. The fire spreads throughout the office building. High winds send cinders into nearby neighborhoods causing additional fires and forcing the evacuation of residents in the area. The fire department calls in all available equipment from the city and surrounding areas to control the numerous fires.

Local TV stations feed the story to their networks and it is carried on the evening news programs, with the suspected cause of the fire mentioned in the reports.
The criteria for these categories are broad because what may seem to be a Level 1 or Level 2 crisis when it first occurs may quickly escalate to a higher level. The Crisis Response Team should be alerted to any sudden crisis that is Level 3 or 4, or that has the potential to reach that level.

Smoldering Crisis

A smoldering crisis is defined as: Any serious business problem that is not generally known within or without the company, which may generate negative news coverage if or when it goes "public" and could result in more than a predetermined amount in fines, penalties, legal damage awards, unbudgeted expenses and other costs. Examples of the types of smoldering business crises that would prompt a call to the Crisis Management Team would include:

a.   Sting operation by a news organization or government agency
b.   OSHA or EPA violations which could result in fines or legal action
c.   Customer allegations of overcharging or other improper conduct
d.   Investigation by a federal, state or local government agency
e.   Action by a disgruntled employee such as serious threats or whistleblowing
f.   Indications of significant legal/judicial/regulatory action against the business
g.   Discovery of serious internal problems that will have to be disclosed to employees, investors, customers, vendors and/or government officials.

A problem past the smoldering stage

Assessing the Severity of a Smoldering Crisis

The following crisis classifications have been established to ensure consistency in assessment of any smoldering crisis situation so that the proper response can be developed to minimize the potential of the crisis going "public" or to reduce the damage to our business if public disclosure cannot be avoided.

Smoldering Level 1

An internal business problem or disruption that can be dealt with and resolved by management responsible for responding to this kind of situation.

Example:
A disgruntled employee who has not been given a raise threatens to disclose internal policies that he feels are illegal or unethical to "the proper authorities" unless his grievances are resolved and he receives a pay increase.

Smoldering Level 2

An internal problem that can be managed by those who are responsible for this area of business, with support from other management or employees who may have to be brought in to assess the situation and help resolve it.

Example:
The disgruntled employee files a complaint with the local government employment agency, which contacts the company for a response to the allegations. He calls his manager to say that he has documents the company certainly would not want other government agencies or the news media to see.

Smoldering Level 3

An internal problem that has the potential of going "public" via the news media and generating negative reactions from government officials, plaintiff's attorneys, competitors, investors consumer activists, labor unions, etc.

Example:
The crisis can still be contained but will require specialized assistance beyond the management capabilities in place to deal with normal business problems. This assistance may be from corporate headquarters, outside legal counsel, and/or consultants who specialize in resolving this kind of problem.

An attorney for the disgruntled employee indicates his client has documents that are highly damaging to the business since they represent illegal or unethical actions. He is willing to settle the dispute for a specified, highly exorbitant, fee. If they are forced to file suit, the documents will be disclosed to the news media.

Attorneys for the employees provide a copy of one of the documents. Company attorneys conclude they were illegally copied by the employee and therefore represent stolen information.

Smoldering Level 4

The situation is very serious and is likely to be disclosed publicly in the very near future. The public reaction will have a significant adverse impact on the business for a period of weeks or months and top management along with numerous employees and outside consultants will have be diverted from their normal activities to resolve this situation. The financial impact will be substantial and will have a direct and indirect effect on operating results.

The dispute and financial settlement cannot be resolved and the employee's attorneys are preparing to file suit, which will be at any time.

A producer for a network television news magazine contacts the company seeking general background information on its business and employment policies for a story they are developing. No mention is made of the disgruntled employee.

The criteria for these categories are broad because what may seem to be a Level 1 or Level 2 crisis when it first occurs may quickly escalate to a higher level. The Crisis Response Team should be mobilized for any smoldering crisis that is Level 3 or 4--or that has the potential to reach that level.

In some instances crisis situations may be either sudden or smoldering, depending on the amount of advance notice and the chain of events in the crisis. Examples would include:

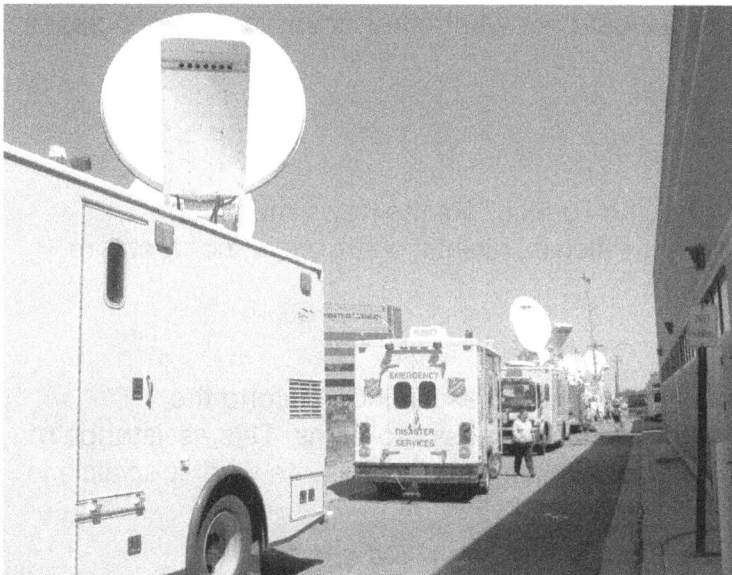

TV trucks on your parking lot means that you're not having a good day!

- Adverse government actions
- Computer tampering
- Anonymous accusations
- Damaging rumors
- Discrimination accusations
- Confidential information disclosed
- Equipment, product or service sabotage
- Industrial espionage
- Disgruntled employee threats
- Investigative reporter contact
- Employee death or serious injury
- Civil Disorder
- Employee involved in a scandal
- Violent police confrontations and arrests
- Lawsuit likely to be publicized
- Extortion threat
- Security leak or problem

- Severe weather impact on business
- Sexual harassment allegation
- Grand jury indictment
- Special interest group attack
- Grass roots demonstrations
- Strike, job action or work stoppage
- Illegal actions by an employee
- Terrorism threat or action
- Indictment of an employee
- Illegal or unethical behavior of an employee
- Major equipment malfunction
- Nearby neighbor, business protest
- Whistleblower threat or actions

You may be able to name a few others!

Most sudden crises also generate "aftershocks" in the form of smoldering crises which occur as the government, media and internal investigations into the cause of the crisis uncover specific problems that were not known previously. Many of those aftershocks are included in the list directly above.

You will need a Crisis Management Program with an "all hazards" approach. The reason is that this type of approach will allow for effective actions by the people determined to have a response role, provide early warning and clear action steps for all of your team members, ongoing assessment by the team of the results of the actions taken and the effects that the emergency has had on the organization and quick resumption of normal business activities when the crisis is over.

Your all weather - all catastrophe Crises Management planning should be built around a four step approach.

Prevention-Communication-Mitigation-Recovery

Let's get started on YOUR plan.

1.   Prevention

In the Chapter 1 discussion about Risk Control Measures you were told that you can either reduce the risk or transfer it. That means that you can identify your level of risk and design barriers that through operations planning like developing policies and procedures and design systems to eliminate or reduce exposure to losses. You can forget all of the planning and buy a lot of insurance to transfer the risk to a third party. **But you can't buy insurance to protect your good name and reputation**. However, insurance is useful during the recovery stage of your crisis plan.

We told you that reducing your company's vulnerability due to any potential crises requires that you develop a system or blueprint that will outline the roles and initiatives that must be addressed. This approach will allow you to act in a consistent manner to fulfill the identified roles and tasks of each team participant. If you have been following the recommendations, you started with our survey of your existing company security systems, rules, policies and practices.

The Crisis Plan starting point is for you as the business owner to sit down with some trusted lieutenants and create a plan structure.

- Who is going to be in charge during a crisis?
- Will you need a command post off site?
- Who will be the official spokesperson for the organization?
- Who are the core members of the Crisis Team?
- What are the human resource and financial considerations?
- What critical assets need to be protected?

- What do we need in terms of operating system redundancy?

The answers, of course will depend on your organization or enterprise type, what resources you have on hand and what will have to be obtained by outsourcing.

The survey you were introduced to from Security Wise Group LLC included having you gather General Administrative Information related to your company record keeping and IT programs. Preservation of accounting records, customer lists and all sorts of proprietary information must be preserved in order to ensure continued operation and post crisis recovery. You should include issues of where and how human resource, payroll and benefits files are stored and how administrative tasks will continue and people will continue to get a paycheck in the event of a crisis. You should list every task that you can think of.

The survey identified written policies, procedures and control programs that currently govern how you do business. The list all of these control functions are important because you need to determine how asset controls and other regulated functions will continue.

You will need to list your identified risks, hazards and potential crises that need to be addressed by the action steps in your crisis plan. This list needs to be comprehensive will no potential disaster or event off the table. An "all hazard" plan really has to work no matter what as long as you have some ability to control the outcome either short range or even just after the dust settles and you can only pick up the pieces of what happened.

Create a list of all critical assets that you would need to preserve or replace in order to continue operations. Depending on the enterprise, the list may be heavily weighted by machinery for a manufacturing facility or by computers in an information technology driven company or inventory and building replacement for the retail sector.

Ultimately, the benefits to be gained from your survey lists are to identify items and issues in need of attention, establishing a list of things that can go wrong in a variety of crisis situations, identifying what financial and personnel commitments you will need to make to manage a crisis and documenting completed items on your plan goals. The survey that you have conducted is a living document that will change as your business changes and must be regularly re-evaluated and kept up-to-date. You internal company audit program should always include key elements of compliance with emergency crisis plan elements.

The survey list process is your first step toward reducing risk exposure vulnerability. The next planning step is to organize the operations response. The management chain is critical to this process. You must ensure that all levels of management become part of the program.

A chain of command is key to developing your viable crisis response plan. Somebody has to have the job of being in control. If you are a small company the buck probably stops with you! If you are the owner or CEO and can possibly pass the buck to a senior trusted manager in your organization you should do so and allow yourself to stand back and see the big picture of what is going on.

Make a senior manager directly responsible to top management and the board of directors if your business is organized that way. Your "Crisis Management Team Director" appointment should have been followed by first creating a specific job description and a performance standard to measure success. It's always a good idea to let the anointed senior manager in on what's expected before they accept the job assignment. Management "buy-in" is a top-down imperative if you expect success and the Owner/CEO and top management must take responsibility for developing measurable goals for the Program Director that are achievable.

Develop and write a mission statement outlining the purpose of the team emphasizing your top down corporate commitment.

Definition and Purpose

The purpose behind every business crisis management plan is the safety, health, and well-being of our employees and customers. Thus, when needed, we must be prepared to respond to situations of crisis with appropriate and timely reactions.

A crises, as you have learned, may take a variety of forms within your company. This includes death of an employee, weather emergencies, criminal acts against the company or it's employees or any other crisis arising that can damage the company reputation and assets. Whatever the situation, Crisis Management leaders need to make the decision of when to call upon the crisis management team and how to formulate an appropriate response.

Generally, each of your business enterprises needs a separate Crisis Management Plan and in order to respond appropriately follow the guidelines developed. The information included below is designed to address crisis response or management.

Within this document, two forms that are not included which are very specific to the individual enterprise is that of a calling tree and a special skills tree. The calling tree is useful during crisis situations to pass important bits of information. Secondly, it is helpful to keep a list of special skills which employees have that are useful in crisis situations. For example, those with emergency medical training, bilingual education, and sign language should be noted and on file as part of the master crisis plan. These two lists are "living" and since they are subject to change need to be regularly updated by an assigned staff or team member.

All staff shall receive comprehensive training on the crisis management plan and will receive a copy of their specific accountabilities and actions to take when the plan is activated.

Your "top down" ownership of the program means just that. Staff or board meetings must set aside specific time on the agenda on a regular basis that includes a discussion of crisis management preparedness as a mandatory item. You have to give it more than lip service and you must make the discussion substantive with participation and decision making occurring to resolve any barriers to completion. It's got to be more than a statistical report and it should include all levels of personnel in the presentation process. Take and preserve notes of all discussions and decisions that are made relevant to the plan and insure that the information flows downhill to all team members.

Crisis management planning issues should be part of your business planning process.

For public companies government regulations, have defined strategic implications for companies. For example, Security and Exchange Commission (SEC) regulations require in the section of the annual report entitled, "Management Analysis and Discussion" a discussion of potential liabilities. Your company response to strategic risks also falls under the Sarbanes-Oxley Act of 2002 that requires Financial and Accounting Disclosure Information.

What is most important is to make your plan part of your corporate culture by communicating compliance through all levels of the organization through company policies and procedures. This can be accomplished through formal adoption of policy at the highest levels of the company. That is why an in-depth analysis of your company operating environment is necessary and important before you develop and implement your Crisis Plan. It makes little sense to require the completion and implementation of a detail heavy plan for an organization that does not have a significant number of written policies and procedures otherwise. The participants will simply not know how to respond.

Preparing Your Plan

Your Crisis Plan needs to address a series of goals. The primary purpose of putting a plan together in the first place needs to focus on prevention first. Fixing what is broken should be your final concern, when all else has failed.

Prevention Is The Real Crisis Plan Purpose

If you have been following along with our recommendations to create a Crisis Plan by now you pretty much know where you are at from a risk position standpoint having used the Security Wise Group survey form, you have performed a SWOT analysis along with the Loss Prevention Survey and you have been looking at your company culture and assets and have begun to develop a vision of where you want to go in terms of Goals and Activities that you will need to pursue.

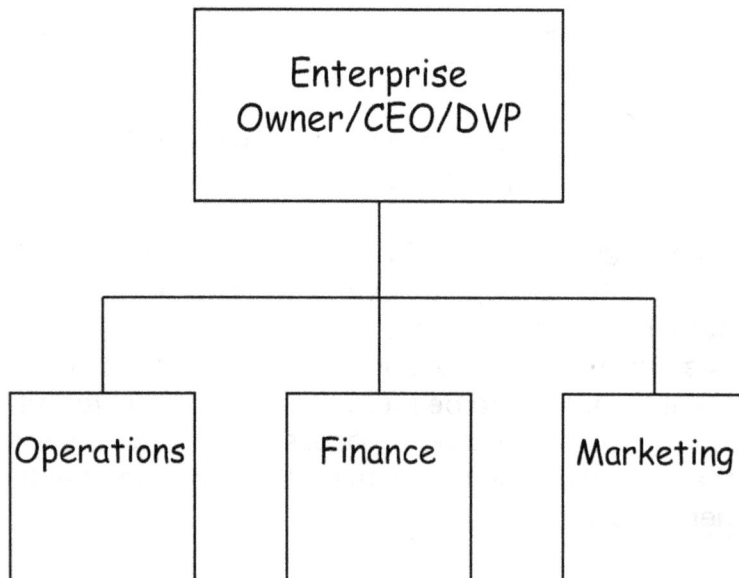

```
            ┌─────────────────────┐
            │     Enterprise      │
            │   Owner/CEO/DVP     │
            └─────────────────────┘
                      │
        ┌─────────────┼─────────────┐
        │             │             │
  ┌───────────┐ ┌───────────┐ ┌───────────┐
  │Operations │ │  Finance  │ │ Marketing │
  │           │ │           │ │           │
  └───────────┘ └───────────┘ └───────────┘
```

The real call to action is to first sit down with all of the key people in your organization and agree on the plan content, who will be responsible for the plan initiatives and when it will be completed.

If you have not taken the time to create an organizational chart and a business function chart that aligns tasks under the direction of your key people, you have some remedial work to do before you create the content of your business plan.

Our illustration shows a typical business organization chart of the primary roles of Operations, Finance and Marketing. In a mid-sized company, these positions can have a number of different titles such as "Director of" or Manager" or might even simply be business partners who have agreed on what the division of labor will be in the organization. The assumption here is that the boss is really responsible for the results of the entire enterprise or at least a subdivision in the case of a larger organization.

Functions To Operate The Business (1)

FUNCTION	MKT	OPS	FIN	Position	Person	Date
Answer the Telephone		x				
Customer Service		x				
Dispatch		x				
Field Service-Architecture Hdwe		x				
Field Service-Auto		x				
Field Service-EAC,CCTV		x				
Field Service-Key Systems		x				
Field Service-Safes		x				
Field SURVEY		x				
Fleet Management		x				
Purchase		x				
Maintenance		x				
Set Up		x				
Hiring/Training		x				
Job Prep		x				
Job Scheduling		x				

Before you can logically create written job descriptions or agreements at any level of the organization, it is important to identify all of the functional tasks that you perform within your company. A number of tasks may cross functional lines and as a rule decisions must be made related to who will be accountable.

As an example of this process, we can offer these three charts that are really one continuous one that divides up tasks. Our example begins with what functions fall into the Operations realm delineating all of this particular organizations' measurable tasks.

Functions To Operate The Business (2)

FUNCTION	MKT	OPS	FIN	Position	Person	Date
Keying Systems Preparation		x				
Lock Services-Bench		x				
Materials Handling		x				
Pick, Pack & Ship		x				
Technical Services		x				
Advertising	x					
Correspondence	x					
Field Sales	x					
Local Sales	x					
Regional Sales	x					
Field Service-Residential	x					
Marketing	x					
Concept/Implementation	x					
Fulfillment	x					
Phone Sales (Proactive)	x					

Operations positions needed to perform all of these functions will vary by organization, but will typically include all of the front line employees engaged in production, customer contact or clerks, line supervisors and the array of managers who are accountable for the performance of their subordinates.

Everyone all the way down the line from top to bottom needs to have a written job description that identifies what role each plays in the completion of the tasks.

Finance is addressed in the third chart and identifies the particular tasks that the group performs in support of the organizations profit plan. With the need to have job agreements/ descriptions for every one of your employees is a very complicated process best achieved in larger organizations by your in house or outsourced Human Resources staff.

Smaller organizations will find that many tasks that are occurring will not be delegated to subordinates because there may not be an actual person to delegate the task to. That means the people responsible for the function have to do it themselves or create a case to add an employee position.

Until you have identified what current employee position in your organization is charged with the responsibility for each functional task list, it is really difficult to create action plans that identify measurable tasks that must be performed in order to meet the goals of the business initiatives that you are trying to achieve.

Functions To Operate The Business (3)

FUNCTION	MKT	OPS	FIN	Position	Person	Date
Promotions	x					
Prepare Proposal	x					
Store Sales	x					
Accounts Payable			x			
Accounts Receivable			x			
Benefits Purchase & Admin			x			
Bookkeeping			x			
Computers & Equipment			x			
Human Resources			x			
Insurances			x			
Inventory			x			
Legal			x			
Payroll			x			
Purchasing-NEW			x			
Purchasing-Rebuy			x			
Prepare Quote			x			
Pricing			x			
Approve Credit			x			
Tax			x			
Workman's Comp			x			

So like Steven Covey tells us in his 7 Habits Of Highly Effective People, "First Things First". By identifying the positional skills that exist in your organization you will know how much of a stretch it will be to change course and begin your transition to proactive planning.

A major piece of your planning process involves the format of the plan itself. It really is important to use tools that everyone understands to create a plan with a distinct process that will allow you to walk your key managers through a process that can then be used subsequently with their subordinates.

The planning format that we like and have used for a number of years is called "SMART Planning". We're not sure where this tool came from so credit will not be given. Coming from the corporate world, I have used it as an operational tool for at least 20 years.

The process takes off when a goal is determined by you and the key members of your organization. For instance, let's say that you want to use your people and resources to begin to transition into a more proactive business Crisis Plan by expanding your loss prevention program to include a new electronic IP camera system that can be remotely monitored by you or a third party service company. The product selection needs to be made, you have to develop a budget to track the cost of installation and determine what an acceptable operating cost in terms of monitoring and maintenance will be.

So you have researched a number of possibilities and have narrowed the selection to a particular manufacturer and model of an IP camera and recording system. You now need to put the process in writing.

So, what is SMART Planning?

The SMART acronym is used in your plan development as a tool to devise a system that you follow through to the completion of the goal. All of your goals are stated in terms of the five steps as you develop your plan

SMART planning
What does it stand for?

Specific

Measurable

Actions

Resources

Time

SMART is an acronym that highlights the key requirements for any desired goal.

As it clearly states in this process, you have to be able to identify your specific goal or objective. The goal has to have measurable benefits to your company and action steps need to be identified to make the goal achievable as well as measurable. Resources to complete the goal must be identified such as security program development, staffing to conduct the purchase and installation process and to roll out the system. Often this is the hardest part of the process as it is likely that your resources have a limit and may seem to be already stretched. It's time to think about letting go of activities that are less profitable and consume more resources than they should.

Finally, all of the actions steps must be time bound with measurable completed action steps by the end of your business year or whatever timeline you have decided is realist and achievable. The rest of the process is to decide who will be responsible for the completion of all of the action steps that you will identify as needed to complete the goal successfully. The plan is completed on worksheets similar to the following example.

Use the form on Page 284 to complete all of your goals that need to be developed into action oriented steps that identify the completion dates for each and who will be responsible and accountable for the completion of the tasks.

This process will be pretty easy to put together if you have completed your business functions form that we showed you earlier in this chapter. Each of your goals will very likely involve operations, finance and marketing to a varying degree and you will need to determine where the resources will be coming from in order to support your goals.

The SMART Plan form works as your template for all of the subordinate tasks that need to be developed and assigned to particular individuals or groups in support of your specific plan goals.

So your proactive planning and

SMART planning
What does it mean?

what are your **S**pecific objectives?

are there any **M**easurable benefits?

what **A**ctions need to be taken?

what **R**esources are required to achieve this?

how much **T**ime is required?

SMART Plan - *(title here.)*

Target: *(Write the target of this document here)*		**Department:**		
Specific	**Measurable**	**Actions**	**Resources**	**Time**
What specific objectives will achieve your target?	*What are the measurable results of achieving your target?*	*What actions need to be completed before your target can be achieved?*	*What resources do you require to complete each of the objectives?*	*What time is needed to complete each of the actions?*

preparation process has identified all of activities that you will implement that are directed at preventing the crisis from happening, reducing the impact of a crisis, mitigate and recover from a crisis. It will include development and implementation of the Crisis Management Program, development and implementation of the Crisis Management Plan, implementing procedures and development and the implementation of Crisis Management/Response Training for all employees.

Plan elements will include exactly what crisis elements will trigger the activation of the plan, the procedures and the organization. Specific plan activities that are implemented in your response plan are directed at saving lives, preventing further damage, reducing the effects of the crisis on your business and support business continuation.

Finally, your plan must include all of the actions steps that can be taken to return your business to normal and include a process of critiquing the crisis to identify plan element changes that must be made to better prevent the possible occurrence of a similar event. Plan Training.

Just because you have published a plan, doesn't mean that it will work when needed unless you have trained all of the participants in the details of their role accountabilities and re-train on a regular basis. Your training Plan needs to be systematic and scripted so all training is presented in a complete form to all groups of managers attending. Training should include lesson plans; performance standards and proficiency testing that ideally include a field exercise to role-play.

A key part of the plan development was to create written job descriptions outlining step-by-step procedures that each team member will follow in the event of a crisis. The script or objective approach is essential to ensure that all of the important plan activities are performed in the sequence needed. You will need visual aids for the presentation as well a method for each team member to carry away their part of the plan in a format easily and readily retrieved when needed.

Finally, you need to document all of the plan creation, implementation and training data since this documentation could be potentially critical to your defense in the event that litigation develops following the crisis. It is not unheard of to be sued for what you did or did not due when a crisis occurs.

Successful response to any crisis depends on your management, response and communication. Response is critical to save lives and property but your ability to communicate can save your business!

No corporation looks forward to facing a situation that causes a significant disruption to their business, especially one that stimulates extensive media coverage. Public scrutiny can result in a negative financial, political, legal and government impact. Crisis management planning deals with providing the best response to a crisis.

Preparing a contingency plan in advance, as part of a crisis management plan, is a major step to ensuring an organization is appropriately prepared for a crisis. Crisis management teams can rehearse crisis plan by developing a simulated scenario to use as a drill. The plan should clearly stipulate that the only people to speak publicly about the crisis are the designated persons, such as the company spokesperson or crisis team members. The first hours after a crisis breaks are the most crucial, so working with speed and efficiency is important, and the plan should indicate how quickly each function should be performed. When preparing to offer a statement externally as well as internally, information should be accurate. Providing incorrect or manipulated information has a tendency to backfire and will greatly exacerbate the situation. The contingency plan should contain information and guidance that will help decision makers to consider not only the short-term consequences, but the long-term effects of every decision.

When a crisis will undoubtedly cause a significant disruption to an organization, a business continuity plan can help minimize the disruption. First, one must identify the critical functions and processes that are necessary to keep the organization running. Then each critical function and or/process must have its own contingency plan in the event that one of the functions/processes ceases or fails. Testing these contingency plans by rehearsing the required actions in a simulation will allow for all involved to become more sensitive and aware of the possibility of a crisis. As a result, in the event of an actual crisis, the team members will act more quickly and effectively.

Communications Issues

A Crisis Communication management plan should be part of an overall safety and emergency preparedness plan and a standard part of your overall strategic planning process. As important as dealing with any emergency situation is dealing with perceptions – what the public thinks happened. This should be planned in the same way you would plan for damage to property or injuries to people. Planning for perception will also protect your company's image/credibility and its ability to recover after a crisis.

Use a company spokesperson

Too often, companies make the mistake of waiting until a crisis occurs to plan a reaction. This gives the company the smallest chance of surviving the crisis without damage. Be prepared ahead of time and your company has the greatest chance to weather the crisis unharmed.

How you communicate your companies positions and response to a crises can give your recovery efforts a big boost.

The following from the American Transportation Association offers some easy to remember guidelines on getting started with your crisis communications plan:

- Predict   Anticipate everything that could go wrong with your company. Identify the issues.

- Position   Decide what your position will be on these issues.

- Prevent   Take preventive measures.

- Plan   In case prevention doesn't work, prepare a plan for dealing with the crisis.

- Persevere   Follow your plan and stick to the positions you have taken. See the crisis through in a thorough and professional manner.

- Evaluate   If the plan is enacted, review the results to determine if there are other steps that can be taken to prevent the crisis from happening again.

These steps will help get your crisis management plan started and keep it vital and updated as your surroundings change.

Issue Identification

Identifying issues is an ongoing process. The crisis team should identify every imaginable issue and list them, starting with the most likely to happen. Crisis issues can generally be put in two categories – man made or natural.

Man made issues include violence, vandalism, accidents, operator error, negligence, defective equipment, poor planning and scheduling, strikes, fire, and illness such as food poisoning. Natural issues include things such as weather, earthquakes and communicable disease.

Some examples of potential issues to consider include motorcoach or plane accidents, robbery, death on tour, strikes, natural disasters, bankruptcy, terrorism or war, and travel scams. Even if such a crisis does not happen to your particular company, but happens to another similar business or industry partner, be prepared to answer questions regarding your readiness should you face the same situation. The crisis team should continually look for potential issues and develop a plan of action should that issue become a reality. That will keep your crisis management plan up to date and vital.

Policy Preparation

When preparing policy statements, the following general principles can help.

- When responding to a crisis situation, the response should be honest, timely and direct. Having a prepared, approved and distributed policy document will help you resist the temptation to say "no comment" or have your company appear uncooperative or secretive during a crisis situation.
- Incorporate your ethical standards into the policy. Do the right thing, being fair to all parties to the best of your ability.
- Think now about how your business practices will be interpreted by the media during an emergency. In addition to specific policy statements, it is important to have background information on your company available. It is your responsibility and in your best interest to provide current, complete information.

Preparing Specific Responses

After issues have been identified, specific responses for each should be prepared. Consider the following checklist when drafting position statements:

- Define the scope of the crisis – local, regional, national or international.
- Establish a unified response – one spokesperson, one person established to distribute statements to the media, etc.
- Keep the message simple, clear, consistent and tailored to each audience.

Understand that the media wants to know three things: what happened, why did it happen and what are you going to do to make sure that it never happens again?

If you understand the media's psyche, you are on your way to finding a solution to the problem. Once position statements have been prepared for each issue identified by the crisis team, include them in your overall crisis management document. In addition, prepare sample press releases for each issue in advance. It will be much easier to modify an existing, approved release than to start from scratch in the middle of a crisis.

In addition to the policy statements and press releases, anticipate questions that will be asked by the media. List the questions with developed answers that the crisis team is comfortable with and continually update the list as new questions are identified.

Finally, the news media must be briefed on a regular basis. All phone calls from the media must be answered quickly and completely. Keep a media log listing the date and time, source, reporter, phone number and the question. Stick to your core message and deliver that message to everyone.

Post-crisis Review

As mentioned previously, the crisis management process does not end once a crisis has occurred and been resolved. Each situation should be carefully evaluated. Look at the media coverage received, the resulting image of your company, short- and long-term programs to rebuild image and review position statements for relevance and necessary revisions.

Only after a crisis management plan has been put to the test can the crisis team evaluate its effectiveness. If a company has been lucky enough not to have a crisis situation in which to test its plan, it should be constantly monitored to make sure the position statements are still relevant and no new issues have arisen. A crisis management plan should be a living document, undergoing constant evaluation and updates.

The bottom line when facing the media and preparing press releases is to be honest and open with any and all questions. Say it like it is. Point out the bad as well as the good and inform them of the steps your company has taken or will take to ensure that such a crisis be avoided in the future. State your company's position and then support that position with fact. Honesty and preparedness will help your company weather the crisis and keep your reputation intact!

We can share some of the following Crisis Management **Lessons From Successes**.

Tylenol (Johnson & Johnson):

In the fall of 1982, a murderer added 65 milligrams of cyanide to some Tylenol capsules on store shelves, killing seven people, including three in one family. Johnson & Johnson recalled and destroyed 31 million capsules at a cost of $100 million. CEO, James Burke, appeared in television ads and at news conferences informing consumers of the company's actions. Tamper-resistant packaging was rapidly introduced, and Tylenol sales swiftly bounced back to near pre-crisis levels.

Johnson & Johnson was again struck by a similar crisis in 1986 when a New York woman died on Feb. 8 after taking cyanide-laced Tylenol capsules. Johnson & Johnson was ready. Responding swiftly and smoothly to the new crisis, it immediately and indefinitely canceled all television commercials for Tylenol, established a toll-free telephone hot-line to answer consumer questions and offered refunds or exchanges to customers who had purchased Tylenol capsules. At week's end, when another bottle of tainted Tylenol was discovered in a store, it took only a matter of minutes for the manufacturer to issue a nationwide warning that people should not use the medication in its capsule form.

Odwalla Foods:

When Odwalla's apple juice was thought to be the cause of an outbreak of E. coli bacteria, the company lost a third of its market value. In October 1996, an outbreak of E. coli bacteria in Washington state, California, Colorado and British Columbia was traced to unpasteurized apple juice manufactured by natural juice maker Odwalla Inc. Forty-nine cases were reported, including the death of a small child.

Within 24 hours, Odwalla conferred with the FDA and Washington state health officials; established a schedule of daily press briefings; sent out press releases which announced the recall; expressed remorse, concern and apology, and took responsibility for anyone harmed by their products; detailed symptoms of E. coli poisoning; and explained what consumers should do with any affected products. Odwalla then developed, with the help of consultants, effective thermal processing that would not harm the products' flavors when production resumed. All of these steps were communicated through close relations with the media and through full-page newspaper ads.

Mattel:

Mattel Inc., the country's biggest toy maker, has been plagued with more than 28 product recalls and in Summer of 2007, amongst problems with exports from China, faced two product recall in two weeks. The company "did everything it could to get its message out, earning high marks from consumers and retailers. Though upset by the situation, they were appreciative of the company's response. At Mattel, just after the 7 A.M. recall announcement by federal officials, a public relations staff of 16 was set to call reporters at the 40 biggest media outlets. They told each to check their e-mail for a news release outlining the recalls, invited them to a teleconference call with executives and scheduled TV appearances or phone conversations with Mattel's chief executive. The Mattel CEO Robert Eckert did 14 TV interviews on a Tuesday in August and about 20 calls with individual reporters. By the week's end, Mattel had responded to more than 300 media inquiries in the U.S. alone"

On The Negative Side - Some Lessons From Losses

On the other hand, Lessons From Losses in crisis management can also be called Impact of Catastrophes on Shareholder Value! One of the key conclusions of a number of studies is that effective management of the consequences of catastrophes would appear to be a more significant factor than not planning for a potential crisis but instead using insurance to hedge the economic impact of the catastrophe.

Bhopal:

The Bhopal disaster in which poor communication before, during, and after the crisis cost thousands of lives, illustrates the importance of incorporating cross-cultural communication in crisis management plans. According to American University's Trade Environmental Database Case Studies (1997), local residents were not sure how to react to warnings of potential threats from the Union Carbide plant. Operating manuals printed only in English is an extreme example of mismanagement but indicative of systemic barriers to information diffusion. According to Union Carbide's own chronology of the incident (2006), a day after the crisis Union Carbide's upper management arrived in India but was unable to assist in the relief efforts because they were placed under house arrest by the Indian government.

Symbolic intervention can be counter productive; a crisis management strategy can help upper management make more calculated decisions in how they should respond to disaster scenarios. The Bhopal incident illustrates the difficulty in consistently applying management standards to multi-national operations and the blame shifting that often results from the lack of a clear management plan.

Ford and Firestone Tire and Rubber Company:

The Ford-Firestone dispute transpired in August 2000. In response to claims that their 15-inch Wilderness AT, radial ATX and ATX II tire treads were separating from the tire core, leading to grisly, spectacular crashes. Bridgestone/Firestone recalled 6.5 million tires. These tires were mostly used on the Ford Explorer, the world's top-selling sport utility vehicle (SUV). The two companies' committed three major blunders early on, say crisis experts. First, they blamed consumers for not inflating their tires properly. Then they blamed each other for faulty tires and faulty vehicle design. Then they said very little about what they were doing to solve a problem that had caused more than 100 deaths -- until they got called to Washington to testify before Congress.

Exxon:

On March 24, 1989, a tanker belonging to the Exxon Corporation ran aground in the Prince William Sound in Alaska. The Exxon Valdez spilled millions of gallons of crude oil into the waters off Valdez, killing thousands of fish, fowl, and sea otters. Hundreds of miles of coastline were polluted and salmon spawning runs disrupted; numerous fishermen, especially Native Americans, lost their livelihoods. Exxon, by contrast, did not react quickly in terms of dealing with the media and the public. The CEO, Lawrence Rawl, did not become an active part of the public relations effort and actually shunned public involvement.

The company had neither a communication plan nor a communication team in place to handle the event.   In fact, the company did not appoint a public relations manager to its management team until 1993, 4 years after the incident.

Exxon established its media center in Valdez, a location too small and too remote to handle the onslaught of media attention and the company acted defensively in its response to the public, even laying blame at times on other groups such as the Coast Guard.

Government And Crisis Management

Historically, government at all levels has played a large role in crisis management.   It is considered to be one of the primary roles of government. Emergency services, such as fire and police departments at the local level, and the United States National Guard at the federal level, often play integral roles in crisis situations.

To help coordinate communication during the response phase of a crisis, the U.S. Federal Emergency Management Agency (FEMA) within the Department of Homeland Security administers the National Response Plan (NRP). This plan is intended to integrate public and private response by providing a common language and outlining a chain-of-command when multiple parties are mobilized. It is based on the premise that incidences should be handled at the lowest organizational level possible. The NRP recognizes the private sector as a key partner in domestic incident management, particularly in the area of critical infrastructure protection and restoration.

A crisis management plan is designed to provide guidelines for a practical communications system that is adaptable for any crisis situation. It should be a working document – continually updated as the industry, the world and your company changes.

One would assume that most companies have responded to the Sept.11 terrorist attacks by making crisis preparedness a high priority. However, according to the American Management Association, a recent survey on Crisis Management and Security showed that 51 percent of the organizations do not have a crisis management in place and 59 percent to not have written policies and procedures for crisis management.

Your worst nightmare could turn out to be what happened to a lot of companies following Hurricane Katrina in 2005. The business in the foreground is gone! Now What?

With the incidents of Sept. 11 the need for such a crisis management plan to be in place and for companies, regardless of size, to be prepared for the unexpected is more important than ever before.

Mitigation and Recovery

Mitigation begins when the crisis is detected, the Crisis Plan is triggered and specific actions must take place by the team members quickly to prevent loss of life or injury and begin the process of reacting to existing conditions that can affect the organization whether planned for or not. The amount of planning you do up front will have a direct impact on how long it will take you to get up and running after the crises. When all is said and done, literally, you get to enter the recovery phase when you can breath a sigh of relief and move on to business as usual. But remember, a new crises can happen, but you can now use your planning and systems that you put in place to lessen the severity and speed the recovery.

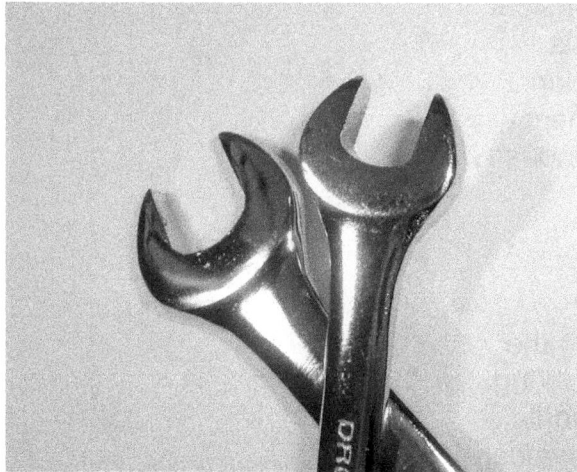

Tighten the connections!

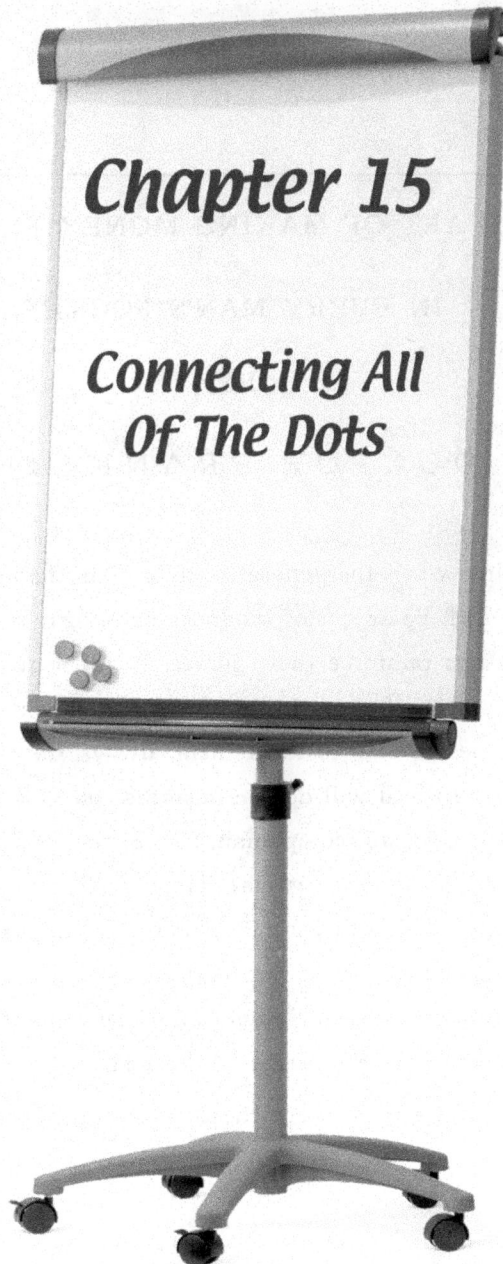

THE ART OF MAKING MONEY PLENTY

IN EVERY MAN'S POCKET

BY

D O C T O R   F R A N K L I N

At this time when the general complaint is that money is so scarce it must be an act of kindness to inform the moneyless how they can reinforce their purses. I will acquaint all with the true secret of money catching, the certain way to fill empty purses & how to keep them always full. Two simple rules well observed will do the business. 1st Let honesty and labor be thy constant companions: 2d Spend one penny every day less than thy clear gains: Then shall thy purses soon begin to thrive, thy creditors will never insult thee nor want oppress nor hunger bite, nor naked freeze thee, the whole hemisphere will shine brighter, and pleasure spring up in every corner of thy heart.

Now thereby embrace these rules and be happy.

B. Franklin. Born Jany. 7th, 1706, O.S. Died Apr. 17th, 1790

Competitive Advantage, you have learned, is about understanding and adopting best practices related to preventing losses. This book has given the reader some food for thought regarding the planning and execution of a new loss prevention program. We hope that the information is useful and that you are able to use it to your best advantage. Since we have raised a number of topics, it seems prudent to spend some time on connecting it all together to show you how all of the tools and policies work together to provide you with a much harder target.

We are also compelled to share with you that regardless of all of your planning and thoughtful program execution, there is always the possibility that a dishonest employee or some other crook will find a way to slip through a protection gap and steal your money. We find that this occurs most often when a policy or procedure that you thought was in place has been either found by your managers to be either too cumbersome to consistently execute or doesn't make sense to them or other wise lacks buy-in and compliance.

We need to return to the 80-10-10 rule and remind ourselves that the 10% of employees who are dishonest are actively looking for these gaps in your program and will test the system in a minor way to see if anyone notices. Then if the opportunity and reward are adequate, you may experience a large theft. Your best defense is to initiate an active internal audit program that reviews policy compliance on a regular basis. The object of the exercise is to eliminate surprises! Finding out that your people are not following policies and procedures needs to be discovered and correct before you have a loss that may then require you to go through a painful recovery process that may include the need to terminate the employment of someone that you like a lot.

The purpose of the cash and systems control audit is not only to test compliance, but also to determine what the possible reasons might be when a gap in your program surfaces on a fairly widespread basis. While conducting security and safety audits, we have often found compliance issues especially when tasks that should be automated by your POS system are instead required by the rules to be completed manually such as a paper check list or signatures or initials on a form. People just hate to be constantly signing or initialing paperwork and simply won't do it if given the choice.

Paper forms are subject to storage and retention policies to be effective. What that means is that you now need a policy that states how another policy must be executed and how proof of the policy execution should be stored for audit purposes! If you are writing policies to control other policies, you might want to take another look at your methods.

You really need to get comfortable thinking outside the box. That means not making assumptions about why the rules are not being followed, but take the initiative of talking to the people that have to comply with it to find out why it's not working and what can be done instead.

Let's look at what problems that you have solved in our loss that occurred in Chapter One and some issues that can arise, even with a well-executed loss prevention program.

First of all, let's assume that you took our advice and got some professional help by retaining the consulting services of a CPP loss prevention professional to help you sort out the issues and priorities of a new loss prevention program.   Most importantly, all of the service providers you needed to implement all of these changes were identified and the CPP helped you with the project management to get the program moving.

There were a number of issues that arose during the analysis of the loss:

REMEMBER WHAT THE POLICE FOUND WHEN THEY INVESTIGATED:

- **There was no forced entry.**

- **They were unable to lift any latent fingerprints.**

- **The safe was loaded on the store hand truck and it and the $12,657 inside was wheeled out the back door.**

- **There were no witnesses.**

- **Store locks had not been changed for years. Many current and former managers potentially had access.**

- **They think it was an inside job but do not have a suspect.**

WHAT YOU NEEDED TO FIX:

1.   You didn't have a system in place to control building access.

You have followed our advice and now have a new key control system with a patented key that can only be replaced by the manufacturer. Each authorized employee has signed for their keys and has acknowledged that they understand the key control policies and the consequences for non-compliance.

A burglary that occurs using a key will now be attributable to an authorized user of which there are only a few for each location. An ounce of prevention has been achieved since few would risk either using their key for a criminal act or giving it to another.

Next year, you plan on replacing interior locksets with stand-alone electronic locks to increase controls on inventory storage.

2.   You didn't have a system in place to detect or deter intruders at night.

You have improved the exterior lighting to your industry standard and the place looks like Yankee Stadium on game night! You know that was a good move, because your nighttime traffic flow has increased and your sales are way up over last year. A somewhat lower level of lighting illuminates all of your buildings at night making illegal entry an event in full view of passersby's and police.

Your new alarm systems can detect an intruder at all possible points of entry and even if they cut a hole in the roof, it will detect them when they walk within any PIR zone. They can't disable the alarm signal from going to the central station because you have installed a radio back up system that alerts the central station even if the phone lines are cut.

You have also arranged for alarm verification service that can bring up your store video system using your DSL line and an Internet connection to determine if the alarm is real or false. And they can record some dandy pictures of the crooks if a burglary is in progress at the same time that the police are notified and given alarm information and a description of the bad guys. Lights, camera and action!

3.   You needed to review your hiring practices.

You now have a better idea about who you are hiring after you heard that only 35% of employers conduct background investigations on their new hires. You also took your attorneys advice and conduct pre-hire drug testing as well as random testing and testing whenever an employee accident occurs. You are doing what you can to ensure that you are hiring and retaining the best.

4.   You needed a new safe.

After taking a look at your existing safes, you found that it was cost effective to switch to a time lock armored car unit. You may not do armored car right away at all of your locations but having the right equipment gives you the flexibility to add the service later if conditions warrant or otherwise makes good economic sense. Yes, they are all bolted to the floor!
Most importantly, you have procedures in place that allows you to have a better working relationship with the new armored car service provider and have had fewer problems with banking issues.

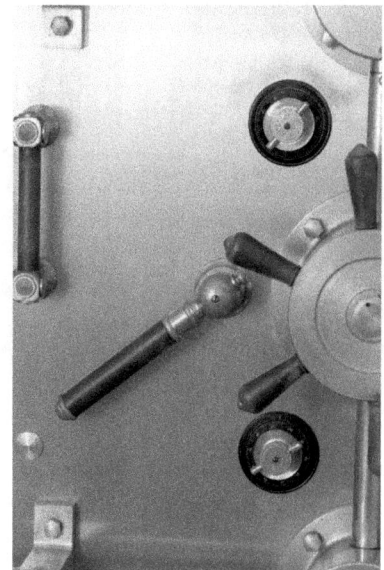

5.   You needed to review all policies and procedures related to security and cash handling.

Putting together an employee handbook and a manual of all of the policies and procedures that your company needed was a major task made a lot easier with the help of your CPP loss prevention consultant who helped you with the writing and program roll-out to your managers and employees. You also found out that by reprogramming your POS system, a lot of unnecessary paperwork could be eliminated and this made your managers very happy and it also made the necessary buy in by your managers and employees easier.

6.   There is a lot of money missing and no suspects.

Alas, the money is still missing and this time the crime went unsolved. There were just too few leads for the police to follow and bring the investigation to a positive conclusion this time.

But if there is a next time, you will be ready for them!

7.   You needed to be able to trust your employees again.

To a large degree, your trust in your employees has been restored but you keep coming back to the fact that where people and money are concerned, you simply cannot afford to trust all of your people. That crooked 10% will always be out there to take advantage. You might take comfort in the fact that you will employ a smaller percentage of the employees, who are dishonest, if you make it harder for them to get away with it. They won't stay if you make their lives too difficult.

We told you that sometimes no matter how well you have executed your loss prevention program you will have losses. The fact is some people believe that they need the money more than they need their job or even self-respect. So they will steal knowing that they will soon be caught, fired and maybe prosecuted. We have had individuals admit to us that they stole to pay for an alarming number of addictions ranging from heroin to horse racing!

Often small losses will occur as a pattern that can be detected fairly quickly if you have a regular cash audit and good inventory controls in place. Signs will surface that might include a spike in inventory cost or reduced sales volume during a day-part where sales have been otherwise growing and trackable to a particular register operator or manager.

If the small losses go undetected, the problem can go from bad to worse as the dishonest employees perceived need to steal grows with time. In our experience, it will grow and the employee will continue to steal until they are caught.

Our best advise to the small to mid-sized business owner is to consult with your CPP Loss Prevention Professional when a loss occurs that has potentially bypassed your prevention efforts. Staying ahead of the crooks is often more "art" than "science" and you must be willing to make program adjustments.

The more time you spend on "the plan" The better the results will be.

Consider how you would solve the following case…

Lessons From Losses - Inventory Theft!

Having a business partner can be a good thing especially if they are putting up some growth capital and want to work as hard as you do. But "unofficial partners" who steal your assets are not.

Tom was a general manager in charge of a corporate owned fast food restaurant in the Northeast. The business did an average volume of $29,000 a week with just fair operations and had an above average food cost variance. Based on some fairly strict food usage recipes practiced by the company allowing for ½% of sales for waste, actual food usage exceeded the theoretical by 2.5%.   So historically, weekly actual inventories showed that more was used than was sold by a significant percentage of sales. In fact, when you convert food cost variance as a percentage of sales to actual dollars, the unaccounted for loss ran about $580 a week. Yes, that equals a little over $15,000 annualized cash loss for the missing food.

Sometimes it occurs in large organizations and small ones too, mediocre performance can be allowed to continue indefinitely due to the inattention of the management above the unit level especially if there are a number of even worse performing stores that need attention.

Also sometimes the solution to the problem surfaces just because someone asks the right questions. In this case a new District Manager on his first visit to the restaurant sat down with the assistant manager on duty and asked; "Why do you think your food cost is so high?"

Startled that no one had ever asked before, the assistant said; "Well, Tom the boss makes food deliveries each week to some local school lunch programs and I don't think I have ever seen him ring in the sales when he returns".

Before talking to the general manager, it was decided to find out what orders were being prepared and delivered to the school lunch program so the schools were contacted and the people in charge of their programs were asked to tell us about any customer service issues that they might have or any comments on the food quality and prices that they were paying. The customer service approach determined that each week, the general manager brought in extra help to prepare a order totaling approximately $350 at each of a varying number of private and parochial schools in the area.   He personally delivered the orders and as far as anyone knew it was just a normal business transaction (food safety issues aside!).

The previous district manager had approved the catering operation and had never really followed up on how much revenue was occurring.

An audit of sales records found that indeed none of the sales had actually been rung into the system. Based on the statements and records provided by the "lunch ladies", a case was presented to the local police who arrested the general manager. First offense theft convictions usually get probation and restitution in that state and that's what eventually happened.

There are a number of tools that restaurant company owners can use to control costs. If you're part of a franchise system, your company can help with the particulars of what works for them. Having said that, there are many more independent operators versus franchises that can help themselves by putting a few easily audited control systems in place.

Portion control is very important in every restaurant. Each product you sell has to have a recipe that requires consistent food product components for every order.

Bun +meat patty +lettuce leaf +tomato slice +cheese slice +special sauce = Cheeseburger!

You can determine the food cost of each component as a portion of the whole unit of measure. You know what you are paying for meat patties per pound, head lettuce and tomatoes by the case, buns by the dozen etc. The idea is to break down the component cost for each item to determine what to sell the finished product for after factoring other operational costs. Your POS system can supply you with a product mix report telling you how many of each menu item that you are selling each day even by the hour if you want.

Once you have an ideal or theoretical food cost and a product mix report, you can track shortages by the day part by conducting targeted inventories at the start of day, shift change and close. You would usually want to target count your major food cost items like meat and chicken by the pound. If the targeted inventory on Tuesday night for instance shows that you are short 8 pounds of meat, you need to ask where the money for 30 sandwiches went!

Setting a standard of food waste is important to your quality of food and service and to track exactly what you are throwing away. All food waste whether due to careless handling, over production on the grill or returned orders can be tracked on a shift report using a special waste bucket for all items to be thrown away. Waste charting is important obviously to determine why it is occurring but even more importantly it is part of your food cost variance.

If it's not in the food inventory and you can't find it in the chart/waste bucket it is very likely that the item was prepared, served, the sale not rung in and the money pocketed by one of your "unofficial partners". Theft of food is a distant second possibility for you to explore. Using the target inventory system will tell you what is missing and when it likely was taken so you can match up the people working to the loss trend information.

Food = Money

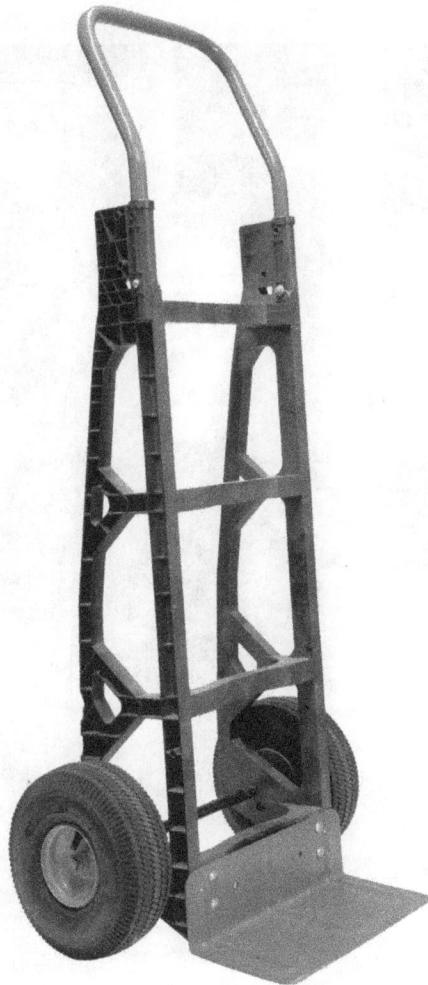

If you implement and execute
a well planned
Loss Prevention Program,
it won't be so easy next
time to break in, jack up the safe
and hand truck it out of the door!

"By failing to prepare, you are preparing to fail".

Benjamin Franklin

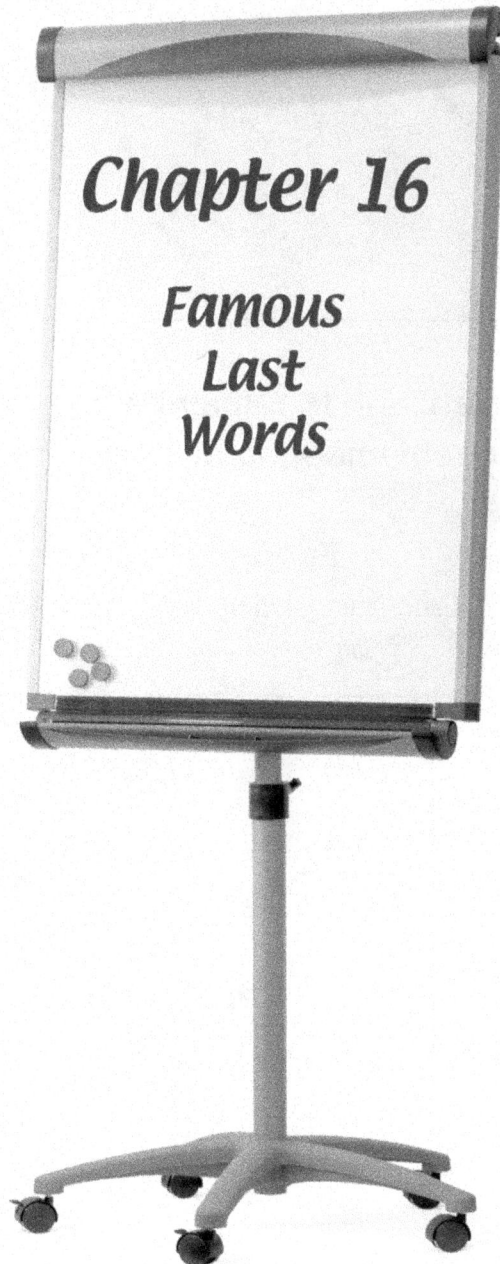

"It is hard enough to remember my opinions, without also remembering my reasons for them!"

Friedrich Nietzsche
German philosopher (1844 - 1900)

The final words regarding all of the things that we have mentioned in this book are to hope that what we have offered to you has been useful. We also hope that our book related to the subject of your business profits should at least offer some ideas that you may not have thought about doing.

The final thoughts we have to share with you are really about Change. Adopting a new business loss prevention plan that migrates from **Reactive To Proactive** may require many of you to drag yourselves and your employees kicking and screaming into the 21st century. Not only will you be adopting a lot of new technology, you will be required to seriously look at new rules that will impact your work flow.

"Change has a considerable psychological impact on the human mind. To the fearful it is threatening because it means that things may get worse. To the hopeful it is encouraging because things may get better. To the confident it is inspiring because the challenge exists to make things better".

King Whitney Jr.

Today's business world is highly competitive and many of us struggle to survive all of the pressures. The way to survive is to reshape to the needs of a rapidly changing world that has to include changing from reactive to proactive business practices in order to maximize our profits.

Organizations go through four main changes throughout their growth Daryl Conner tells us. Where is your organization on the cycle?

1.   Formative Period
A lot of experimentation and innovation taking place and changes of creativity and discovery are needed to overcome obstacles and accomplish breakthroughs.

2.   Rapid Growth Period
Change is focused on defining the purpose of the organization and on the mainstream business.

3.   Mature Period
Changes are needed to maintain established markets and assuring maximum gains are achieved.

4.   Declining Period
To survive, changes include tough objectives and compassionate implementation. The goal is to get out of the old and into something new. Success in this period means that the four periods start over again.

Change Acceptance

A good organization is always changing, leaders need to concentrate on having their people go from change avoidance to change acceptance. There are five steps accompanying change

(Conner, 1993):

  * Denial - cannot foresee any major changes
  * Anger at others for what they're putting me through
  * Bargaining - work out solutions, keep everyone happy
  * Depression - is it worth it? doubt, need support
  * Acceptance - the reality

This is why you and your employee's first reaction to change is often to resist it. People get comfortable performing tasks and processes in a particular manner. It's known as your "comfort level". The comfort part provides you with the security that you are in charge of your environment. Some of the things that cause you to fear change include a dislike of a disruption of your life, looking like a fool by not being able to adapt and learn new technologies like the first time you sat in front of a computer. You and your employees may fear that your jobs might become harder, and you can lose of control.

Leading the Change

It helps a lot to be able to change your questions from "Why do we have to do this?" to "What new opportunities will this provide?"

By spelling out the benefits, you will not only comfort your employees, but help to convince yourself too!

Martin Luther King did not say, "I have a very good plan," he shouted, "I have a dream!" You must provide passion and a strong sense of purpose of the change.

There is a story circulating around the Internet that describes an animal behavior study purported to have occurred at an unspecified university. As most of you know, there are a lot of unverified stories and urban legends floating around the Net. In a moment we'll tell you about the story, but first we have to tell you that we do not know if it is true or not. But, you can put the following into the category of being a parable or a fable. A parable tells a story that guides the reader through a set of circumstances that in the end states a lesson to be learned.

The story of the animal study goes like this...

A group of researchers start with a large cage containing five monkeys. Inside the cage they hang a banana on a string from the center of the ceiling and place a stepladder underneath. The experiment requires the monkeys to be moved from the cage each night, into their sleeping quarters, and the banana is replaced to keep the reward fresh and attractive. A very desirable reward and tools to access the reward has been created and implemented.

Before long, a monkey will go to the step ladder and start to climb towards the banana. As soon as he starts up the ladder, the researchers spray all of the monkeys with ice-cold water. The climbing stops! After a while, another monkey makes an attempt to go up the ladder with the same result; all the monkeys are sprayed with cold water. This repeated process might take several days. Eventually, the lesson will be learned to the point when another monkey tries to climb the ladder, the other monkeys will consistently try to prevent it from even taking the first step!

Next, the researchers stop with the cold-water treatment. They then remove one monkey from the cage and replace it with a new one. The new monkey sees the banana and wants to climb the ladder. To his surprise and horror, all of the other monkeys attack him. After a number of attempts and attacks, he knows that if he tries to climb the ladder, he will be enthusiastically assaulted!

Next, the researchers remove another of the original five monkeys and replace it with a new one. The newcomer goes to the ladder, tries to climb and is attacked. The previous newcomer takes part in the punishment with indignant glee because if he can't have the banana, neither can the newcomer! So it goes on and, they replace a third original monkey with a new one, then a fourth, then the fifth. Every time the newest monkey takes to the ladder, he is attacked.

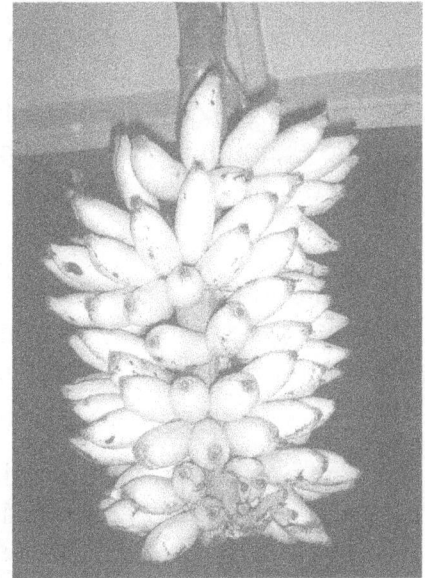

When all of the original monkeys have been replaced, the fact is none of the newer monkeys have ever been doused with cold water. Consequently, none of the monkeys know why they are beating the newcomer or why they are not permitted to climb the ladder!

Nevertheless, no monkey ever again approaches the ladder to try for the banana. Why not? Because, as far as they know that's the way it's always been done!

And that is how a company policy begins. And that type of company policy, like our parable, can stifle the creativity and innovation you need to be successful. We call it the "Paradigm Parable" (OK-we made that up). It is a false set of rules, beliefs or resistance to change that prevents you from growing your business.

You end up stuck in a box!

Those of us that have extensive experience working for large companies will immediately recognize what is going on here. Many large companies rigidly compartmentalize the necessary operational departments that often do not communicate well with one another and erect barriers to progress by establishing all kinds of protocols that must be hurdled before any innovative change is agreed upon, let alone implemented.   Protecting turf and managing careers becomes the primary activity!

Boy, can I tell you some war stories!   But guess what, small and medium sized business operators can fall into the same trap of rigidly defining their operation parameters that preclude innovation and growth because of failing to change with the industry trends.   As you know staying on top of your game requires a lot of hard work and an extensive dialog with your customers to see what they *need* versus trying to sell them what you have. That includes your operations procedures and policies that must proactively reflect your risk environment as your business grows.

Remember that we told you that rules have to make sense if you expect them to be followed.

Your examination can certainly look at the reason that a policy that you have deemed important to maintaining an audit trail is not being followed and whether the best path is disciplinary action or simply changing the policy to one that makes sense to the people who have to execute it. It is certainly okay to ask your employees why it does not make sense and what would.

Are you part of the problem or part of the solution? Are you locked into conducting your business the same way year in and year out because that is what you have always done? Have you resisted learning and adopting new technologies because it is outside your normal comfort zone?

The real point of this entire story is that if you want the reward, you have to use your tools to climb the ladder to get it. Notice that you can't get the reward by going sideways, you have to go up, *that is where the banana is!* The tools that you can use to create your blueprint and execute your loss prevention plan can be found in this book.

It's all about communication and asking the right questions so that you can arrive at the right solutions that make sense to your enterprise.

The results of our survey, when reviewed by professionals, can supply you with a written report outlining the appropriate needs and loss exposures that you should address to prevent losses and become more profitable. Even if you don't have access to professionals you can get a lot of expertise from certified consultants and even get started yourself by taking the Survey and applying it to your unique business situation. The key is to go from **Reactive To Proactive.**

There you have it. We hope that you now have the tools and the understanding that you need to take positive advantage of the system and maximize your Competitive Advantage!

By the way... Enjoy Your Banana!

We think that your **Competitive Advantage** by adopting some of our recommendations will materialize very quickly, in some cases, depending on how many best practices are part of your company culture. And some will take a while to achieve.

Please remember, that everything that we have offered to you may not be cost effective or otherwise appropriate to your business type or environment. The items that are always "low hanging fruit" are the best practices that often have little cost and maximum positive benefit such as taking care of your employees through good compensation, training, supervision and encouragement and investing in programs and equipment that make sense for your business and have an identifiable return on investment.

We have shown you a number of forms and tools that you are welcome to use in your business as you develop your loss prevention program. If you like, as a special gift to the buyers of this book, send me an E-mail request and I will reply with a form copy of your choice in PDF format that you can copy and use.

Bill Wise CPP is a Certified Protection Professional and President of Security Wise Group LLC. Prior to founding SWG in 2004, he previously worked over 26 years as a security professional for large retail companies. His experience ranges from directing security and safety operations at hotel and convention complexes to the position of Regional Loss Prevention Manager for two Fortune 500 companies for over 24 years where he developed and implemented successful loss prevention strategies, policies, procedures and products. He is active in professional organizations as a Vice President for the Eastern States Criminal Investigators Association, a member of the American Society for Industrial Security, a member of the American Society of Safety Engineers and is certified by the Pennsylvania State Self Insurance Program.

Bill is also the author and publisher of ***Selling Security- Reactive Based Service To Proactive Marketing and Sales*** (2008 ISBN 9780615186023)

You can reach Bill at the Security Wise Group LLC website (www.securitywisegroup.com) or by E-mail at bill@securitywisegroup.com.

Your comments, praise and complaints are welcome!

Is it time to upgrade your business security program?

Competitive Advantage A to Z

Symbols

80-10-10 Rule 127
9/11 attacks 103

A

Abuse of company property 129
Access control points 22
Access controls 21
Accident 236, 238
Accident Prevention and Planning 251
Accident prevention committee 251
Accounting losses 229
Accounting procedures 9
Accounts receivable and accounts payable 184
Actions you can take 240
Acts of terrorism 39
Administrative error 229
Adverse government actions 276
Advice from counsel 228
AFTER A ROBBERY 215
Aftershocks 277
Aggravated assault 50
Alarm access codes and safe combination 76
Alarm central station monitoring 89
Alarm company 39, 89
Alarm components 94
Alarm electrical codes 89
Alarm installation issues 89
Alarm service providers 23
Alarm system maintenance 91
Alarm systems 297
Alarm systems priorities 97
ALCOHOL & DRUG ABUSE 198
Alert button 112
All hazards approach 277
American Management Association 291
American National Standards Institute (ANSI) 37
Anchor the safe 219
Animal study 306
ANSI accreditation 37
ANSI American National Standards Institute 71
Anti-globalization 269
Applications contain fabrications 121
Appropriate gloves 242
Armed robberies 269
Armed robbery 16
Armored car banking services 57
Armored car companies 157
Armored car company 148
Armored Car Drop Log example 160

Arrange counters 222
Arrange displays 222
Arrests 49
Arrests of juveniles 49
A SERIES OF UNFORTUNATE EVENTS 15
ASIS board-certified professionals 38
ASIS certification programs 37
ASIS International 20, 37
Assault 131, 228
Assessing Crime Risks 41
Association of Certified Fraud Examiners 182
ATM machines 56
Attorney knowledgeable in labor laws 119
Audio recording 109
Audit feature 22
Auditors 187
Audit Trail 141
Authority to get the job done 241
Auto dialers 66
Automatically renewing contracts 158
Automatic window openers 216
Automation considerations 148
Avoid Lifting and Bending 247
Awareness programs 235

B

Back (Money) Window 110
Back Dock 113
Back door 15, 80, 110, 111
Back door alarm 95
Back door hazards 236
Back door local alarm 93
Back door viewing device 81
Background checks 125
Back Safety 247
Back up power supplies 73
Bad banking procedures 213
Bank all registers 145
Bank frequently 219
Bank registers 143
Bankruptcy 187
Bank service company 164
Barricade traffic areas 246
Before You Open For Business 210
Best practices 169
Best response 285
Better attendance and lower turnover 122
Bill of lading 231
Biometrics 73
Bonding 31
Booster bag 221

Broadband DSL or cable 90
Bubble or housing 109
Bureau of Labor Statistics 247
Burglar-resistant glass 84
Burglar alarm protection 22
Burglar alarm system 112
BURGLARY 216
Burglary 15, 24, 43, 55, 296
Burglary offenses 217
Burglary protection 92
Business bankruptcies 31
Business environments 235
Business survey tools 19
Buy and bust 115
Buying a safe 55

C

C-stores 61
Cabinet locks 81
Cameras address the front registers 111
Camera systems 24
Cancel your coverage 235
CAP Index 49
Carry ladders 246
Carts and dollies 247
Cash 23
CASH CONTROL SYSTEM 142
Cash drawers 55
Cashier training 225
Cash Management Programs 162
Cash Manager 141, 142, 145
Cash policy violations 132
Cash pull 141
Cash shortage 193
Cassettes for safekeeping 164
Catastrophic loss 30
Caught in the act 223
CCTV standard 109
CCTV systems 24
Central station 112, 114
Certified Protection Professional 9, 19, 37, 39
Certified Public Accountant 189
Chain of command 278
Chambers of commerce 45
Change Acceptance 305
Change the combination 219
Changing business locks 76
Changing locks 218
Chemical Hazard Awareness Program 237
Citations and fines 22
Civil Disorder 276
Civil liability 24
Claims handling 264
Claims with high potential costs 238
Clean as you go 250
Clear assignments of responsibility 241

Closed circuit television system 104
Cobb City Lock and Supply 62, 82, 95, 112
Coded keys 72
Coin and change deliveries 159
Collateral damage 270
Commercial burglaries 216
Commercially packaged chemical 256
Commercial sprinkler system 96
Common sense dictates 214
Communicate hazard information 257
Communicate the hazard 256
Communication 277
Communications 285
Company Property 196
Company spokesperson 285, 286
Competitive Advantage 9, 308
Complies with ISO/IEC 17024 37
Comply with federal regulations 122
Composition of the population 47
Compound-locking device 244
Compulsive gamblers 193
Computer fraud 31
Computerized accounting systems 230
Conducting a loss prevention survey 41
Conduct interviews 119
Confidence tricks 200
Consolidation of cash deposits 163
Consult with your attorney 228
Contact information 20
Contact switches 92
Contaminating chemicals 110
Contingency plan 285
Control building access 296
Control of banking charges 163
Control panel 89
COPE 227
Counseling of register operators 146
Counter camera 110
COUNTERFEIT 226
Counterfeiting 31
CPP certification 37
Crash bar 80
Creating a disaster plan 269
Creation of the program 41
Credible complaint 236
Crime 19
CRIMECAST 48
Crime loss vulnerability 20
Crime protection insurance 31
Crime rate 41, 46
Crime reporting practices 47
CRIMES AGAINST YOUR CUSTOMERS 228
Crime Scene 271
Criminal acts 272
Criminal attacks 269
Criminal histories of applicants 124
Crisis Management 272

Crisis Management/Response Training 284
Crisis Management Plan 279
Crisis Management Program 277
Crisis Management Team 274, 277
Crisis Management Team Director 279
Crisis Plan 277
Crisis situations 276
Critical assets 277
Critical Control Points 141
Cultural factors and educational 47
Customer Liability 25
Customer Liability Claim 31, 235, 238
Cut false alarms 91

D

Daily Credit totals 165
Data Mining 149
Define the scope 287
Deliveries 213
Delivery piece count 230
Department Of Homeland Security 38, 108
Deposit drop log 157
Deposit ticket 160
Deposit transfers 159
Deposit transit bags 160
Description of the incident 228
Description of the robbery 215
Description of what happened 262
Design barriers 277
Detection and delay technology 176
Detect or deter intruders 296
Determine the hazards 256
Deterrence marketing 220
Dial safe 58
Digital cameras 110
Digital camera systems 24
Digital Video Recorders 105
Dining room 110
Disaster plans and response 250
Discrimination 130
Discrimination accusations 276
Disgruntled employee 275
Dishonest employees 127
Dishonesty 31
Disorderly Activity 227
DISORDERLY ACTIVITY/ VIOLENT PERSONS 227
Disorderly conduct 131
Dispute resolution 158
Documented Patented Key Control Technology 78
Door closer hardware 82
Door contacts 95
Door contact switches 94
Do the right thing 287
Double dead-bolt lock 80
Drawer shortage 145
Drilling attacks 66

DRUGS & YOUTH 51
Dual controls 141
Dummy or non-working cameras 24
DVR 105

E

E.-coli 269
Economic conditions 47
EEOC complaint 128
Electrical equipment 243, 245
Electrical Safety 245
Electrical tools and equipment 245
Electronic access control systems 73
Electronic key 56
Electronic locks 56, 58
Embezzlement 31, 181
Embezzlers 184
Emergency medical procedures 250
Emergency response agencies 273
Employee's Right To Know Act 256
Employee death or serious injury 276
Employee dies 236
Employee Dishonesty Coverage 32
Employee Handbook 129
Employee injuries 238
Employee Involvement 239
Employee lockers 172
EMPLOYEE SCREENING 119
Employee Search Guidelines 196
Employee theft 9, 191
employee training programs 235
Employers 256
envelope account 157
Equipment & Machinery 243
Establish a unified response 287
Established accountability 141
Ethical issues 134
Evaluate 286
Ex-employees 216
Exception reports 149
Excessive line item voids 151
Excessive phone calls 132
Exercise due diligence 124
Expert advice 37
Exposed To Burglary 217
Exposure to robbery 214
Exterior doors 23
Eye protection must be worn 242

F

Facts about commercial burglaries 83
False alarms 22
False Insurance claims 200
Falsification of company records 132
FBI 45, 108
Federal and State OSHA 236

Federal Bureau Of Investigation 45
Felony 181
FEMA 291
Fidelity Crime Insurance 31
Fights 228
Finance 281
Fine count banking services 157
Fine count verifications 162
Fingerprints 15
Fire 31
Firearms 43
Fire extinguisher 250
Fire prevention 250
Fire Protection 244
Fire pull stations 96
flood 31
Focus on apprehension 220
Follow all safety requirements 240
Food cost variance 229, 300
Food poisoning 287
Forced entry 296
Forcible entry 217
Forensic Science Division of the FBI 108
Foreseeable 109
Forgery 31, 200
Formative Period 305
Fraud 152, 200
Fraud and embezzlement 32
Fraud detection 202
Freight-receiving window 113
Front (Food) Window 110
Front Counter 110, 113
Front Door 111
Fuzzy bank robbery video 108

G

General Liability Claims 251, 262
General Manager 142
Goals and Activities 280
Good Housekeeping 242
Good surveillance 219
Gordo's Fast Food 60, 80, 92, 109
Grade 1 Heavy Duty locks 71
Grade 2 Commercial Duty Locks 71
Grade 3 Light Commercial Duty Locks 71
Grand jury indictment 276
Grand larceny 181
Grocery stores 230
Gross misconduct 129
Ground-fault circuit interrupter (GFI) 245
Guards 25
Guard service company 173
Guessing the combination 65

H

Handling voids 142

Hand Tools 243
Hand truck 15
Hazard communication program 256, 257
Hazard identification 235
Hazardous chemicals 257, 272
Hazardous conditions 252
Hazardous materials 237
High frequency 236
High inventory variance 141
Hiring 15
Hiring new employees 119
Hiring practices 297
Hold a meeting 240
Hold people accountable 235
Hold register operators accountable 145
Hold up alarm buttons 90
Hold up alarm switches 93
hold up button 94
Horn or siren 89
Hosted IP video service 114
Hosted Video Solution 114
Hot Phone 112
HR Section 25
Human resource 271, 277
Human Resources 281

I

IC Cores 72
ICM (Institute For Crisis Management) 272
Identify and list hazardous chemicals 256
Identify hazards 26
Identity theft 123, 200
Illegal drugs 130
Image stabilization 103
Implementation plan 41
Implement standard accounting 136
Impulse robbery 57
Inadequate security 108
Inappropriate behavior 130
Incident Investigations 260
Incident report form 170
Individual combinations 22
INDIVIDUAL KEY HOLDER AGREEMENT 79
In lieu of prosecution 224
Inside job 296
Inspect what you expect 75
Insubordination 131
Insurance carrier 235
Insurance policies 32
Intelligent Safes 163
Intelligent video system 177
Interactive hosted guard service 175
Interactive systems 112
Interchangeable removable cores 72
International Organization for Standardization (ISO)
    37

Interruptible surge protected power supply 58
Inventory 31
Inventory losses 229
Inventory Theft 299
Inventory variance 21
Investigating incidents 260
INVESTIGATIVE GUIDELINES 193
Investigative reporter contact 276
IP address 176
IP system 175
Issue Identification 286

J

Job safety and health 239
Joint employee-management safety committee 239

K

Keep the message simple 287
KEY AND SAFE CONTROL 76
Key controls and systems 76
Key Control System 77
Key Log 78
Key Pad 93
Key pad 95, 96
Key strategies 218

L

Ladder Safety 246
Larceny 44, 181
Larceny-theft offenses 44, 50
Late night operations 216
Latent fingerprints 296
LAW ENFORCEMENT EMPLOYEES 50
Leading the Change 306
Leave together 214
Legal counsel 191
Less litigation 123
Less theft 123
Liability coverage insurance 235
Liability exposure 31
Liability insurance 173
Liability litigation 41
Lighting Makes A Difference 219
Live video 114
Local alarm/Chime 93
Local TV stations 274
LOCATING SAFES IN YOUR BUSINESS 59
Lock manipulation 65
Lockout device 244
Lockout device and tag 244
Lock out switches 243
Locks 15
Locksmith firms 39
Locksmith trades 39
Loiterers 227
Loitering and other undesirable activity 110

Loss analysis 236
Loss Prevention Managers 10
Loss prevention managers 37, 235
Loss prevention professional 21
Loss Prevention Program 9, 39
Loss Prevention Survey 20, 280
LOSS REPORTING 170
Loss reporting system 170
Loss Run 237
Loss thresholds 147
Lost customer property 172
Lot lights should be on 214
LOWERING CORRECTLY 248

M

Management Commitment 239
Management decisions/indecision 272
Management Theory 231
Manager Meeting 251
Managing Your Lock & Key System 77
Mandatory drug testing 131
Manual cash handling 162
Marketing 281
MASTER KEY, Grand Master 77
Material Safety Data Sheet 256
Material Safety Data Sheets (MSDS) 237
Measurable goals 251
Measure and reward success 236
Mechanical Patented Key Control 72
Media attention 215
Minimize outside activity 211
Minimum of two people 214
Minimum standard 71
Misdemeanor 181
Missing deposit 194
Mission Statement 129, 239
Misuse of company computer equipment 133
Mitigation 277
Modes of transportation 47
Modifier number 235
Money 15, 31
Money and Security Coverage 32
Money missing 298
Money rooms 157, 159
Money safes 22
Monitoring and recording 111
Monthly safety inspection 251
Motion interrupt 175
MSDS book 237
Multiple charge voids 151
Multiple victims and injuries 236
Must be enforced consistently 128
Must receive a written copy 128

N

National Response Plan (NRP) 291

National Retail Federation (NRF) 182
National Retail Security Survey 182
Natural disasters 272
Nature of injury 262
Negative publicity 270
Negotiating refunds 160
Network management 114
News media 288
Night depository 211
Non-disclosure agreement 134
Non-profits 32, 186
No sale following a cash void 150
No Unwritten Policies 146
NYPD 270

O

Office 111
Oklahoma City bombing 103
On-property first aid 238
Only authorized persons 224
Operating system redundancy 278
Operations 281
Opportunities 30
Opportunity 32, 127, 190
Organizational chart 280
Organized retail crime 183
OSHA citation 256
Outdoor cameras 110
Over/short report 159
Over/short standard 147
Overhead rolling steel doors 82

P

Parking lot cameras 112
Passive infrared-switched flood 219
Passive Infrared detectors 96
Passive infrared sensors 93, 94
Patented Key Control System 77
Pathological gambling 192
Pattern recognition 152
Percentage of sales 21
Performance standards 284
Perimeter protection systems 176
Personal injury 249
Personal injury Lawsuit 220
PERSONAL PROPERTY 172
Personal protective equipment 236
Pete's Food and Beer 61, 82, 94, 111
Philadelphia Police Department 46
Physical risk of injury 220
Pick pockets and unruly individuals 110
PIR (passive infrared) sensors 23
Placement and use of camera systems 108
Plaintiffs attorney 41, 42
Plan 286
Plan activities 284

Plan Development 254
PLANNING A KEY CONTROL SYSTEM 71
PLANNING YOUR CCTV INSTALLATION 103
Plan Training 284
Point of sale cash register 23
Police 15
Police departments 22
Police report 228
Policies and procedures 277, 297
Policies and Procedures Manual 129
Policies must be written 58, 128
POLICIES THAT YOU NEED 91, 107
Policy compliance 295
Policy Preparation 287
Policy statement 240
POLYGRAPH 196
Population density 47
POS 164
Position 286
Possession of a firearm 131
POS system 143, 145
POS system balances 165
Post-crisis Review 288
Pre-opening robbery prevention 210
Predict 286
Predictive analytics 203
Predictive models 202
Premises liability claim 41
Premises liability issues 262
Prepare deposits 143
Preparing Specific Responses 287
Preparing Your Plan 280
Presenting recommendations 41
Prevent 286
Prevent accidental start-ups 243
Preventative maintenance 107
Prevention 213, 221, 277
Prior criminal conviction section 125
Privacy laws 109
Proactive planning 283
PROBABILITY 17
Probability and Severity 17
Procedures 18
Process for Retrieving Keys 78
Productive employees 124
Proficiency testing 284
Profit margin 235
Programming level key 57
Progressive disciplinary policy 195
Prohibition on copy of keys 74
Prohibition on lending keys 75
Project manager 41
Proper Lifting 248
Property crime 50
Property crimes 42, 44
Property damage 228
Proprietary information 134

Prosecute shoplifters 222
Protection of assets 119
Protective housing-cameras 106
Protect your cash 153
Protests and demonstrations 269
Provision for periodic key audits 75
Psychological counseling 215
Psychological counselors 271
Psychological trauma 215
Public relations experts 271
Pull cash 143
Purpose is robbery prevention 110
Purse snatching 228

Q

Quality Control department 231

R

Racial harassment 130
Random checks 112
Rapid Growth Period 305
Rationalization 190
Re-locker 66
Reactive To Proactive 305, 308
Reasonable care 24, 41, 263
Reasonable person 263
Receiving 113
Record keeping & Capability of Audit of keys 78
Recovery 277
Reduce 18
Reinforce good behaviors 235
Relying on the consensus 121
Rely on the applicants statements 120
Rely on what the recruiter tells you 121
Remote operators 112
Reportable accident 238
Report any injury 242
Reporting of lost or stolen keys 74
Residential burglaries 217
Respiratory equipment 242
RESTITUTION GUIDELINE 224
Restrain the disorderly 227
Restricted keyway 72
Retail shrinkage 229
Return Fraud 225
Return Fraud Survey 225
Return of non-defective 226
Return policies 225
Returns without a receipt 150
Reverse negative trends 236
Reward 127
Right To Know Act 237
Ringing in employee purchases 142
Risk 18, 127
Risk Analysis 16
Risk Control Measures 277

Robbed On The Way To The Bank 212
Robbery 24, 31, 43, 215, 228
Robbery Defined 209
ROBBERY PREVENTION 209
Robbery trends 43
Routine inspection 236
Rules and policies 119
Rules and procedures 235

S

Safe 15, 297
Safe burglary 31
Safe cracking 67
Safety 235
SAFETY Act 38
Safety awareness 235
Safety awareness programs 235
Safety Coordinator role 238
Safety inspections 26
Safety loss exposure 235
Safety policy 235
Safety practices 9
Safety procedures and policies 239
Safety programs 25
Safety shoes 242
Safety Station 242
Safe warranties 58
Safe work environment 235
Said to contain 157
Sales deduct items 147
Sales Room 113
Sarbanes-Oxley Act 280
Screen your applicants 124
Sealed cassettes 157
Securities 31
Security 297
Security and Exchange Commission (SEC) 280
Security Equipment 18
Security guard company 174
Security guards 173
Security lighting 219
Security personnel 25
SECURITY PROGRAM CONSIDERATIONS 170
SECURITY SERVICES 173
Security tapes 159
Security Wise Group LLC 278, 309
Self-insured 235
Serious violent crime 41
Service Counter 111
Severe weather response 250
SEVERITY 17
Severity of a Smoldering Crisis 274
Severity of a Sudden Crisis 273
Sexual harassment 130
Shift deposits 157
Shim plates 218

SHOPLIFTING 220
Shoplifting 223
Shoplifting apprehension 220
Shoplifting losses 220
SHORT CHANGE ARTISTS 225
Shrinkage 21, 194
Signature acknowledging key 74
Signed admission 222
Significant financial risks 220
Significant loss of cash 130
Siren/Horn 93
SIU 201
Slip and fall 262
Slip and Fall Injury Prevention 249
Slip resistant shoes 250
SMART acronym 283
SMART Planning 282
Smart Safes 163
Smash and grab 218
Smoldering Crisis 274
Solicitation 133
Solid core doors 84
Sources of ignition 244
Spills such as grease 243
Stability of the population 47
Standard employment applications 119
State fire codes 80
Statement of consequences 75, 128
Statistical Analysis of Voids 151
Steps to prevent injuries 249
Stock deliveries 231
Stock receivers 230
Strengths 29
Strike, job action or work stoppage 276
Strobe light 93, 94
Strobe lights 95
Substance abuse 198
Sudden crisis 272
Sudden Level 1 273
Sudden Level 2 273
Sudden Level 3 273
Sudden Level 4 273
Suffolk County Police 270
Supply chain 229, 269
Survey tools 19
Survey Yourself 19
Suspect 15
SWOT 29
SWOT analysis 29, 280
Synergy 29
Systems control audit 295

T

Take care of your employees 215
Taking an active part 240
Tamper-evident plastic bag 211

Technical skills 29
Termination 130
Terrorism threat or action 276
Test safes to worst-case scenarios 55
TEST YOUR ALARM SYSTEM 98
Theft 16, 24, 129
Thinking outside the box 295
Threats 31
Time and attendance violations 132
Time delay change fund safes 61
Time lock compartment 211
Top down ownership 279
Train all employees 58
Trained employees 243
Training 30, 241
Training and information program 257
Training tools 235
Transfer 18
Transfer the risk 277
Trespassers 177

U

U.S. Census Bureau 45
UCR 42
UL's safe attack tests 55
Under-ring of keyed items 150
Under counter drop safe 61
Underwriters Laboratories or UL 55
Uniform Crime Report (UCR) 42
Unlawful entry 43, 217
Unsafe act 241
Unsafe condition 241
Unwritten Rules 58

V

VAGRANTS & LOITERERS 227
VANDALISM 226
Vandalism 83, 175
Variance report 162
Video surveillance system 114
Video verification 175
Violation of cash control policies 130
Violation of safety policies 131
Violation of safety rules 134
Violation of security policies 132
Violent crime 50
Violent crimes 215
VISITOR ACCESS CONTROL 224
Voids before opening 151

W

Warehouse 113, 230
Warehouse environment 112
Warning Devices 18
Warning Signs of Stolen Goods 115
Waste or mismanagement 229

Weaknesses 30
Wear protective clothing 246
Weather disasters 269
Web-browser 114
Weighing the cash 147
Well-lighted secure building 218
What shoplifters use 220
When the key must be returned 74
While You Are Open 211
White collar crime 32
Wi-Fi 114
Wine and Beer Coolers 111
Wireless installation 93
Wire transfer fraud 31
Witnesses 15, 270, 296
Workers Compensation 25, 26, 31, 235, 249, 251
Workers Compensation claims 238
Workers Compensation Fraud 199
Working alone 214
Workplace violence policies and rules 125
Work rules 31
Worst case scenario 16, 30, 31, 269, 271
Write off a loss 160
Written and acknowledged policies 58
Written business plan 169
Written hazard communication program 256
Written job descriptions 281, 285
Written Key Control Policy 78
Written manifests 164
Written policies and procedures 23
Written procedures 22
Written report 260
Written Rules 135
Written statements 228
www,fbi.gov/ucr 42
www.nrf.com 182
www.osha.gov 236
www.securitywisegroup.com 309

Z

Zero disabling injuries 239
Zero tolerance policy 129

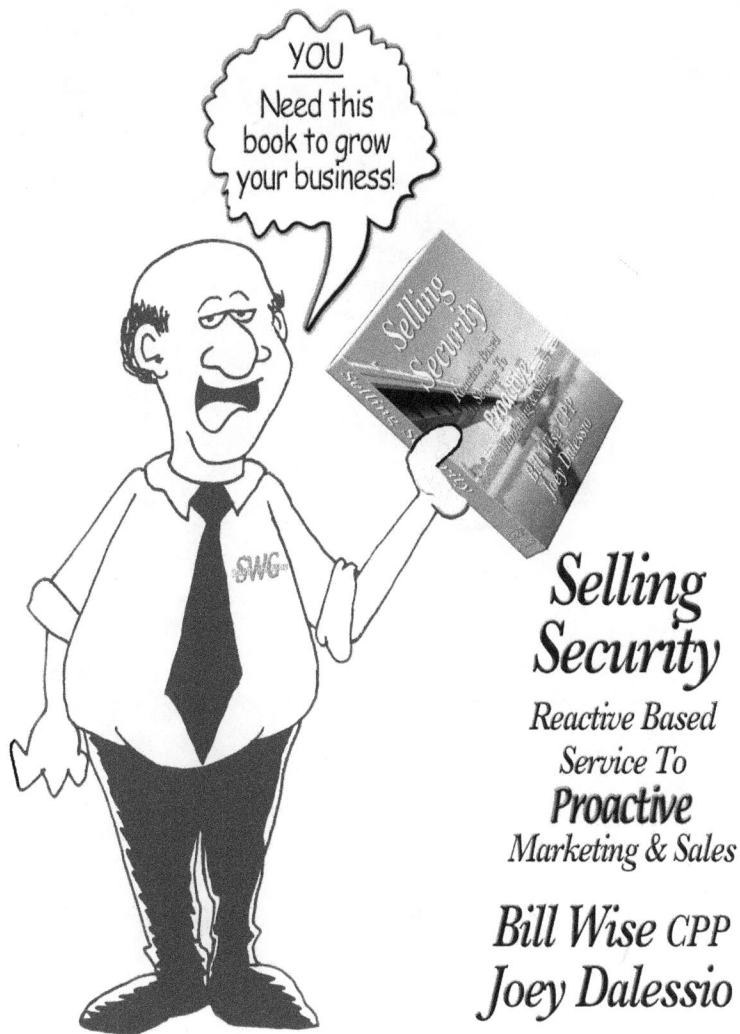

www.ingramcontent.com/pod-product-compliance
Lightning Source LLC
Chambersburg PA
CBHW080512220326
41599CB00032B/6061